D0523960

Northern Ireland: Politics and the Constitution

Northern Ireland: Politics and the Constitution

Edited by
Brigid Hadfield

Open University Press
Buckingham · Philadelphia

Open University Press
Celtic Court
22 Ballmoor
Buckingham
MK18 1XW

and
1900 Frost Road, Suite 101
Bristol, PA 19007, USA

First Published 1992

Copyright © Brigid Hadfield and The Contributors 1992

All rights reserved. No part of this publication may be
reproduced, stored in a retrieval system or transmitted
in any form or by any means, without written permission
from the publisher.

British Library Cataloguing in Publication Data

Northern Ireland: Politics and the Constitution.
  I. Hadfield, Brigid
  320.9416

  ISBN 0–335–09963–7
  ISBN 0–335–09962–9 pbk

Library of Congress Cataloging in Publication Number Available

Typeset by Type Study, Scarborough
Printed in Great Britain by St Edmundsbury Press Ltd
Bury St Edmunds, Suffolk

Contents

List of contributors

Antony Alcock, Professor, Faculty of Humanities, University of Ulster at Coleraine

James Casey, Professor, Faculty of Law, University College, Dublin

Brice Dickson, Professor of Law, University of Ulster at Jordanstown

Sydney Elliott, Senior Lecturer, Department of Political Science, Queen's University, Belfast

Adrian Guelke, Lecturer, Department of Political Science, Queen's University, Belfast

Brigid Hadfield, Reader in Law, School of Law, Queen's University, Belfast

John Loughlin, Lecturer, Department of Public Administration, Erasmus University of Rotterdam

Paul Maguire, Lecturer, School of Law, Queen's University, Belfast

Edward Moxon-Browne, Reader in Politics, Department of Political Science, Queen's University, Belfast

Clive Walker, Senior Lecturer, Director of the Centre for Criminal Justice Studies, University of Leeds

R. A. Wilford, Lecturer, Department of Political Science, Queen's University, Belfast

Acknowledgements

Editing a volume of collected essays is not easy, and without willing collaboration it is impossible. My thanks, therefore, go first and foremost to the individual authors without whose patience and tolerance this book would not have been completed. A word of thanks must go especially to Rick Wilford, for his invaluable assistance in helping to 'bridge the gap' between lawyers and political scientists.

My thanks are also due to Dr Ray Cunningham, commissioning editor of the Open University Press, whose insight into and interest in this work, beginning with a conversation at a conference in Sheffield in January 1990, have been much appreciated.

My thanks also go, last but not least, to my secretary, Mrs Nancy Bowman, whose willing and cheerful assistance have made my work so much easier.

The chapters were all written between autumn 1990 and spring 1991, just as the long-projected talks about devolution to Northern Ireland and about the nature of an Irish dimension were scheduled to begin. It is the lot of anyone writing about Northern Ireland to be confronted constantly with the possibility of changes which may overtake, sometimes immediately, much of what has been written. Conversely, writers may stay their hand waiting for developments which do not materialize or which do not materialize as expected. It is, nevertheless, our collective hope that this book will serve to inform what will undoubtedly be a continuing debate about the form of government in and for Northern Ireland.

Introduction

Brigid Hadfield

The purpose of this book may be stated simply: its aim is to facilitate an exchange of ideas between lawyers and political scientists on the issue of Northern Ireland and its form of government. Much has been written about Northern Ireland, particularly over the past twenty years, both ephemeral and scholarly, from a wide variety of angles, within a wide variety of disciplines, serving a wide variety of purposes and working towards a wide variety of conclusions – or towards none. Little, however, has been achieved from a cross-disciplinary perspective. Each contributor to this book, therefore, was requested to write with an audience of both lawyers and political scientists in mind in order to enhance awareness of the insights and knowledge which the one discipline might bring to the other. It has long been recognized that the two disciplines are not discrete, but a combined consideration of matters of common concern is not often attempted.

A similar, although not identical, venture to this, but for the United Kingdom constitution as a whole, is to be found in Jowell and Oliver, *The Changing Constitution*. In their preface, the editors state:

> As editors we have resisted imposing any ideological or theoretical framework on this book and have confined our role to the selection of issues that we feel merit close examination as current problems of constitutional law. To explore these issues we have selected authors (both lawyers and political scientists) who are specialists in the law and practice of modern government. These authors will of course bring to their discourse values and perspectives of their own. For this kind of work we feel that such diversity is more useful to the reader than conformity to an editorially imposed pattern.[1]

This is the approach that has been adopted here. The first four chapters consider the evolution of the Northern Ireland constitution and the factors which have been or will be influential in its development. This continuing evolution is considered not only in terms of the law and the formal institutional changes, but also in terms of the policies and commitments of the various political parties. Chapter 3, on consociationalism, contains a warning against over-concentration on the 'top-tier' institutions at the expense of other changes – for example, in education and employment – which might influence the course of events. Chapter 4, on Northern Ireland and the European Community, introduces the theme of 'external' influence – that is, an influence from outside Northern Ireland, Great Britain or the Republic of Ireland – albeit one which will become increasingly internalized.

Chapter 5, on policy administration within the context of the institutional framework delineated in the earlier chapters, develops the theme of public accountability in an increasingly bureaucratic, depoliticized system of public administration. Chapter 6, on the electoral system, considers choice and participation in the context of voting and electoral boundaries. These two topics relate to popular involvement at the two ends of the continuum – the choice of the people in whom state power will be vested and the actual implementation of chosen policies.

Consideration of electoral systems frequently leads to debates on the *legitimacy* of the institutions elected by one system rather than another. In divided societies debates on legitimacy can also arise with regard to those institutions which have the task of enforcing and upholding law and order in the state. Consequently, Chapters 7, 8 and 9 deal with policing and the role of the Army and of the judiciary in Northern Ireland.

Finally, Chapters 10 and 11 broaden the perspective by considering, respectively, comparative material from other divided societies in Western Europe and some of the problems and issues which can arise within a state which possesses a written constitution. For the latter purpose the Republic of Ireland clearly, in the context of this book, lent itself as the most appropriate case study.

No overall conclusions are drawn from the eleven chapters, neither for Northern Ireland specifically nor more generally, although it is hoped that many of the issues considered here will be regarded as being of more general relevance and interest. Devolution, proportional representation, the influence of the European Community, the powers of local government, the status of the judges, policing in a divided society, the merits and the demerits of a written constitution – all these matters are currently of widespread interest throughout the United Kingdom. Northern Ireland and the issues it raises should not be marginalized.

Note

1 J. Jowell and D. Oliver (eds), *The Changing Constitution* (2nd edn), Clarendon Press, Oxford, 1989, p. v.

Chronology of events

The events listed here have been selected for their significance to the themes discussed in the ensuing chapters.[1] Most of the events mentioned here are also discussed further in the book.

1800
Acts of Union between Great Britain and Ireland.

1886
First Home Rule Bill (defeated in the House of Commons).

1893
Second Home Rule Bill (defeated in the House of Lords).

1914
Government of Ireland Act. This provides for the establishment of one all-Ireland parliament and government, Ireland remaining within the United Kingdom. The Act is suspended on the outbreak of the First World War and never comes into operation.

1920
Government of Ireland Act.

1921
Parliament and government of Northern Ireland begin operating under the 1920 Act.
(December) Articles of Agreement for a Treaty between the British Government and the Sinn Fein leaders.

1937

New Constitution of the Irish Free State. Articles 2 and 3 claim sovereignty over the whole of the island of Ireland.

1949

Irish Free State leaves the Commonwealth. Under the Ireland Act 1949 (an Act of the Westminster Parliament) provision is made for it to be known as the Republic of Ireland. The Act also gives a guarantee to the Northern Ireland Parliament with regard to the status of Northern Ireland.

1965

First meeting between the Prime Minister of Northern Ireland (Terence O'Neill) and the Taoiseach (Séan Lemass) at Stormont.

1967

Northern Ireland Civil Rights Association formed.

1968

Civil rights protest marches begin.
(5 October) Violence occurs at a march in Londonderry.

1972

(March) Northern Ireland (Temporary Provisions) Act prorogues the Parliament of Northern Ireland and suspends the Northern Ireland government, introducing direct rule.
(September) Conference on the future form of government for Northern Ireland is held at Darlington between the Secretary of State for Northern Ireland and representatives of the Official Unionist Party, Alliance Party and Northern Ireland Labour Party (other parties refuse to attend).
(October) Government's discussion document on 'The Future of Northern Ireland' is published. NIO *The Future of Northern Ireland. A Paper for Discussion*, HMSO, London, 1972.

1973

(March) Border poll is held, voting overwhelmingly in favour of Northern Ireland remaining part of the United Kingdom.
(June) Elections for the new Northern Ireland Assembly.
(July) Northern Ireland Constitution Act.
(November) Agreement is reached between the Secretary of State and the leaders of some Northern Ireland parties on the establishment of a power-sharing Executive.
(December) Sunningdale Agreement reached between British and Irish governments and Northern Ireland Executive-designate.

1974

(January) Power-sharing Executive and Assembly with devolved powers begin operating under the terms of the Constitution Act 1973.

(February) Anti-Sunningdale unionists win 11 of the 12 seats at the (Westminster) general election.

(May) Strike by (loyalist) Ulster Workers' Council; unionist members of the Executive resign; the Executive collapses; the Assembly is prorogued; Northern Ireland Office ministers take over the functions of the Executive.

(July) Direct rule is reintroduced under the Northern Ireland Act 1974.

1975

(May) Elections are held to the Constitutional Convention elected to consider which form of government would have widespread acceptance throughout the community.

(November) The Convention publishes its report, the majority rejecting power-sharing and calling for a (virtual) return of the 1920 system of government.

1976

(February–March) The Secretary of State reconvenes the Convention to reconsider its report. Its sittings are concluded without reaching any recommendations acceptable to Westminster.

1979

(November) Publication of a White Paper: *The Government of Northern Ireland: A Working Paper for a Conference.*

1980

(January–March) The 'Atkins Conference' – a series of (ultimately) inconclusive meetings on a future form of government for Northern Ireland between Humphrey Atkins, Secretary of State for Northern Ireland, and the leaders of the DUP, SDLP and Alliance Party. The OUP does not accept the invitation to attend, although it does submit a detailed paper.

(July) Publication of a White Paper: 'Proposals for Further Discussion'.

(May and December) Summit meetings between the British and Irish Prime Ministers.

1981

(November) The Anglo-Irish Intergovernmental Council is established.

1982

Northern Ireland Act 1982 provides for elections to a new Assembly. Elections are held in October. The Assembly is boycotted by both SDLP and Provisional Sinn Fein. The Assembly had two statutory functions: first, to formulate proposals for (rolling) devolution which would command cross-community support (this was not achieved); second, to scrutinize the operation of direct rule (this the Assembly did).

1983
(May) New Ireland Forum – consisting of the nationalist parties, North and South (Fianna Fáil, Fine Gael, Irish Labour Party and SDLP) – begins its deliberations in Dublin on Northern Ireland.

1984
(May) New Ireland Forum Report published.

1985
(November) The Anglo-Irish Agreement is signed, and later approved by both Westminster and the Oireachtas and lodged at the United Nations. The Anglo-Irish Intergovernmental Conference is established.

1986
(June) The Assembly is dissolved.

1989
(January) In a speech to the Bangor (Co. Down) Chamber of Commerce, the Secretary of State for Northern Ireland, Peter Brooke, says: 'It does appear . . . that common ground exists about the major issues which talks between the political parties [in Northern Ireland] would need to address. There needs to be devised workable and acceptable arrangements for the exercise of devolved powers over a range of matters. There needs to be agreement on democratic institutions which would give appropriate weight to majority and minority aspirations and views. There is the question which is addressed by the Anglo-Irish Agreement: how the legitimate interest of the Irish Government in matters within Northern Ireland, particularly as regards the minority community, are to be acknowledged, without the dilution of UK sovereignty or the status of Northern Ireland as part of the United Kingdom. And there is the question of a local political contribution to security matters.' Talks about talks on 'new arrangements for exercising political power within Northern Ireland' come onto the agenda.

1991
(March) The Secretary of State announces a three-month timetable for talks about devolution to begin at the end of April, during which time the Anglo-Irish Intergovernmental Conference and its secretariat are to be effectively suspended. The talks are to have three elements: talks between the Northern Ireland political parties; talks between Belfast and Dublin; and talks between Westminster and Dublin.

Note

1 For a full chronology, see W. D. Flackes and S. Elliott, *Northern Ireland: A Political Directory 1968–88*, Blackstaff Press, Belfast, pp. 1–57.

Postscript

The inter-party talks did begin, but faltered and eventually collapsed in July 1991 by which time the time-table laid down for discussion had fallen far behind schedule. The talks had only reached the first of the three projected stages, that is, on the future form of government for the province, the other two stages being concerned with its relations with the Republic of Ireland and relations between London and Dublin.

At the time of writing (July 1991) it is not at all clear whether or when the talks will resume.

The Northern Ireland constitution

Brigid Hadfield

'What you see is what you get' is a term from the realm of the computer, but it also seems apposite for the Northern Ireland constitution. Northern Ireland is a part of the United Kingdom but it is also a place apart. A consideration of the constitution of Northern Ireland must be placed within, on the one hand, the borders provided by both the territorial claim to Northern Ireland in the Republic of Ireland's 1937 Constitution, and, on the other, the United Kingdom's declared willingness to cede Northern Ireland, a part of its own national territory, should the condition of majority consent be met. It is, however, not in itself sufficient to take into account these external factors. Account must also be taken of the fact that within Northern Ireland there are two separate communities or identities, which even in the absence of the external factors would still have to be considered in the construction of its institutional structures and the formulation of its laws. The link between the external and the internal factors is that the larger of the two communities within Northern Ireland supports the union with Great Britain and also opposes a union (of whatever nature) with the Irish Republic, while the smaller of the two communities by and large supports the (re)unification outside the United Kingdom of what is often referred to as 'the island of Ireland'. These two communities are traditionally identified by religious labels (Protestant and Roman Catholic), political labels (unionist and nationalist, or more specifically, loyalist and republican) or national labels (British and Irish, or Ulster-British and Ulster-Irish), although these terms are not totally interchangeable. It is the purpose of this chapter to consider both the external (or exogenous) and internal (or endogenous) factors in terms of the influence which they have had upon the construction and evolution of the Northern Ireland constitution.

The history of the constitution divides into two quite distinct sections, the first spanning the period 1920–72.[1] Under the terms of the Government of

Ireland Act 1920, Westminster intended to establish two parliaments and governments in Ireland with extensive devolved powers, but subject to the supremacy of Westminster, where power to legislate on matters of imperial and national concern was to be retained. The all-Ireland dimension in the 1920 Act consisted of the establishment of a Council of Ireland, with provision made for it to be transmuted into one all-Ireland parliament with potentially very extensive powers. Under section 2(1) of the 1920 Act, the functions of the Council, pending the eventual establishment of the all-Ireland parliament, were the bringing about of harmonious action between the Northern Ireland and Southern Ireland parliaments, the promotion of mutual intercourse and uniformity in relation to matters affecting the whole of Ireland, and the administration of those services which could be dealt with uniformly throughout Ireland. The Act also established a common High Court of Appeal which actually sat from December 1921 to December 1922, hearing a total of nine cases. The all-Ireland dimension, however, either did not become operative or ceased to be operative as a result of the talks between Lloyd George, the British Prime Minister, and the leaders of Sinn Fein (which had already established its own parliament in Dublin in 1918), which culminated in December 1921 in the Articles of Agreement for a Treaty, commonly called the Treaty. It and the related legislation led to the establishment of the twenty-six county Irish Free State with Dominion status. The six counties of Northern Ireland remained within the United Kingdom and for it and it alone the 1920 Act, as amended, came into operation.

The 1920 Act established a bicameral Northern Ireland Parliament, originally elected by a system of proportional representation. Section 14(5) of the Act empowered the Northern Ireland Parliament after three years from the day of its first meeting (in 1921) to alter this system. This power was exercised in 1929, the first-past-the-post electoral system replacing the original. (A similar change had already taken place in 1922 for Northern Ireland local government elections.) To the Parliament was transferred or devolved the power to make laws for the peace, order and good government of the province. There was no enumeration of transferred powers, but included were education, planning, local government, law and order, the civil and criminal law, minor but not major taxation, the appointment of magistrates and judges other than to the Supreme Court, and health and social services. Section 4 of the Act precluded the Northern Ireland Parliament from legislating on those matters of imperial and national concern, which remained the responsibility of Westminster, and section 5 prohibited the enactment of laws interfering with religious equality.

The Crown was represented within Northern Ireland by the Governor, who discharged the normal ceremonial functions associated with the Crown. The executive power, however, was effectively located in the Prime Minister, the leader of the largest party in the Northern Ireland House of Commons and, therefore, invariably a Unionist, and his single same-party Cabinet, who individually headed the Northern Ireland departments or ministries.

Throughout the life of the Northern Ireland Parliament, Westminster retained its inherent sovereign power in and over Northern Ireland, a position reinforced by the provisions of sections 75 (which saved its supreme authority), 6(2) (which provided that in the case of a conflict of laws passed after 1921, the Westminster Act prevailed) and 12(2) (which enabled the Governor to reserve a Bill rather than give to it the Royal Assent). The force of section 75, however, was weakened by Westminster's desire for non-involvement in Northern Ireland affairs, a constitutional convention that it would not legislate for Northern Ireland without the latter's (full-blooded or half-hearted) consent and a ruling in 1923 of the Speaker of the Westminster House of Commons that no question could be asked there on matters transferred to the Northern Ireland Parliament. Section 6(2) was largely evaded by the insertion into the Westminster Act of a provision deeming that Act to have come into force *before* 1921; in case of a conflict, therefore, the Northern Ireland Act would prevail. Section 12 became a dead letter after 1922 when the Governor reserved the Bill abolishing proportional representation in local government elections. In the face of threats of resignation from the Unionist government (which in the event of an election would have been returned to power), and in spite of pressure put upon Westminster by the (then) Provisional Government of the Irish Free State, the Royal Assent to the Bill was eventually given. Section 12 was never invoked again.

This system was thus marked by a desire for non-involvement in Northern Ireland affairs by Westminster which left the continuously Unionist government 'master in its own house'. Northern Ireland was possessed of all the trappings of a 'mini-state' and, whatever the strict legal form, the appearances gave rise to suggestions that Northern Ireland was akin to a province or a state in a federal system or was gently moving towards Dominion status.

During this period, there was some cross-border co-operation between North and South – for example, on fisheries and railways – but, from a Northern point of view, there was little or no concern with what is now termed the 'Irish dimension'. The schedule to the Ireland (Confirmation of Agreement) Act 1925, which was the last major piece of legislation amending and supplementing the Articles of Agreement for a Treaty of 1921, spoke of the desire, in light of the 'improved relations now subsisting' between the governments and peoples of Great Britain, Northern Ireland and the Irish Free State, to 'avoid any causes of friction which might mar or retard the further growth of friendly relations between the said Governments and peoples'. The Act recorded the formal agreement between Great Britain and the Free State that the extent of Northern Ireland should be such as was fixed by section 1(2) of the 1920 Act, namely the six counties of Antrim, Armagh, Down, Fermanagh, Londonderry and Tyrone.

This stance on the part of the Irish Free State was changed in its new Constitution of 1937 – although the 1937 provisions almost certainly reflected more accurately the climate of opinion in the South. Articles 2 and 3 of the

1937 Constitution respectively proclaim that the 'national territory consists of the whole island of Ireland, its islands and the territorial sea', but that 'pending the reintegration of the national territory', the laws of its Parliament would apply only within the Irish Free State.

When in 1949 the Irish Free State, becoming the Republic of Ireland, left the Commonwealth, section 1(2) of the Ireland Act of that year (an Act of the Westminster Parliament) declared that Northern Ireland remained a part both of the Dominions and of the United Kingdom and affirmed that 'in no event will Northern Ireland or any part thereof cease to be' such a part 'without the consent of the Parliament of Northern Ireland'.

In response to this the Dáil Éireann unanimously passed a declaration in May 1949

> Solemnly re-asserting the indefeasible right of the Irish nation to the unity and integrity of the national territory. Re-affirming the sovereign right of the people of Ireland to choose its own form of Government and, through its democratic institutions, to decide all questions of national policy, free from outside interference . . . [Calling] upon the British Government and people to end the present occupation of our six north-eastern counties, and thereby enable the unity of Ireland to be restored and the age-long differences between the two nations brought to an end.[2]

Some would argue that this stance, labelled by them 'irredentist', ignores the preferences, loyalties and identity of virtually 1 million people living in those six counties. Others would counter-argue that the inflexibility lay not in the Dáil but in the Northern Ireland Parliament (in itself regarded as anathema), which failed to give due regard to approximately one-third of the people living under its jurisdiction – although some of the major criticisms, because levelled against local government in the province rather than against the Parliament, were of passive rather than active discrimination. The criticisms made of the Parliament are most neatly summarized by the disparaging quotation of the remark of the Prime Minister Viscount Craigavon (James Craig) in 1934: 'All I boast of is that we are a Protestant Parliament and a Protestant state'.[3] More specific Roman Catholic/nationalist grievances included (allegations of) gerrymandering, unfairness in the allocation of public housing, discrimination in employment in both the public and private sector, policing, the Special Powers Act and its operation, and political bias on the part of (particularly) the magistrates and county court judges.

The dominant features, thus, of the system which existed from 1921 were, first, the conferment upon Northern Ireland of many of the trappings of statehood; second, a desire for non-involvement on the part of Westminster in 'internal' Northern Ireland affairs; third, the (effectively) permanent exclusion from the devolved government of any representatives of the minority community within Northern Ireland; fourth, a perceived and/or actual failure of the substantive laws to provide both equal protection for the two communities and remedies for the redress of grievances; and fifth, mutual antipathy, at least at the institutional level, between the (Protestant) North and the (Roman Catholic) South. The (unannounced) visit of the Taoiseach, Séan Lemass, on 14 January 1965 for talks with the Northern Ireland Prime Minister, Terence O'Neill, was the first of its kind and caused a division of opinion within the unionist ranks.

By 1972 events over the previous five years had had such a cataclysmic effect that the scene was to change beyond recognition. The Northern Ireland Civil Rights Association was established in 1967. Modelled on the then National Council for Civil Liberties and influenced by the American Civil Rights campaign, it sought the repeal of those laws and the ending of those practices which discriminated against the minority community. Though its first demonstration in County Tyrone to protest against discrimination in the allocation of public housing passed off peacefully, the second demonstration in October 1968 in Londonderry did not – and, crucially, the world and national media of communication were alerted. The 'nationalization' and 'internationalization' of the Northern Ireland issue had begun.

A detailing of the rapid sequence of events has necessarily to be selective, but there would probably be general agreement that the following are of not inconsiderable significance. First, between 1968 and 1972, a series of legislative and other measures was introduced by the Northern Ireland Parliament and government either on its own initiative or in response to active prompting by Westminster: electoral reform; the establishment of the 'Ombudsman'; the disbandment of the Ulster Special Constabulary (the B Specials); the enactment of the Prevention of Incitement to Hatred Act (NI); the institution of a Ministry of Community Relations; the creation of an independent Police Authority; the institution of the Northern Ireland Housing Executive (responsible for all public authority house building and allocation); and the reform of the whole system of local government. Second, the Westminster government became increasingly involved in Northern Ireland affairs, particularly law and order. Violence in the Roman Catholic Bogside area of Londonderry in the wake of the Protestant apprentice boys' march on 12 August 1969 led to the deployment of British troops in the province, first in Londonderry and then, almost immediately, in West Belfast. The convention of non-intervention by Westminster, already weakened, now disappeared. Paradoxically, however, although the Army was originally welcomed by the Roman Catholics of the Bogside and West Belfast, the implementation of security measures, most especially the imposition of a curfew on the Falls Road in West Belfast during 3–5 July 1970 and, later, the shooting dead of thirteen people in the Bogside by soldiers of the First Parachute Regiment on 30 January 1972 – which became known as 'Bloody Sunday' – led to a considerable amount of alienation between the Army and the minority community. Third, the Northern Ireland political parties began to fragment. Fourth, the Provisional IRA, formed in 1969, began its campaign of violence, the 'armed struggle', in 1970. The Ulster Defence Association (a loyalist paramilitary organization whose military arm, the Ulster Freedom Fighters, is proscribed) was formed in 1971. By 1972, the Ulster Volunteer Force, also a loyalist paramilitary organisation, also proscribed, is thought to have had a membership of around 1,500. A vortex of violence engulfed the province. The number of deaths in the four years from 1969 to 1972 was 13, 25, 174 and 467, respectively. Fifth, the government of the Irish Republic, led from 1966 to 1973 by Jack Lynch of Fianna Fáil, put Article 2 of the Irish Constitution into the forefront of the debates about Northern Ireland. At first this was done somewhat emotively. In a broadcast in Dublin on 13 August 1969, during the clashes in the Bogside, he stated that the current situation was 'the inevitable outcome of policies pursued for decades by successive [Northern Ireland] governments'; that the 'Irish government can no longer stand by and see innocent people injured and perhaps worse', and that the Irish Army would set up border field hospitals for those injured in the North. He called both for a United Nations peacekeeping force to be sent to Northern Ireland and for negotiations with Britain about the future of Northern Ireland, 'recognising that the re-unification of the national territory can provide the only permanent solution for the problem'.[4] Although such statements and others – for example, his calling for the end of internment without trial, which had been introduced in August 1971 – were resented by both unionists and, at first, the British government as being an interference in the internal affairs of the United Kingdom, Edward Heath, the British Prime Minister, invited Jack Lynch to bilateral talks in early September 1971 and then later that month to tripartite talks including Brian Faulkner, then Prime Minister of Northern Ireland.

The second – and quite distinct – phase in the history of the Northern Ireland constitution was, however, about to begin. The Westminster government, insistent on removing all law-and-order powers from the devolved institutions, found the latter resistant to the proposal, but it was not a case of irresistible force and immovable object and at the end of March 1972 the Northern Ireland Parliament was prorogued, the government was suspended and all legislative and executive powers were transferred to Westminster. Direct rule and the search for a new constitution had begun.

The salient features of direct rule (which, apart from the first five months of 1974, has been in existence since March 1972) may be briefly described but their consequences – an almost complete absence of representative participation and of accountability – are at best disquieting and at worst deplorable. Under direct rule,[5] the vast majority of laws which are made for Northern Ireland take the form of Orders in Council. These are a form of delegated legislation and when introduced into the House of Commons by the Secretary of State for Northern Ireland cannot be amended at all. If in content they are a parity measure, making the law in Northern Ireland the same as that in Great Britain, they will become law unless opposing backbenchers can procure and win a debate on the issue. Otherwise, they will become law once the government has secured the approval of the House. Either way, however, the amount of time made available for the debate of these Orders, either on the floor of the House (in which case it takes place late in the evening and misses much media coverage) or in a Standing Committee, is very limited. Clearly these constraints severely limit any non-governmental input into the formulation of laws for Northern Ireland, although the situation is ameliorated by the fact that for approximately half of the Orders in Council the government will circulate to all interested, including the political, parties a copy of the proposed Order inviting comments which can be taken into account before the Order is formally laid before Parliament. The Order in Council procedure is not used for Northern Ireland on matters of national concern or for those matters the exercise of which had proved divisive when legislated on by the Northern Ireland Parliament, for example, emergency or special powers.

As far as executive power is concerned, virtually all decision-making is either possessed by or subject to the direction and control of the Secretary of State for Northern Ireland – agriculture, education, economic development, the environment, health and social services, law and order, security. He, or one of the junior ministers, appears in the rota for House of Commons Question Time. There is, however, no Select Committee on Northern Ireland affairs, although the other departmental Select Committees have the relevant responsibilities of the Secretary of State within their remit – a power only occasionally exercised. The Northern Ireland Committee, a Standing Committee having only deliberative powers, has, for various reasons, played only a small part in the scrutiny of decision-making for the province. This overall situation is exacerbated by the fact that the substructure of local government as it exists in Great Britain is largely absent in Northern Ireland. The local authorities – the district councils – possess very limited powers, their main concerns being refuse collection, leisure centres, the crematorium and graveyards. Much power is instead located in non-elected, nominated boards – for example, the Education and Library Boards, the Housing Executive, the Health and Social Services Boards and the Police Authority.

The only factor which can be used to justify such a situation is that it is a temporary expedient. Although it would be possible to reform direct rule (retaining the principle that Westminster is as responsible for Northern Ireland affairs as it is for the other regions of the United Kingdom, but injecting greater amounts of participation and accountability), the main emphasis has been on the formulation of a system of devolved government for the province. For the first five months of 1974 a new system of devolution was in operation – the only break in direct rule since March 1972 – and, although it was short-lived, it did reflect the essence of what is still Westminster's approach to Northern Ireland. This system was introduced under the terms of the Northern Ireland Constitution Act 1973 (and related legislation), which provided that both the Northern Ireland Parliament (then standing prorogued) and the office of Governor should both cease to exist – the trappings of the 'mini-state' were dismantled. In place of the Parliament, there was established a unicameral Assembly – the change in terminology is of significance, too – elected by a system of proportional representation. The Secretary of State was given a central role to play in the formation of an 'Executive' (not 'Cabinet'), the composition of which had to reflect wide support throughout the community – this is commonly referred to as 'power-sharing'. The Executive was headed by the 'Chief Executive' – not 'Prime Minister'. The Assembly was given wide power to legislate on a range of internal matters – education, the environment, agriculture, health and social services, economic development – but any laws (termed 'Measures' not 'Acts') which discriminated on the grounds of religious belief or political opinion would be void. Power to legislate on matters which might prove divisive was withheld from the Assembly. Similar provision was made with regard to executive action. The other notable provision in the Act designed to ensure that there would be greater equality of treatment was section 20, which established the Standing Advisory Commission on Human Rights, to advise the Secretary of State 'on the adequacy and effectiveness of the law for the time being in force in preventing discrimination on the ground of religious belief and political opinion'.

By this time, however, it was also patently clear that the issue was not solely one of the formal mechanisms of government or of civil rights; it was also about the status of Northern Ireland. As the 1973 Act abolished the Northern Ireland Parliament, the provision of the Ireland Act 1949 – which precluded any change in the status of Northern Ireland without the consent of that Parliament – was replaced by section 1 of the 1973 Act, the 'constitutional guarantee', which required 'the consent of the majority of the people of Northern Ireland voting in a poll' held for the purpose. There was also a North–South Irish dimension in the Act – section 12 enabled a Northern Ireland executive authority to consult on any matter with any authority of the Republic and similarly to enter into agreements or arrangements in respect of any devolved matter. Supplementary to the Act, however, was what is known as the Sunningdale Agreement of December 1973, made between representatives of the Westminster and Republic of Ireland governments and of the Northern Ireland Executive-designate. The Agreement provided for the establishment of a Council of Ireland, consisting of a Council of Ministers (seven representatives each from the Northern and Southern governments), with 'executive and harmonising functions and a consultative role', and a Consultative Assembly (thirty members each, chosen by the Assembly and the Dáil, respectively) with 'advisory and review functions'.

The Sunningdale Agreement was not implemented; the power-sharing Executive and devolution lasted for only five months. In the general election of February 1974, eleven of the twelve members returned to Westminster for Northern Ireland were strongly opposed to both the proposed Council of Ireland (particularly) and to power-sharing. Eventually in May 1974, loyalist opposition culminated in the Ulster Workers' Council strike, which effectively halted much of industry and led to power cuts and the limiting of oil and petrol supplies. A fortnight into the strike, the unionist members of the power-sharing Executive resigned and direct rule, as described above, was reintroduced into the province and has continued ever since.

What, of constitutional significance, has happened since then? With regard to thinking on devolution, the answer is 'probably very little'. Devolution remains the preference of both the British and Irish governments, and indeed of many of the political parties within Northern Ireland. The phrase 'power-sharing' is now used less frequently, but 'participation and partnership' and 'cross-community consensus' embody a very similar principle, and it is clear that any future devolved system in the province will involve 'power-sharing' or a close equivalent. That this much is clear is reflected in, for example, the provisions of the Northern Ireland Act 1982 which reiterated the 'widespread acceptance throughout the community' criterion – the phrase which is also used in Article 4(b) of the Anglo-Irish Agreement which states the commitment of both British and Irish governments to a devolved system on that basis.

The likelihood of a new devolved system being established depends, first, upon whether the unionists will accept a 'partnership' devolved government and upon whether the nationalists – and the British and Irish governments – will settle for anything significantly different. It also depends upon the issue of the Irish dimension, strongly resisted by unionists and insisted upon as essential by the Social Democratic and Labour Party, the main constitutional nationalist party. The Irish dimension, however, has an East–West (London–Dublin) axis as well as a North–South axis, and it is in this respect that the most significant developments have taken place since the early 1970s. Inevitably intertwined with the issue of the Irish dimension is the issue of the status of Northern Ireland. The formal starting point on this for the British government is the 'constitutional guarantee' in the 1973 Constitution Act (as read with Article 1 of the Acts of Union of 1800, which proclaimed the union to last 'for ever'); that for the Irish government is Articles 2 and 3 of the 1937 Constitution. The Sunningdale Agreement of 1973 contained a parallel Article 5 on the issue. The Irish government 'fully accepted and solemnly declared' that there could be no change in the status of Northern Ireland without majority consent. This consent principle was also accepted by the British government which, for its part in Article 5, stated that 'the present status of Northern Ireland is that it is part of the United Kingdom'. It continued, however, to provide that 'if in the future the majority of the people of Northern Ireland should indicate a wish to become part of a united Ireland, the British Government would support that wish'. This is of significance in two respects. First, it is an accretion on the 'constitutional guarantee' in the 1973 Act which contains only a negative proposition; it does not state what necessarily should happen if a border poll were to express consent for change. That is, it seems to narrow Northern Ireland's 'options' to two – membership of the United Kingdom or of a united Ireland. Second, the British Article 5 indicates a willingness on the part of the Westminster government to cede a part of its national territory – hardly a common occurrence on the world stage. As it transpired, however, it was the Irish Article 5 which was challenged in the courts on the grounds that it conflicted with Articles 2 and 3 of the 1937 Constitution. In *Boland* v *An Taoiseach*[6] the Irish Supreme Court stressed that the phrase 'status of Northern Ireland', unspecified in the Irish Article 5, referred only to the *de facto* status of Northern Ireland: it did not, and could not lawfully, derogate from the Irish Constitution's claim to jurisdiction over the province.

By the late 1970s, prospects for devolution to Northern Ireland seemed remote. There was thus no framework on or from which to build a North–South Irish dimension. In 1981, therefore, the British and Irish Prime Ministers instituted the Anglo-Irish Intergovernmental Council, the remit of which was to facilitate at the institutional level contacts between the two governments on matters of common concern, including cross-border co-operation. This was followed in November 1985 by the Anglo-Irish Agreement, which established the Anglo-Irish Intergovernmental Conference which can meet at both ministerial level (the Secretary of State for Northern Ireland and the Irish Minister for Foreign Affairs) and official level. The main aims of the Agreement, and of the Conference specifically, are to provide equal recognition to and protection for both communities in Northern Ireland; to provide a means (the Conference) through which the Irish government could (particularly pending devolution) act as a 'guarantor' of the interests of the nationalist community in Northern Ireland; and to facilitate cross-border co-operation on security, economic and cultural matters.

The Irish dimension consequently now has three formal aspects – the East–West dimension (the Council, dealing with matters of common concern to the United Kingdom and the Republic), the North–South dimension (the Conference, dealing with matters of common concern north and south of the Irish border); and the internal Northern Ireland dimension (again, the Conference, to which the Irish government can put its views and proposals particularly on issues of concern to the minority community).

This must be placed against Article 1 of the Agreement, which deals with the status of Northern Ireland and contains a joint affirmation of the two governments that 'any change in the status of Northern Ireland would only come about with the consent of a majority of the people of Northern Ireland'. This article was supposed to act as a counter-weight to the strengthening of the Irish dimension in and with regard to Northern Ireland by providing a guarantee to the unionists that the status of Northern Ireland *within the United Kingdom* would remain as long as there was majority consent for this. Article 1, however, did not, because of the Irish Constitutional requirements, spell this out, both leaving the unionists to argue that Article 1 reflected a serious weakening of the United Kingdom government's approach to the status of Northern Ireland and leaving some nationalists to argue that Article 1 reflected the first recognition by a government of the Irish Republic of the 'legitimacy of partition'.

In *McGimpsey* v *Ireland*,[7] however – a case brought by two Northern unionists before, ultimately, the Irish Supreme Court – the Court ruled that Articles 2 and 3 of the Irish Constitution reflect a claim as a matter of legal (not merely political) right to the entire national territory, the whole of the island of Ireland, and that the reintegration of the national territory is a 'constitutional imperative'. Consequently, Article 1 of the 1985 Agreement could only lawfully be construed as constituting a recognition of the *de facto* situation in Northern Ireland, *without* involving an abandonment of the claim to the reintegration of the national territory. This judgment served only to intensify unionist anger against the Agreement.[8] On the nature and form and import of the Irish dimension, the 'what you see is what you get' factor is stronger than with regard to any other aspect of the Northern Ireland constitution.

The current position with regard to the Northern Ireland constitution is not a particularly satisfactory one, from whatever angle one looks. At the heart of direct rule there is undoubtedly a political vacuum: lack of accountability and lack of participation. Improvements could be made even in the absence of devolution – if there were the political will to do so.[9] There has also been too much uncertainty about some fundamental matters for too long – for example, is the Anglo-Irish Agreement a terminus or a staging post? If the latter, then along which route and to what destination are the two governments travelling? If the former (at least for as long as there is majority consent), has the Irish dimension reached its apex (or could there be yet further developments?), leaving the form of a devolved system of government the only issue to be resolved? Certainly these are issues which must be directly addressed in any talks about the future form of government for Northern Ireland. The chances of the government(s) and the representatives of the Northern Ireland political parties, however, ever finding a formula which maximizes the interests of both segments/sections of Northern Ireland are rendered much harder by the conflicting allegiances of the two internal segments, which means that forms of internal government become inextricably intertwined with questions of status.

Ireland is often called the 'land of saints and scholars'. This is, in many ways, still an accurate description, but often it seems that the Northern Ireland question has defeated them all.

Notes

1 For a fuller account, see B. Hadfield, *The Constitution of Northern Ireland*, SLS, Belfast, 1989.

2 Quoted in J. Whyte, *Interpreting Northern Ireland*, Clarendon Press, Oxford, 1990, pp. 118–19.

3 Quoted in C. O'Leary, S. Elliott and R. Wilford, *The Northern Ireland Assembly*

1982–1986, Hurst, London, 1988, p. 20. Cf. Article 44 of the Irish Constitution 1937 which says: 'The State recognises the special position of the Holy Catholic Apostolic and Roman Church as the guardian of the faith professed by the great majority of its citizens'. This provision was repealed in 1972.

4 Quoted in P. Buckland, *A History of Northern Ireland*, Gill and Macmillan, Dublin, 1981, pp. 133–4.

5 I have dealt more fully with particularly the legal aspects of direct rule in Hadfield, *The Constitution of Northern Ireland*, ch. 5 and Appendix V; and in B. Hadfield, 'Direct Rule, Delegated Legislation and the Role of Parliament' in J. Hayes and P. O'Higgins (eds), *Lessons from Northern Ireland*, SLS Publications, Belfast, 1990, pp. 9–30.

6 *Boland* v *An Taoiseach* [1974] IR 338.

7 *McGimpsey* v *Ireland* [1990] ILRM 441.

8 Mr Peter Brooke, the Secretary of State for Northern Ireland, in November 1990 stated that 'it is not the aspiration to a sovereign united Ireland against which we set our face, but its violent expression . . . The British government has no selfish, strategic or economic interest in Northern Ireland'. Quoted by Charles Haughey, the Taoiseach, at the Fianna Fáil Annual Conference, March 1991.

9 See, for example, Hadfield, *The Constitution of Northern Ireland*, ch. 8.

2

Why devolution?

Paul R. Maguire

The story of how devolution came to Northern Ireland in 1920 and how it operated during the period 1920–72 has been told many times.[1] It remains relevant and instructive. For our purposes, two essential points from it may be repeated here. First, devolution to Northern Ireland arose out of a historical fluke. Neither unionists nor nationalists in Ireland wanted it; on the contrary, they wanted to avoid it. Unionist concern was to resist 'home rule' for Ireland as a whole and particularly to prevent the province falling within the jurisdiction of a Dublin home-rule parliament. Nationalists wanted home rule for the island but for them any talk of the partition of Ireland and separate institutions in the North was anathema. Wanting to grant home rule to Ireland but being driven by unionist pressure to exclude the North-East of the island from it, the British government legislated for devolution to both North and South, each area with its separate institutions. As Buckland has said of the legislation: 'The Act was basically a device adopted by the British government and Parliament anxious to get rid of the Irish Question and yet obliged to redeem pledges to Ulster unionists'.[2] The proposed institutions only took root in Northern Ireland, Southern Ireland soon becoming a Dominion and later a Republic.

Second, the operation of devolution in Northern Ireland ended in failure. At the worst of times, the unionist majority in the province governed in its own interest and to the detriment of the minority. At the best of times, the devolved institutions lacked the political consensus across the historical community divide to sustain them. For over fifty years, allegations of discrimination and bias against, and repression of, the minority were widespread, and many of these allegations were justified. When a civil rights movement to redress minority grievances led on to inter-communal violence, this resulted in the deployment of the British Army, in aid of the civil power, in 1969. The slumbering national government was woken up. By 1972 London's need to control security in the province meant that it had to ask the government of

Northern Ireland to agree to powers in this sphere, which legally were vested in the devolved authority, being returned to the centre. When the devolved authority refused to accept this and resigned, the British government, exercising its undoubted legal right, prorogued the Parliament of Northern Ireland and ended devolution. Direct rule of Northern Ireland by Westminster began. Devolution for Northern Ireland at this point looked dead and buried, and few would have thought that after 1972 there would be any sustained interest in it. Expectations pointed away from devolution. Unionists would surely find nothing more acceptable than rule from Westminster? Similarly, one might have expected nationalists to prefer London to Belfast rule: surely the latter would be the last thing they would want? And to the British government, the responsible power internationally accountable for the calamitous situation in Northern Ireland, the idea of entrusting power again to provincial politicians cannot, it might have been thought, have had much appeal. Yet the focus of political debate about the future government of Northern Ireland since then has not substantially centred on forms of government from the centre. Instead, much of the time, it has been directed to the restoration of devolution. Time after time the body has been exhumed and attempts made to breathe life into it. Why? What are the arguments being deployed to support a return to devolution? In this chapter, after considering the demand for devolution, it is proposed to identify and consider these arguments. The purpose is not to pass judgement on the future viability of devolution; rather, it is to seek to explain why it is desired. Understanding the latter may, it is hoped, provide a foundation for conclusions concerning the former.

The demand for devolution since 1972

The stance of three main groups needs to be considered in the assessment of the demand for devolution: the British government; the Irish government; and the political parties in Northern Ireland.

As far as the first is concerned, it is clear that a policy of redevolving power to institutions in Northern Ireland has held sway. That this is so is evident from a series of papers published on the future government of Northern Ireland in 1972, 1973, 1974, 1979, 1980 and 1982.[3] Moreover, the Anglo-Irish Agreement signed in 1985 records the British government's support for devolution in Northern Ireland on a basis which would secure widespread acceptance throughout the community. At the time of writing (mid-1991), the Secretary of State has obtained the agreement of relevant other parties to the establishment of formal talks whose aim, *inter alia*, is to arrive at a situation in which devolved power could again be transferred to regional institutions.

As regards the Irish government, it is probably correct to say that its approach has varied from time to time. Three periods are worth distinguishing:

1972–9, 1979–85, and 1985 to the present time. In the first of these, Irish governments of all political shades supported a policy which had two limbs to it: first, the establishment of a partnership or power-sharing devolved system in Northern Ireland in which the traditional minority would have a full part to play; and second, the creation of an appropriate institutional recognition of what at that time was referred to as 'the Irish dimension'. Consequent to this broad policy, both Irish government and opposition were in support of the power-sharing and Sunningdale package put together in 1973, with devolved power actually being transferred at the beginning of 1974. When the package came apart in mid-1974, Irish government policy was directed to re-establishing a similar arrangement and this remained the case until the election of Charles Haughey as Fianna Fáil leader and Taoiseach in 1979. From then until 1985 interest in Northern devolution waned. The emphasis was placed instead on Anglo-Irish intergovernmental structures, a process begun by Haughey and continued by Garret FitzGerald when he was Taoiseach. While this approach faltered because of the Falklands war, and while for a period the field was occupied by the New Ireland Forum which had nothing to say about the idea of devolution to Northern Ireland – its conclusions supporting a series of more or less nationalist options – by 1985 the intergovernmental strategy was back on course, leading in November to the signing of the Anglo-Irish Agreement. Though initially rejected by Fianna Fáil, which were then in opposition, the Agreement has represented Irish Government policy since, despite the return of Fianna Fáil to power in 1987. In its terms, the Agreement commits the Irish government to support devolution for Northern Ireland, albeit devolution within the context established by the Agreement itself. The strength of that commitment, however, is open to debate. At the time of writing, a gap is proposed in the meetings of the Anglo-Irish Intergovernmental Conference to enable talks between relevant parties to proceed with the aim mentioned earlier.

The attitudes of the political parties in Northern Ireland can broadly be seen by reference to manifestos or position papers at times of inter-party negotiation or discussion, that is, in 1972–3, 1975–6, 1980, and 1982–6. Inevitably there have, over time, been some changes in the composition of the 'constitutional' political spectrum[4] but, notwithstanding these, it is possible to distinguish four main groups: the Democratic Unionists (DUP); the Official Unionists (OUP); the Alliance Party; and the Social Democratic and Labour Party (SDLP).

The position of the DUP after the breakdown of devolved government in 1972 was that 'Northern Ireland should cease to have any separate legislature or executive of its own, but be fully integrated with the rest of the United Kingdom'. But by 1975 this position had altered. Since then, either as part of a unionist coalition or in its own right, the DUP has consistently and vigorously argued for devolution.

In contrast, while the OUP strongly supported redevolution in 1972 and, as part of a unionist coalition, in 1975, after this it became ambivalent, some of the leading spokesmen adhering to a policy of devolution, some advocating only a very weak form of devolution, and others, led by Enoch Powell, calling for integration. Since 1986 OUP support for devolution has been intermittent, though an OUP representative, Jack Allen, appears to have been in favour of it at the Duisburg talks, an informal gathering of representatives from Northern Ireland's political parties held in Germany in 1989, and, more recently, the party has indicated its willingness to participate in the Secretary of State's proposed discussions, referred to earlier.

The Alliance Party has consistently adhered to a policy of redevolution, as is clear from its submissions to the Darlington Conference held in September 1972 (which three out of seven local parties invited by the Secretary of State attended), its participation in the power-sharing executive in 1974, its manifesto for the Convention election in 1975, its participation in the Convention in 1975–6, its submission to the Atkins inter-party talks in 1980, and its involvement in the 1982–6 Assembly. After 1986 it also published its proposals for the future, which centred on devolution.

Finally, the SDLP position has progressed on lines not dissimilar to those along which the Irish government's thinking has progressed. While the language used in 1972 was that of the creation of an interim system of government for Northern Ireland in which there would be an Assembly and Executive drawn from it, under the joint responsibility of the British and Irish governments, the party was actively involved in the power-sharing Executive in 1974 and was a supporter of the Sunningdale package. In 1975 its manifesto for the Convention election proposed the establishment of 'a powerful and representative Northern Ireland Assembly' and an administration in which both sections of the community could participate to the full. It also sought recognition of both Irish and British dimensions. After initial hesitation, the party did take part in the Atkins conference, but only on condition that there be discussions with the Secretary of State to deal with arrangements for an Irish dimension to any agreed partnership form of devolution. In 1982 the SDLP decided to contest the election to the proposed Assembly but not to take any seats, if elected. This was because it considered unworkable the rolling devolution proposal legislated for in the Northern Ireland Act 1982, and, in any event, as far as the party was concerned the plan lacked a sufficient Irish dimension. Instead of going to the Assembly the SDLP became involved in the proceedings of the New Ireland Forum, which sat for the first time on 30 May 1983 and reported on 2 May 1984. As would be expected, the SDLP supported the Anglo-Irish Agreement. Since 1985 there has been interest in the SDLP in devolution within the framework of the Agreement or a suitable Anglo-Irish agreement to supersede it. The SDLP has agreed to enter the formal inter-party talks noted earlier.

Overall, it may be concluded that the concept of devolution has played a significant part in the thinking of all the groups concerned at some time, if not throughout the period under review. What, of course, has been lacking has been agreement both on the ways in which minority rights are to be safeguarded in the internal operation of devolution and on the relationships between the devolved institutions and the two governments involved.

The arguments for devolution

In discussing the arguments addressed in favour of devolution, reliance has been placed mainly, but not exclusively, on the stances adopted by the relevant parties: not exclusively, because it is necessary at times to seek to interpret party postures. This is so because very often what parties state is the form of devolution they desire, and only in passing do they state their reasons for preferring a devolutionary model in the first place. Why this is so is itself interesting. The assumption must be that either the parties themselves have not addressed, head-on at any rate, the question why there should be devolution, or they regard candour in this respect, for reasons perhaps related to negotiation, as unnecessary or even counter-productive. Whatever the reason, the result is that in what follows lines of argument may be exposed which are implicit rather than explicit in their thinking.

For the purpose of exposition, it is proposed to look at the arguments for devolution in two categories: those in which all concur and which (to some degree) are incorporated into the parties' thinking, and those which do not share this characteristic, that is those arguments which appeal only to a limited selection of the interested parties. Of course, the differing strands of argument will at times overlap but, it is hoped, not to a degree which negates the value of isolating one from the other for the purpose of analysis.

Common arguments

Accountability
One of the major arguments used by all who support devolution is that government in Northern Ireland today under direct rule is unaccountable and that devolution would restore accountable government to the province. There are two central strands in this argument.

The first relates to a distortion in the structural shape and responsibilities of government produced as a consequence of direct rule. Until shortly before its introduction, three differing levels of administration could be identified in the province (the central, the regional and the local level), and each had its own political institutions (Westminster, Stormont[5] and elected local authorities). Ironically, one of the last actions of the Stormont regional legislature had been to reform local government institutions following upon the recommendations of the Macrory Report.[6] In essence, many former local government functions were, for accountability and decision-making purposes, transferred to the regional level (in some areas via the agency of Area Boards), leaving behind a local level of administration, in the form of district councils, which had few powers. Consequently, with the political (though not legal)[7] demise of regional government, not only was this level lost to the system but the local level which remained was a shadow of what local government had been. The direct rule administration became, at a stroke, responsible for all that occurred in government in the province beyond the tiny responsibilities of district councils and was only held accountable for all these powers at Westminster.

Secondly, if this accountability problem is not bad enough, it is clear that it is made worse by virtue of the procedural operation of direct rule at Westminster, as described in Chapter 1. The arrangements are such that 'no-one would dream of inventing [them] as a long term way of governing any sizeable community'.[8]

More responsive government

All parties which seek devolution, to a greater or lesser extent, promote the argument that the existence of local devolved institutions would create government which would be more responsive to the needs of the province than that provided by Westminster. The notion of 'more responsiveness' is multi-faceted. In principle, decision-making should become speedier; decisions should be based on greater understanding and appreciation of local needs; priorities can be more closely modelled upon local requirements; non-conformity with national norms can be facilitated; and the decision-making process itself can present multiple opportunities for local participation.[9] As a result the decision produced, it is argued, will be a better one than would be produced otherwise. This conclusion, however, is open to argument. Much will depend on the extent of the list of subjects transferred. It is plain that some decisions are more appropriately taken at the centre. This may be because the matter at issue is national rather than regional in character, or it may be that the centre is better placed, by dint of expertise, skill or resources, to prescribe a cure for a regional ill. As Calvert has argued: 'It by no means follows that institutions controlled by the group affected and obviously concerned with the group's interests will be best placed to secure them effectively'.[10] Much will also depend, especially in a divided society, on whether power is exercised fairly. One of the major criticisms aimed at the practice of devolution in Northern Ireland for fifty years was that decision-making lacked objectivity and was tainted by discriminatory motivations. Finally, much will depend on the capacity of the devolved institutions, even where dealing with a transferred matter, to deliver in response to the need which has been recognized. In non-financial areas, assuming legislative devolution, the ability to reflect local rather than national values is likely to be substantial though not absolute, but in areas which require public expenditure, the ability to deliver is likely to be heavily circumscribed. A devolved administration can only be responsive in proportion to its financial capacity.

Should there be a restoration of devolution, it seems clear that there will be little room for manoeuvre in relation to finance. In fact, it is difficult to envisage anything other than an expenditure-based system[11] of financial allocation being employed, with the consequence that ultimately the national government will be engaged in a continuing process of monitoring and assessing needs and services in the province against a backdrop of parity or equality of treatment with Great Britain. The problem is that, if carried to extremes, this approach would smother local freedom to act independently. Of course, a case can be made for giving the devolved authorities power to levy additional funds from local sources, but the product of local fund-raising would have to be on top of and not at the expense of the revenue allocated as a result of the expenditure-based system. Otherwise, the region's population would be shouldering an additional burden in order to relieve the national exchequer from having to transfer funds earmarked on the basis of need for Northern Ireland.[12] In any case, the product of resort to local 'top-up taxation', in the absence of any new substantial revenue-creating source, is likely to be small. Another approach would be to distinguish actual from potential parity. The latter has been described as the situation in which 'the provincial government is placed in a position financially where it can if it so desires provide services to national standards but it is free to choose to do otherwise'.[13] The revenue allocated to the region continues to be based on an assessment of need, but how the money is in fact spent between competing local services is at the direction of the regional institutions. While technically complex, this proposal produces valuable local discretion but within the sphere of public welfare services — for example, the health service and cash social services — public opinion may not easily accept any diminution in national standards.

The regeneration of the political process

The argument which is commonly advanced by all devolution supporters is based on the premise that without devolution political life in Northern Ireland functions in a vacuum. Several factors have predisposed the parties concerned to accept this premise. First of all, attitudes have been conditioned by the existence of devolution in the province for so long. But second, and of more importance, local political parties are products of and largely shaped by the constitutional debates of a century ago. Most of the parties are peculiar to Northern Ireland. They have only limited interest and appetite for national politics. Their appeal and concern is predominantly local and inward. Consequently, the political stage which appeals most to them is the provincial one. Third, while direct rule continues, in addition to the problems of accountability, the fact is that the rewards of political life in Northern Ireland are meagre. There are no glittering prizes to be had in the powerless fora of local government, the district councils. The relatively small number of professional politicians elected to Westminster for Northern Ireland constituencies find they have little of a decision-making role and little prospect of one. This breeds frustration at best and hopelessness at worst. The overall effect of these factors, the argument holds, is to eat away at the vitality of the political life of the province. The able stay out of politics. The public become scornful of politicians and the political process. Political parties find it increasingly difficult to survive. This would be of concern in any society, but it is of special importance in Northern Ireland, where there is an evident struggle in progress between the ballot box and the bullet. With terrorists of all hues conveniently placed and eager to fill it, Northern Ireland, it is concluded, cannot afford a political vacuum.

The remedy, therefore, must be a proposal which regenerates the political process: a strong and vibrant form of devolution. Suggestions which undershoot this goal, such as local government reform, would not be sufficient to meet the mischief because they would only partially fill the vacuum or would be inadequate as a counter-weight to the potential dominance otherwise of subversive forces.

While Northern Ireland's political parties have perhaps been cautious not to press this argument too strongly, for fear of accusations that what they are after are 'jobs for the boys', it is notable that the Secretary of State for Northern Ireland on 5 July 1990 called attention to it. Addressing the House of Commons, he said:

> Without a regional political forum, elected representatives in Northern Ireland are left with little opportunity to influence the decisions of the government or to exercise powers that are available to politicians elsewhere in the United Kingdom or the Republic of Ireland ... The present weakness of local political involvement in the government of Northern Ireland is not a satisfactory long term arrangement, and it causes a local power vacuum which terrorists and their supporters attempt to exploit to their advantage.[14]

Particular arguments

Securing the Union

Central to the thinking of many unionists who would like to see devolution restored is the view that the existence of local devolved institutions, ultimately controlled by unionists, is the best means of politically securing the Union. Much of the force of this conviction derives from experience with the operation of the Stormont system. Though devolution was reluctantly agreed to, once the government and Parliament of Northern Ireland were up and running with trappings of power, inviting comparison with Dominions, unionists soon appreciated that the new 'constitution' of the 1920 Act strengthened their hand both against the British and the Irish administrations. Their own administration, based on electoral dominance within Northern Ireland, had henceforth to be reckoned with, a bleak prospect as viewed from Dublin. And politically it was difficult for London, having just established the devolved institutions, to ignore them. In fact, after early skirmishing between Belfast and London in 1922 over the proposed abolition of proportional representation in local government elections, resulting in a London climbdown, the national government effectively (financial matters apart) adopted a policy of non-interference in matters within Stormont's delegated authority, a policy which survived until 1968. During this period unïonists felt that the existence of their own Parliament offered the best available bulwark against the 'sellout' over their heads of Northern Ireland by London to Dublin, the scenario which was their greatest fear. In fact in 1949, as mentioned in Chapter 1, the Ireland Act formalized in statute what already most unionists regarded as the reality when it stated 'that in no event will Northern Ireland or any part thereof cease to be part of Her Majesty's Dominions and of the United Kingdom without the consent of the Parliament of Northern Ireland'. In these circumstances Lawrence, as late as 1965, felt able to remark that 'constitutional security was rooted in the soil of devolution',[15] and for many unionists this remains the case today. But this argument is surely weaker than it was. The affirmation of 1949 has been repealed and replaced by one which involves no reference to a veto on change in Northern Ireland's status resting with a local legislature; instead the veto is given to the people of Northern Ireland speaking by a majority in a border poll – 'the constitutional guarantee'. It is unlikely that in the future any United Kingdom government would be prepared, in the context of devolution to the province, to operate a non-interference policy again. After the breakdown of devolved government in a context in which allegations of abuse of governmental power were widespread, and after twenty years of continuing violence, which has provoked international as well as national interest, central government would surely feel bound to superintend the working of any devolved institutions established. Such institutions, moreover, are likely to be clearly identifiable as subordinate ones. The outward appearances of a national legislature, very largely enjoyed by the Parliament of Northern Ireland, increased its political credibility, but if the Assemblies since 1972 are any guide, national policy has been to scale down appearances, with the result that the emphasis falls more on the regional, than the national, role. No one argues that the existence of local authorities helps to secure the Union and a form of devolved government which resembles an upper-tier local authority would, for this purpose, offer little more. Clearly, those unionists who favour this argument for devolution have an interest in a form for it which is strong not just in terms of powers but also in terms of appearances.

Interestingly, the episode of the making of and opposition to the Anglo-Irish Agreement, so intensely disliked by unionists, is one which on reflection cuts both ways in the context of its impact on this argument. Devolutionists can point to the dangers of putting faith in the national Parliament when it so overwhelmingly approved the Agreement, while integrationists can point to the fact that while the Agreement was under construction and then under debate, a unionist-controlled elected Assembly, albeit with no power other than the power to debate, was in being and could not stop it. However, it is perhaps of note that the Assembly until dissolution became the engine of unionist opposition to the Agreement after it was signed, and even those unionists most associated with the integration option deserted Westminster in favour of the Assembly during this period.

Maintaining the balance of the 1920s

A particular argument in support of devolution which appeals chiefly to the UK government, but not exclusively to it, is that devolution to Northern Ireland was a crucial element in the settlement offered in the 1920s and that there is simply no, or little, scope to do other than seek to restore it. Any attempt to do otherwise, this argument holds, would involve the taking of unjustifiable risks of opening up old wounds or inflicting new ones, so that even when an immediate restoration of devolved administration is unavailable, the situation must be kept in neutral by the operation of direct rule, a procedure which maintains the form but not the substance of devolution.[16]

The strength of this argument depends somewhat on the extent to which it is true to regard the grant of devolution to Belfast as a crucial element in the settlement of the 1920s. After all, at least in terms of the 1920 Government of Ireland Act, the scheme legislated for was stillborn in other respects, with both the proposed devolved institutions in Southern Ireland and the Council of Ireland never operating. But what seems clear is that at this juncture the United Kingdom government had a very limited range of options open to it. It could seek to coerce unionists and proceed with home rule for Ireland as a whole; it could confine home rule to what became the Republic of Ireland and continue to govern the North from Westminster; or it could provide devolution to both North and South. When the last option was chosen and became impracticable because of the separatist tendencies of the South, the structures of devolved government in Northern Ireland were maintained rather than providing government as before from Westminster. The advantages of doing so were several. The decision to exclude Northern Ireland from the Dominion status later agreed for the rest of Ireland was taken not by the British but by Ulstermen in the Parliament of Northern Ireland.[17] Hence the resolution of the 'Irish Question' could be viewed (from Britain anyway) as a matter for Irishmen, North and South. The domestic affairs of Ireland were removed from Westminster and this was of importance, not only because it helped to decongest Parliament but also because it symbolized British disengagement from Irish affairs. If Northern Ireland were to have been governed from Westminster, with the South having its own separate relationship, Britain could not have thought of the Irish Question as being settled and would have been clearly seen to have a continuing presence in Ireland. This it did not want, so that the existence of devolution to Northern Ireland was of considerable importance. While that experiment in devolution broke down, the relationships forged in the 1920s have altered little over time. Sentiments in both parts of Ireland have remained constant, and British desire to avoid retrenchment in Irish affairs is arguably a continuing underlying theme of national policy. This explains the reluctance of successive Northern Ireland Secretaries of State to embrace the integrationist position and the constant return to initiatives to discover ways forward to devolution. Similarly, the reassurances to unionists of Northern Ireland's status as part of the United Kingdom may be seen in this light. The overriding fear is that unravelling the settlement of the 1920s would be likely to reproduce the pressures of that time without measurably increasing the room for manoeuvre.

Of course, even if it is accepted that in the 1920s Britain wanted to keep the affairs of Northern Ireland at arm's length, circumstances have changed. After twenty-two years during which the United Kingdom government has been intimately concerned with governing Northern Ireland, is it realistic now to think of Britain not having a continued presence in Ireland or, in view of happenings in Northern Ireland during this period, of the Irish Question as having been settled? And, whether Britain likes it, is it not now clear that, for all practical purposes, it is fixed with continued responsibility for Northern Ireland? These questions suggest that the arguments for maintaining the basic lines of settlement agreed in the 1920s may be overstated but, even if this is so, this does not necessarily mean that other realistic options are available, although it does suggest that, if devolution is again possible, Britain will not be as distant from it as it was in the past. An important subtheme of the argument for maintaining the balance devised in the 1920s is that through devolution a measure of political reconciliation may be achieved in the province, given at least a form of devolution which commands wide cross-community support. As non-devolution proposals tend to be regarded as leading to a political victory of one side over the other (integration equals unionist victory over nationalists; any all-Ireland proposals being the opposite), and structurally offer meagre prospect of the growth of trust and confidence between local parties, it is easy to see the appeal of this view which is endorsed by the United Kingdom government and would be accepted by some nationalists and unionists alike. However, while in the short term co-operative devolution, if put into practical operation, might achieve greater acceptance than other competing proposals, questions are always bound to arise about the direction in which such a system would lead in the long term. For this reason many unionists and nationalists, who do not wish to get on a vehicle unless they can see in advance it is going to the destination they seek, are suspicious of proposals on these lines.

Devolution as part of a new settlement
Many nationalists support this argument. They realize that immediate

movement towards an all-Ireland solution to the problem of Northern Ireland is unobtainable so instead they argue for a new settlement, which includes devolved government for Northern Ireland while it remains in the United Kingdom, but which leans towards, or is orientated in the direction of, an eventual unification of the island. As a means of promoting that goal, devolution will have a role to play at several levels. First, devolved institutions in Northern Ireland would emphasize and accentuate the province's separateness from Britain. To that extent, they should be encouraged. Second, provided nationalists in the North have a significant role to play in them, devolved institutions should be valuable both in the short term and strategically: in the short term, they provide a constructive role in looking after the needs of the nationalist community; and strategically, nationalist involvement in the processes of devolution may force unionists to come to terms with them. At its height this might mean that unionists might consider the merits in the course of time of a broader constitutional accommodation with nationalists within a united Ireland. At a lower level, the operation of devolution would probably involve unionists being in greater contact with Dublin in the context of cross-border co-operation. Third, the superintendence of the devolved structures should provide a role for the Irish government within a framework similar to that established by the Anglo-Irish Agreement. Both governments together would supervise and scrutinize the activities of the devolved government and perhaps create an atmosphere in which unionists would become more open to overtures from the South. Certainly, to nationalists, devolution without intergovernmental support and input would be hazardous, as the degree of control exercised by unionists over any institutions established is likely to be substantial and such institutions would, therefore, heighten unionist potency.

A share of the power

Many unionists want devolution for the simple reason that it would put a slice of political power into their hands, as the local majority: it would make them masters of their own house for practical domestic purposes. Looked at from this perspective, the alternatives to devolution are not inviting. Both integration and direct rule repose power at Westminster and there unionists (indeed Northern Ireland's MPs as a whole) are but a small minority, unlikely to be involved in government. The mentality behind this argument can be observed from the words of the late Harold McCusker MP:[18] 'At the moment . . . we're invited up to Stormont like serfs to talk with their master . . . We're knocking at the door, going in as beggars'. Hence, a reason for devolution is 'to get out of the position of always going cap in hand looking for something'. In light of the financial relationship mentioned earlier, it might be thought that, even with devolution, going to the national government in a subservient posture might not be entirely a thing of the past, but at least under this argument Northern Ireland would be administered by politicians whose electoral mandate is locally produced.

Conclusion

What emerges from examining the arguments put forward for devolution in Northern Ireland is that while there is broad agreement on the need for government to be locally accountable and responsive, and for elected regional institutions to regenerate the political process in the province, beyond this the different parties involved have different motivations which cause them to favour devolution. And it seems clear that it will often prove to be the case that the reason why one party wants devolution is the direct opposite of the reason why another seeks it. Some unionists may see in it the chance for greater constitutional security within the United Kingdom, while some nationalists may regard it as a preliminary or staging post along the road to national unification. Others still may see in it the best chance of promoting political reconciliation or as the only practical option, save for direct rule. The motivation involved, it also seems clear, will have an important impact on the type of devolution proposal advanced. Constitutional security is linked to the notion of strong devolution *à la* Stormont. 'New settlement' devolution conjures up a picture of active intergovernmental supervision. And the reconciler's form of devolution will be bound to power-sharing or stiff acceptability hurdles within the operation of the system in order to provide protection and participation for minorities.

In discussion about devolution for Northern Ireland, therefore, it appears unlikely that any agreement would emerge among the relevant groupings precisely as to the purposes served or desires to be met in providing devolution. Party realization of this may, indeed, be the reason why arguments about the 'why' question are often understated, if stated at all, in political literature. To seek such agreement may, therefore, be a mistake. However, this does not mean that aspirations and motivations should be swept under the carpet. They do have an important effect both on perceptions and positions and require to be understood. What may be desirable is a willingness on the part of the relevant actors to agree not to make devolution conditional on general acceptance of any particular view of the purposes it can serve. Rather there is a need to see it as a model capable of accommodating diverse ambitions, or one better capable of doing so than the available alternatives.

That devolution as a form of government may have the capacity to cope with such diversity is a matter which has stimulated some controversy. Writing in 1936, Nicholas Mansergh stated, in the context of government in Northern Ireland, 'that no scheme of devolution is likely to satisfy a demand for self government prompted by national sentiment'.[19] If by this he meant that a region dominated by a separatist ambition will never accept devolution as the continuing form of government, then he is probably right. The case of the proposed devolution to institutions in Southern Ireland in 1920 is one in point. But in Northern Ireland the nationalist point of view is a minority one. While some nationalists may see devolution only as a stage in a process which leads to their goal, this should not be seen as a factor which ought necessarily to preclude the adoption of a devolution model, if indeed the majority of those who seek it have their own non-nationalist (even unionist) reasons for doing so. Thus Mansergh is probably being unduly pessimistic when he goes on to say that the value of devolution 'disappears once the unity of the State is questioned'.[20] If this were so, it would suggest that devolution is inappropriate for any region where any sizeable grouping questions the unity of the State. On this basis, there should be no devolution for Wales, Scotland or Northern Ireland and the concept is relegated to being valuable only for the purpose of securing better government within a state in which no nationalist ambitions have to be accommodated. This is surely to define its value too narrowly. Against the background of the unitary state, devolution offers scope for political pluralism, a spreading of power within the state, which, in the case of Northern Ireland, in view of the facts of historical difference and geographical separation, may be of particular worth. Likewise, the process of constructing devolved institutions and of prescribing how they are to work presents opportunities for architectural imagination, negotiation and compromise which are themselves valuable. The future occupants of the devolved institutions under construction have their points of agreement as well as their points of difference, and appreciating what these are may enable a degree of comfort to be provided which may not easily be found in the context of proposals other than devolution. Not too heavy an emphasis should be placed on the points of difference. After all, those between 'bulwark unionists' and 'new settlement nationalists' may be viewed as focusing more on how each wishes to see devolution regarded and the direction in which each may wish to see it develop, than on the actual substance of the institutions as initially devised, although the two may not be wholly unrelated. Against this, there is perhaps not sufficient emphasis placed on the points of agreement which, it may be argued, provide enough in common to cement the elements of a proposal together. There does appear to be evidence of a desire for a form of devolution which gives a real measure of power and responsibility to the devolved institutions. And, notwithstanding the problems of finance discussed earlier, the need to offer scope for local initiative, if the aims of responsiveness and regeneration are to be realized, is unlikely to be a matter of contention. Equally, the goal of obtaining a more accountable system of government than is presently available is widely shared. It is these last factors which have prevented the idea of devolution for Northern Ireland resting in peace. Until the arguments for devolution discussed in this chapter no longer have application, or relevance, it would be unwise to disregard the role devolution may yet play in relation to the future government of Northern Ireland.

Notes

1 For the most recent discussion of it, see B. Hadfield, *The Constitution of Northern Ireland*, SLS, Belfast, 1989, in particular chs 1–3.

2 P. Buckland, *Ulster Unionism and the Origins of Northern Ireland 1886–1922*, Gill and Macmillan, Dublin, 1973, p. 125.

3 See Northern Ireland Office (NIO), *The Future of Northern Ireland. A Paper for Discussion*, HMSO, London, 1972; *Northern Ireland Constitutional Proposals* (Cmnd. 5259), HMSO, London, 1973; *Northern Ireland Constitution* (Cmnd. 5675), HMSO, London, 1974; NIO, *The Government of Northern Ireland: A Working Paper for a Conference* (Cmnd. 7763), HMSO, London, 1979; NIO, *The Government of Northern Ireland: Proposals for Further Discussion* (Cmnd. 7950), HMSO, London, 1980; and NIO, *Northern Ireland: A Framework for Devolution* (Cmnd. 8541), HMSO, London, 1982.

4 These changes occurred mainly in the period 1972–80; a useful account of political developments in this period is C. O'Leary, S. Elliott, and R. Wilford, *The Northern Ireland Assembly 1982–86*, Hurst, London, 1988, ch. 3. See also Chapter 6, below.

5 The government and Parliament of Northern Ireland were, from 1932 onwards, housed at Parliament Buildings, Stormont, Belfast.

6 P. Macrory, *The Review Body on Local Government in Northern Ireland* (Cmd. 546), HMSO, Belfast, 1970.

7 The Northern Ireland (Temporary Provisions) Act 1972, which ushered in 'direct rule', retained the legal forms of devolution but effectively suspended its operation.

8 Mr Brooke, Secretary of State for Northern Ireland, *HC Debs*, vol. 175 (1989–90), col. 1141.

9 Accessibility, however, can also have disadvantages. Speaking of the operation of the Government of Ireland Act 1920, Buckland remarks 'Governments and politicians rarely led, but were at the mercy of so many pressures that calm political discussion and detached and efficient government became virtually impossible' (P. Buckland, *A History of Northern Ireland*, Gill and Macmillan, Dublin, 1981, p. 26).

10 H. Calvert (ed.), *Devolution*, Professional Books, London, 1975, p. 16.

11 An expenditure-based system is one in which expenditure requirements are measured first and the subordinate government is furnished with the income necessary to meet them.

12 For a discussion of some of the possibilities, see 'Principles and Problems of Devolved Public Finance' in *Fourth Report of the Devolution Report Committee*, HMSO, Belfast (13 March 1986) NIA 242, Appendix Paper II.

13 Ibid., p. 31.

14 Peter Brooke, *HC Debs*, vol. 175 (1989–90), col. 1144.

15 R. J. Lawrence, *The Government of Northern Ireland: Public Finance and Public Services 1921–64*, Clarendon Press, Oxford, 1965, p. 76.

16 As to how the legal forms of devolution are maintained, see Hadfield, *The Constitution of Northern Ireland*, ch. 5.

17 The Anglo-Irish Treaty of 1921 gave Dominion status to Ireland as a whole but enabled Northern Ireland to vote herself out of the Irish Free State within one month of the Treaty's ratification. Both Houses of the Parliament of Northern Ireland unanimously took this course on 7 December 1922.

18 Quoted in P. O'Malley, *The Uncivil Wars*, Blackstaff Press, Belfast, 1983, pp. 154–5.
19 N. Mansergh, *The Government of Northern Ireland*, George Allen & Unwin, London, 1936, p. 16.
20 Ibid.

3

Inverting consociationalism?
Policy, pluralism and the
post-modern

R. A. Wilford

The challenge of governing segmented societies is one of the less tractable issues confronting policy-makers and theorists alike. Students of the enduring conflict in Northern Ireland will be familiar with the litany of options that have been orchestrated to promote durable political structures for the region. To recite them is to rehearse a chorus of more or less grand designs each of which has attracted some support, yet none has proved capable of producing cross-community harmony. Full integration with Britain, unification of the island of Ireland, joint sovereignty, independence, repartition, a federal Ireland or, more imaginative yet, a federation of the British Isles (the 'Iona' variation), all have been mooted as the way out of the impasse.

This is not the place to reconstruct and evaluate each of these alternatives, nor to essay in detail the Anglo-Irish Agreement (AIA) and the process of bilateral discussions it has formalized. Rather than explore the high ground of constitutional policy-making itself, this chapter is intended to survey a less elevated terrain which, however, after the manner of politics in Northern Ireland, is inevitably joined to the wider matter of the province's constitutional status.

A permanent feature of British policy since the introduction of direct rule has been the restoration of power-sharing or, more precisely, a consociation. The more variable feature has been the so-called 'Irish dimension', now insti-tutionalized via the AIA's Intergovernmental Conference and its supporting Secretariat. However, the AIA is essentially a process of dialogue and consultation. To that extent it defines a challenging mission for its proponents since it is open to a variety of conflicting and largely hostile interpretations. Is it concerned with conflict management or conflict resolution? Does it signify a long-term intention on the part of the British to withdraw, or does it represent a continuation of the British guarantee by other means? Does it mean that the Irish government effectively only aspires to unification, or should the refusal to amend the *de jure* claim to all of the island be interpreted as conclusive evidence of undiminished irredentism? It is the existence of such conflicting perceptions that compounds the uncertainty about Northern Ireland's future.

Though dogmatists claim to see only too clearly what the AIA represents – either a giant step along the Dublin road or the maintenance of the British presence – others perceive a more conventional purpose: the restoration to Northern Ireland of a consociation, albeit engineered by unsubtle means.[1] Until recently such confusion seemed to provide an alibi for inaction, yet the AIA has succeeded in concentrating minds wonderfully. The tortuous route to the discussions embarked upon by Peter Brooke in January 1990 seems to have been deftly traversed, such that, at the time of writing, devolution is once again emerging onto the agenda.

Though this prospect is disarming (!), it is also possible to discern a course towards a future which, while imperfect, may yet produce stability. Moreover, it seems to be a path which has neither a predetermined constitutional end nor one which is contingent upon the success of any talks concerning the restoration of some form of local Assembly. It appears to have been constructed so as to encourage the recognition among its inhabitants that Northern Ireland is possessed of a plurality of cultural identities rather than a mere duality of conforming stereotypes. To that extent it casts formal policy-makers as exponents of inclusive, post-modernist attitudes, not just the arbiters of mutually exclusive modernist prejudices.

The consociational fix

Since the introduction of direct rule, six British governments, four Conservative and two Labour, have struggled with the seemingly bewildering nature of Northern Ireland. Each of the constitutional initiatives that has been tried, from the power-sharing Executive of 1974 to the Anglo-Irish Agreement of 1985, has been influenced by two precepts: power-sharing and the accommodation of the 'Irish dimension'. While the latter has had a fluctuating significance, the former has been a consistently reiterated theme of British policy. In effect, it has been interpreted as meaning the restoration to Northern Ireland of a devolved (and singular) form of coalition government, a consociation.

The model of consociational democracy was the work of the Dutch political scientist, Arend Lijphart.[2] It was specifically elaborated as a means of governing segmented societies and as such has provided the intellectual underpinning of institution-building in and for the region. The other element, the involvement of the Irish Republic, has, since 1985, enjoyed a renaissance reminiscent of the heady days of the 1974 experiment's flirtation with the Council of Ireland. But the AIA, besides affirming a joint commitment to the restoration of a devolved power-sharing institution, also implies something of a new approach to the problems besetting Northern Ireland: one that may yet turn the *idée fixe* of consociationalism on its head.

Lijphart's motive in designing the consociational model was to explore how deeply divided societies, ill suited to the imperatives of majoritarian democracy, could be governed in a manner that promoted political, economic and social stability. The key to his alternative conception was the forging of elite accommodation within the context of mutually alienated and recriminatory communities.

Lijphart identified four institutional characteristics of a consociation, the presence of which would permit effective (if constrained) democratic government to take place. The first was a power-sharing coalition comprising parties that enjoy more than simple majority support and which, at elite level, thereby transcends communal divisions.

The second was the provision for segmental autonomy. Lijphart subscribes to the idea that high fences promote neighbourly relations. By enabling each segment to enjoy autonomy over matters of central concern to its identity, whether religious, national, ethnic, ideological or linguistic, potentially eruptive issues are 'walled in' to largely self-governing communities. Such cultural segregation facilitates the integrity and the stability of the wider political system.

The third institutional feature relates to the representativeness of the public realm. Lijphart proposed that the principle of proportionality must apply in the public sector. To that end he advocated proportional representation in elections, in executive and legislative committees, in public employment and the proportional allocation of public spending. The implementation of this principle was intended to ensure that no one community enjoyed any perceived unfair material advantage over another (or others), thus avoiding a possible cause of grievance, conflict and potential instability.

The final element in the equation concerns the decision-making process and structures at the highest level. Consistent with the stress on accommodation and conciliation that underpins the model, Lijphart rejected simple majoritarianism in favour of a mutual veto or concurring majority principle, thereby ensuring that the minority community (communities) could protect its (their) most deeply felt interests.

Whether one regards this model as painfully contrived or a sane and pragmatic recipe for durable and stable mechanisms of governance, it conveys a rather bleak view of humanity. The jealous regard for identity afforded by high fences, proportionality, and the exercise of a mutual veto betoken an endemic distrust between relevant peoples. This is most apparent in relation to segmental autonomy, which signifies a hands-off approach to intra-communal affairs. More, rather than the promotion of social contact between or among communities, it argues the virtues of segregation, in the process threatening to cast them in marble. Its saving grace is the opportunity which consociational democracy affords for effective government to proceed through the internalization of the politics of accommodation at the elite level. Representative elites function as the guarantors of national or ethnic identity, while their respective communities go about the business of consolidating those identities in parallel milieux.

Where there are multiple sources of identity, that is to say, a genuine plurality of segments, the prospects for wider social and political stability may, paradoxically, be enhanced. Consider the other situation, which is commonly understood to characterize Northern Ireland: a society within which there are two segments, a large majority and a significant minority, divided by mutually reinforcing and exclusive national and religious affiliations. In such a bifurcated society, where difference is equated with division, any 'gain' by one community, whether material or symbolic, is experienced as a significant and threatening 'loss' by the other. Further, that the minority community is numerically large, accounting for approximately 40 per cent of the total population, spatially concentrated in relatively few areas and in receipt of widespread external and irredentist support, lends it a significance that may not obtain where there is a plurality of more or less coequal segments.

Besides citing the institutional attributes of consociational democracy, Lijphart also identified a set of conditions conducive to its creation and maintenance. In addition to a multiple balance of power which does not apply in Northern Ireland, he instances the condition of a multi-party system founded upon segmentation. However, the desired condition of symmetry between party and segment is missing, given the division within the majority community between unionists and loyalists and that within the minority between nationalists and republicans. The third background condition, that of relatively small population size, does obtain, as does that requiring relative segmental isolation in the shape of residential and much consequent social segregation. The remaining conditions – a common external threat, a common national identity, the lack of extreme material inequalities and a prior tradition of political accommodation – are all conspicuous by their absence.

Thus, in theoretical terms the prognosis for a workable consociation is decidedly unpromising. If nothing else, the reliance placed upon elites to engage in the politics of accommodation is extremely heavy, especially given the underlying and chronic condition of mutual distrust. Where violence begets violence, as in a cycle of tit-for-tat killings, the strains that develop within such a coalition and, more crucially, between leaders and followers within each segment can quickly become unsustainable. In such a context political elites are required to demonstrate that they are keepers of the relevant true faith; heretics have no place in the midst of clamant believers.

The AIA: Coercing a consociation?

What price, then, a devolved power-sharing arrangement – or, rather, what price a *voluntary* consociation? One recent author, Brendan O'Leary,[3] discussing the prospects of a political settlement for Northern Ireland, argues that besides repartition, the thinkable alternatives amount to either consociational democracy or no local democracy at all, save that provided at one remove through the blunt arrangement of direct rule. A survey of the other options mentioned earlier, though intellectually engaging, swiftly exhausts their feasibility. Yet voluntary consociation has patently failed, disabled by the unwillingness or the inability of elites to accommodate one another and/or to deliver their supporters.

Contending that voluntary consociation is unlikely to be realized, O'Leary perceives the Anglo-Irish Agreement as a means of *coercing* local elites, essentially those from within the 'unionist bloc', into the acceptance of power-sharing. The conscious abandonment of the principle of voluntarism by Britain represents, on this view, a belated recognition that sweet reasonableness is not about to descend on internal political leaders: time for a diplomatic version of banging (primarily unionist and loyalist) heads together: enter the Anglo-Irish Agreement.

While the long-run implications of the AIA are, I believe, open-ended, the fact remains that its authors have underwritten the achievement of agreed devolution on a consociational basis as a biddable and shorter-run goal. As O'Leary notes, to that end the AIA brandishes a stick at unionist and loyalist leaders in the form of the institutionalization of the Irish dimension, but it also proffers a carrot.

Articles 4(b) and 4(c) declare the joint policy of both governments to be the restoration of devolved powers, provided any such proposal secures widespread acceptance throughout the community: a form of words invariably understood to imply power-sharing along consociational lines, although the precise form this would take is a matter of some conjecture. Such an outcome would entail a corresponding diminution in the scope of the AIA's peripatetic Intergovernmental Conference (IGC) together with its Belfast-based Secretariat, through which bilateral discussions and measures are processed by Irish and British officials. The sufficiency of this inducement to the majority's political leaders is as yet uncertain. As for the SDLP, the AIA represents a tangible advance. For more than ten years it has made clear that any political settlement must comprise power-sharing as well as a formal role for the Republic in representing the interests of the minority population within Northern Ireland. In the zero-sum terms through which the politics of the region is ordinarily perceived, to the majority the AIA meant that the Republic and the nationalist population in Northern Ireland had gained at their expense.

The Anglo-Irish strategy represents an attempt to transform the internal politics of the region from a zero-sum to a positive-sum condition, wherein all benefit from the prize of peace, stability and reconciliation. On O'Leary's reading of the AIA, these ends can only be served by the achievement of consociation while, at the same time, each government underwrites Northern Ireland's conditional constitutional status, thereby refusing to close the door on eventual unification. This push to what O'Leary terms 'coercive consociationalism' loosely translates as a version of forcing the participants to be free. If there are no constructive moves towards an internally agreed settlement then the direct rule system, critically modified by the AIA, remains operative.

Almost six years on, this imputed strategy shows some sign of success in the shape of talks planned for the early summer of 1991, thereby keeping the spectre of devolution in view. While testimony to the adroitness of Peter Brooke and the surprising suppleness of other key actors, the major problem with this strategy is the onus that it places on the internal political elites to reconcile their mutually exclusive constitutional aims, coupled with their ability to carry their supporters with them.

The British government, through its Northern Ireland Secretary, has certainly kept alive the consociational flame despite, or more probably because of, the apparently coercive nature of the AIA. Indeed, O'Leary's reading of the dynamics of the AIA has much to commend it. However, it is also possible to observe the outlines of a different if concurrent strategy which is not in any way hindered by the failure to secure agreement among local political elites. Furthermore, it may be a more far-sighted strategy that makes redundant an attempt to create an orthodox consociation, whether coerced or not.

Internal policy and consociation

Consociationalism, as developed by Lijphart, was not intended as an end in itself, but rather as the prelude to the evolution of a more normal polity and society. As such, the formulae it contains amount to a series of confidence-building measures at elite or 'tree-top' level that can, over time, trickle down and infuse segmented communities with mutual trust and a readiness to accommodate one another. However, in Northern Ireland such an outcome has proven elusive. While the AIA commits both governments to the pursuit of a devolved arrangement, a local Assembly coupled with a power-sharing institution would at best be grafted onto a body politic that, in the current climate of popular sentiment, would be inhospitable to such an institution. In such circumstances, a repetition of the events of 1974 when the power-sharing Executive was toppled by a near-insurrection would be little short of disastrous.

At this point what becomes clearer is the need to generate sufficient grassroots support upon which amenable leaders could rely, rather than to depend upon elite accommodation atop mutually exclusive and distrustful communities. Perhaps it is here that we can begin to apprehend the outlines of a new approach which turn the classic model of consociation on its head.

It has long been the case that devolved power-sharing is the second best option for both the majority and minority populations in Northern Ireland. Though it should not be overstated, this has meant that, among policy-makers, there has been a certain taken-for-grantedness about popular opinion, hence the emphasis on fostering dialogue at elite level. However, certain recent policy initiatives suggest a more considered effort by both the Irish and British governments to promote inter-communal contact and understanding.

Let us look briefly at two policy initiatives that, without too great an imaginative leap, can be viewed in this light: the new fair employment legislation; and developments in the field of educational policy. If nothing else, each of these initiatives seems to controvert the Lijphartian dictum that segmented societies must accept that neighbourliness is determined by the height of boundary fences.

The fair employment initiative

The issue of religious discrimination in employment in Northern Ireland has long bedevilled the region, both before and since the introduction of direct rule, although its true extent during the Stormont regime remains the subject of some speculation.[4] The passage of anti-discrimination legislation in 1976, implemented the following year, was an attempt to end this pernicious practice. However, in 1985 the British government took the view (during the process of negotiating, but prior to the signing of, the AIA) that current law and policy needed to be reviewed.

For a considerable period the outcome of that review was uncertain. Moreover, there are grounds for doubting that the government freely chose to embark on such a course, and for believing that it was impelled to do so in the face of internal and, from the British perspective, ominous mounting external criticism of existing law. Whatever the precise weight and combination of reasons, new legislative proposals were forthcoming and, after some four-and-a-half years in the making, eventually emerged from Parliament in July 1989 and began to be applied in January 1990.

The Fair Employment Act 1989, which adds to and amends that of 1976, is rooted in a commitment to equal opportunity rather than in a purely procedural concern with equity but represents less than the full-hearted embrace of positive – or, as critics would term it, reverse – discrimination. Its stated goal is to achieve 'fair participation' within the workforce rather than, as the preceding White Paper stated,[5] a 'more representative distribution in the workforce': to that extent it falls far short of the principle of proportionality prescribed by Lijphart as an institutional feature of consociationalism (though he confined its application to the public sector). Where the legislation appears to represent the consociational idea is in its insistence that all employers, whether in the private or public sector, are to record the religious composition of their workforces: that obligation is consistent with segmentalist, or as it is put in Northern Ireland, sectarian thinking.

The Act, which prohibits both direct and, unlike its predecessor, indirect discrimination, rejects quotas but does endorse the use by employers of goals and timetables as performance indicators by which 'fair participation' can be at least assessed if not accurately measured. Thereby hangs a problem, of course: what is 'fair participation'? The Standing Advisory Commission on Human Rights (SACHR), in its 1987 report on religious discrimination in employment, recommended that the government should adopt a target ratio of 1½ : 1 Catholic-to-Protestant male unemployment within a five-year period, reducing it significantly from the 2½ : 1 ratio that existed at that time.[6] This was rejected by the government in favour of the more elastic goal of 'fair participation' and an emphasis on procedural rather than substantive equality. Though critics of the legislation emphasize the woolliness of this goal, consider the alternative.

In a region with the weakest economy in the UK and where jobs are at a premium, any excursion by government into the labour market that sought actively and explicitly to favour the job prospects of a disadvantaged minority would invite trouble. While the legislation is at one level about the pursuit of social justice, the endorsement of preferential treatment for Catholics would, in such a chronic economic situation, serve only to inflame intercommunal relations. Thus, while acknowledging that anti-Catholic discrimination exists and by prescribing affirmative action measures short of quotas, the government's policy serves a number of ends.

First, it tackles an indefensible restrictive practice, seeking to rid the labour market of an insidious and distorting rigidity. Second, by framing its new policy in terms of equality of opportunity it manages to square the ideological circle. A government that prides itself on its commitment to deregulation requires a coherent justification for what might otherwise be construed as an unwarranted interference in the free play of market forces. Appeals to fairness and equality of individual opportunity which the new legislation voices are fully consistent with ideological beliefs that prize individual self-reliance. On the political front there are other ends served. Most obviously the legislation is a tangible response to Article 5(a) of the AIA. This specified that the IGC would consider measures to prevent and avoid economic and social discrimination in Northern Ireland. Equally critically, the legislation also relieves external pressure emanating from the USA in the form of the MacBride Principles campaign.

This campaign has its roots in a lengthy effort by the Irish National Caucus (INC) to draw the attention of American public opinion to the existence of religious discrimination in the province. It began with a successful effort in the late 1970s to ban the sale of US-made weaponry to the RUC and evolved via an unsuccessful lobby of Congress to prevent the purchase by the US Air Force of transport aircraft manufactured by Short Brothers. While the immediate objective of that campaign was not realized, it did succeed in propelling the issue of discrimination against Catholics onto the Congressional and wider public agenda.

In the early 1980s, Short Brothers was very much the stalking horse for the INC's campaign. During Congressional hearings before the House and Senate Armed Services Committee its National Director, Séan McManus, had accused the company of a notorious record of blatant discrimination against Catholics; as a public-sector enterprise, this inevitably implicated the British government in the allegation. Stung by the adverse publicity that had been generated by the hearings, Short Brothers agreed a series of measures with the Fair Employment Agency (FEA) designed to attract job applications from within the minority community. This buoyed the INC which, concurrent with the hearings, had secured Congressional support for legislation modelled upon the 'Sullivan Principles'. These had been developed in 1977 by Leon Sullivan, a veteran civil rights campaigner, and took the form of a corporate code of conduct for US companies with undertakings in South Africa.[7] The code, which embraced measures according preferential treatment to 'Africans', was advanced by a shareholder resolution campaign. Failure to adopt the Principles would both tar US companies with the brush of apartheid and threaten disinvestment by individual and institutional shareholders. Such disincentives had persuaded such firms of the wisdom of adopting the code and thus the campaign had been remarkably successful. Having alerted Congress to the existence of discrimination in Northern Ireland during the course of a 1981 hearing sponsored by the Ad Hoc Congressional Committee for Irish Affairs, the INC sought to generate a similar code for US companies with a presence in the province. After a faltering start which produced a code that was inconsistent with existing domestic law in Northern Ireland, by the late autumn of 1984 the INC and others had devised a set of principles that did not run foul of the 1976 Fair Employment Act.

The emergence of the ecumenical and politically diverse MacBride lobby, against the immediate background of embarrassing reports by the FEA disclosing the continuing existence of discriminatory practices in the private and, most worryingly, the public sector, gave the government real cause for concern. Its self-presentation as the dispassionate arbiter of the inequalities and divisions within the province was undeniably tarnished by the growing awareness that existing law was unequal to the task. Its discomfiture was compounded by the availability to the Secretary of State, Douglas Hurd, in January 1985 of raw data from the 1983–4 *Continuous Household Survey* demonstrating,[8] among other things, the 2½:1 unemployment ratio of Catholic to Protestant males. These data did not, however, enter the public domain for a further six months, by which time the MacBride campaign had begun to accrue increasing support for its corporate code.

The campaigners adopted a three-pronged approach to the promotion of the Principles: shareholder resolutions; Congressional legislation; and state and municipal legislation and ordinances. It is this last tactic which has been most successful. By the end of 1990 a dozen states and more than thirty major cities had adopted the Principles, committing their legislators to invest pension and retirement funds in only those US companies that had implemented them and threatening to disinvest from those that refused to incorporate them into company policy. The prospect of disinvestment, coupled with the undeniably bad publicity that flowed from the unflattering comparison with South Africa, clearly cautioned the British government to act. However, it was almost two years after the publication of the Principles that the first official response to them appeared and then only in the form of a consultative document. Such tardiness enabled their adversaries to engage in a proactive campaign throughout the United States while the government was forced into a rather weak defensive posture.

Latterly, as its proposals began to take on a more concrete form, the British government has been able to mount a counter-attack arguing, with the support of the SDLP among others (though excluding the current Irish government), that the new legislation renders the MacBride Principles redundant. However, the campaign in the USA shows no signs of abating as its proponents intensify their efforts to give them legislative form in all states and to consolidate those municipal and state laws already adopted.

The 1989 Act is not without its detractors both within and, most significantly, outside the province. While it does serve a number of reasonably obvious goals, not least the attempt to counter external pressure designed to delegitimize the British presence, the legislation may convey a more discreet social purpose: one that is suggestive of a fresh, if not entirely novel, approach to the achievement of political stability in Northern Ireland. If the top-down approach to the restoration of local democracy has failed, why not adopt a coherent bottom-up strategy? Among other things, this requires the active promotion of inter-communal contact, not its arrest *via* an unswerving commitment to segmental autonomy. That is to say, the fair employment legislation can be construed not only as an attempt to secure social justice but also as a means of advancing desegregation.

The workplace is an appropriate context within which to embark on such a course. The adoption of employment procedures that promise to disadvantage neither community whether at the point of hiring, promotion or lay-off and that prospectively bring together representatives of each in greater numbers and frequency should occasion greater social intercourse. Experimentation has shown that prolonged and intense contact, especially where it entails co-operation in problem-solving, can assist markedly in overcoming mutual distrust, incomprehension and suspicion, thereby significantly reducing stereotypical behaviour among all parties. Such programmes, which are decidedly long-term in their nature, could facilitate not merely better workplace relations but could conceivably spill over into other realms with perhaps positive implications for the wider condition of social stability.

Is such a strategy feasible? By itself, no. Among other things, it would require massive investment in order to provide full – or, at least, fuller – employment. The assurance that employer practices are non-discriminatory only becomes meaningful where there is a real prospect of actual employment. Moreover, the existence of a government averse to increased injections of public spending places the onus on the private sector to generate employment, although the heavy reliance on the public sector in Northern Ireland for the provision of jobs lends it more than a purely symbolic significance. However, it is also the case that the new measures are in part designed to attract inward investment, especially from the USA. Removing the apprehension among potential external investors that by setting up operations in the region they would be guilty of propping up a discriminatory regime, cannot but help create the conditions for economic revival.

The overt objective of the fair employment initiative is, then, to assist in the promotion of social justice and, in so doing, to help improve the internal economic condition of the region. Although it may seem somewhat quixotic, the new policy can also be viewed as an attempt to promote desegregation. While not a stated goal of the new policy, by demonstrating to fellow workers that their new, or newly promoted, colleagues are not all dyed-in-the-wool loyalists or republicans, Pavlovian impulses may be countered. This is not to claim that all workplaces will become fully integrated – although that ought to be more than a mere aspiration in the public sector, especially the Civil Service – nor is it to suggest that the legislation does more than permit desegregation to occur. A more determined approach at what might be termed 'pressure cooker' integration would entail the strict implementation of quotas and religion-specific tie-break procedures. But, just as the new education reforms fall far short of enforcing integration, so the employment measures are more permissive than mandatory in relation to the mixing of the working population.

Fingers burnt by the earlier failed experiments in integrated housing, policy-makers are now less ingenuous. And yet, one effect of the fair employment policy – intended or not – will be a greater incidence of more representative workforces. At the risk of tilting at another windmill, or seeming unduly Panglossian, it is conceivable that frequency of contact in employment may, in the longer run, produce more stable relations between Catholics and Protestants. Should increased levels of workplace integration develop from the implementation of the new measures, both local elites and policy-makers may be freed from the inhibitions of undiluted consociational thinking. Creating the space and the opportunity for workplace desegregation to occur could thereby afford the opportunity for more 'normal' politics to evolve.

Education policy

When the 1982 Northern Ireland Assembly got under way, its primary role was to subject the administration of transferred matters to a measure of local political scrutiny. This was achieved through a system of statutory committees modelled along the lines of the departmental Select Committees established at Westminster in 1979. Among the six such committees was one concerned with administration, expenditure and policy on education. During its lifetime it embarked on a wide range of inquiries, but there was one topic that was conspicuously absent from its agenda: integrated education.[9]

The committee's neglect of this matter could perhaps be explained in terms of the desire among its members to avoid conflict: integrated education is highly contentious, because it appears to pose a fundamental challenge to the prized identities of both communities in Northern Ireland and, more particularly, confronts the hegemony of the Catholic Church over its congregation. Moreover, Lijphart's prescription of segmental autonomy requires that distinctive communities enjoy control over policy that is central to those identities. At the communal level, an integrationist education policy is inconsistent with consociational philosophy.

Such reticence did not typify the initial proposals for educational reform by the first Stormont government in 1923 or the British administration's attempt to forge a national educational system in the nineteenth century. While the respective motivations for these early attempts to promote mixed schooling may have been questionable, this is less evident in the case of the ill-fated power-sharing Executive of 1974, which did ally itself with proposals to promote integrated education.

In an Assembly debate on 30 April 1974 the Executive's Education Minister, Basil McIvor, expressed his 'basic belief that the mixing of school children would contribute to the reduction of community tension'.[10] This was fully in accord with the Executive's economic and social aims which proposed to introduce, with parental consent, a series of pilot experiments in integrated education. The proposal was given a cautious welcome by those party spokesmen who were present and reiterated when the main estimates of the Department of Education were debated on 8 May 1974. McIvor summarised the role of mixed schooling thus:

> We are seeking to build a Northern Ireland in which the two communities can live in harmony . . . We owe it to our children . . . to create a climate in which they cannot easily inherit the irrational hatreds of the past . . . which have blighted the lives of so many . . .[11]

The demise of the Executive sounded the death-knell of early, officially sanctioned experiments in integrated education. Yet the idea did not wither, but was taken up by a number of voluntary organizations which began to mobilize support for the integrated school movement within the wider population.[12] The pressure for the sanction of government was slow to build and, for a lengthy period, consigned to the margins of society where, if considered at all, it was regarded as the preoccupation of a group of well-meaning but naive and misguided cranks. Yet the Cinderella status of the movement was to alter with the introduction of wide-ranging educational reforms by the current Conservative government.

The renewed signal in the direction of integrated education was made in September 1987 by the then minister with responsibility for education, Dr Brian Mawhinney. It took the form of a revitalized initiative, 'education for mutual understanding' (EMU), which set aside resources to promote that goal in the training of teachers and the enhancement of inter-school contact. To promote EMU and related cross-community contact programmes, a Central Community Relations Unit (CCRU) was created in the Northern Ireland Office to advise the Secretary of State on all aspects of the relations between the two traditions in Northern Ireland. The Unit works with the Department of Education for Northern Ireland (DENI) which has statutory responsibility for formulating and sponsoring policies for the improvement of community relations.

The attempt to promote harmonious inter-communal relations was not new to Northern Ireland. Many voluntary groups had sprung up since the onset of 'the troubles' with that express purpose and had been supported by grant aid from government. Moreover, while EMU had made its first faltering appearance in Northern Ireland in the early 1980s, Mawhinney's announcement did mark a new departure. It represented a coherent attempt to alter the substantive content of children's education and, more recently, offered both positive official encouragement and the means by which integrated educational institutions would be put on a sound financial footing.

There are two distinct but related aspects of the new educational reforms that dovetail neatly with the renewed emphasis on community relations – and which, in the process, challenge Lijphart's requirement of high fences. The first relates to the substantive content of education, by introducing a core curriculum in six areas of study together with six further cross-curricular themes which are integral to the compulsory subjects.[13]

As in Britain, the *raison d'être* for the reforms was presented as raising educational standards and enabling parents to enjoy more choice and involvement in their children's education. But, in introducing the measures to Parliament, Mawhinney made plain the second and wider purpose they served: 'We intend . . . that the school curriculum should play its part in fostering greater understanding, tolerance and respect across the community divide.'[14] To that end the reforms reiterated the importance of EMU, stressed the theme of 'cultural heritage', introduced a common history curriculum and a core syllabus for religious education, and enabled children to study Irish in addition to, or instead of, one of the major European languages.

The legislative proposals came in the wake of the cross-community contact scheme begun in 1987 with an initial annual budget of £200,000. By 1989, with some 600 school, youth and community groups participating in the programme, funding was increased to £650,000. While this is a modest level of support, the then Secretary of State, Tom King, provided an effective riposte to the charge that this was mere window-dressing. At a reception for community workers he left his audience in no doubt as to the grand design: 'The CCRU is laying the foundations for a challenging change in attitudes. Young people have a crucial role in helping to promote community understanding and tolerance in our divided society'.[15]

Throughout his speech King adverts to '*community* togetherness' and the need to '[un]shackle animosities within the *community*',[16] suggestive of a renewed stress on those features of Northern Ireland that can unite rather than inevitably divide. The official message appears to be thus: Northern Ireland is one organic community within which there are realizable, mutually enriching and plural traditions, not a society riven by unbridgeable cleavages and implacably unyielding segments. Such sentiments were expressed clearly by Mawhinney in announcing a £1 million Cultural Traditions Programme for 1989/90:

> It is crucially important to recognize and understand that there is much in our heritage and culture that we share. We also want to ensure that the diversity in our heritage and our traditions do not become a wedge dividing the community and to show that sincerely held views need not be threatening or divisive.[17]

In February 1989 the message was reinforced with the expansion of the Cultural Traditions Programme and the creation of a new charitable organization, the Community Relations Resource Body, together with a Cultural Traditions Group, based at the Institute for Irish Studies at Queen's University, Belfast, whose terms of reference are to 'widen the appreciation of Northern Ireland's rich and diverse cultural heritage'.[18] These bodies are not to confine themselves to the fostering of cross-community contact among children but are also to include adults within their remits.

But, of course, it was towards the young, specifically schoolchildren, that the educational reform package was primarily directed. Combined with the cross-community contact scheme, it is intended to 'help forge lasting friendships between children and young people'. To that end it was incumbent upon government not merely to fund voluntary efforts 'to generate greater mutual trust, understanding and respect' but also to venture into the realm of integrated education. Thus, and for the first time, the Education Order in Council places a duty on DENI to encourage and facilitate integrated education. 'Integrated schools', stated Mawhinney, 'will make a very positive contribution to breaking down the sectarian divisions'[19] – or, if you will, knocking holes in Lijphart's fences.

The government proposed two routes towards the promotion of integrated schools. First, the legislation enables an existing school, of either denomination, to opt out of its existing status and become an integrated institution, thereby qualifying for 100 per cent capital funding. Second, the Order makes it possible for the government to provide financial support to new integrated schools *ab initio*. Both are hefty shoves in the direction of integration, but in each case it is for the parents of the relevant children to decide whether it should take place, to what extent and how quickly. Thus, there is no wholesale imposition of integrated status: consistent with the government's ideological stance, the matter is left to parental choice, in the first case via parental ballot. Yet the funding provision for such a change in status is a positive incentive, as is the assurance that integrated schools will enjoy equal legitimacy alongside controlled and voluntary schools.

However, even this cautious approach prompted the Catholic hierarchy to mount a legal challenge, arguing that the 100 per cent capital funding provision for integrated schools effectively discriminated against Catholic schools which receive 85 per cent of their capital costs from the government. Though the legal challenge was unsuccessful and is now the subject of an appeal, it does underline the sensitivity of education and the anxiety that the pursuit of integration will inevitably bring secularization in its wake and a consequent loss of influence by the Church.

Recognizing that the growth of integrated schooling is likely to prove somewhat protracted, the government has ensured that both EMU and cultural heritage will become compulsory cross-curricular themes. These themes, in harness with the provision for religiously mixed schools, seem to amount to a 'belt and braces' approach towards the achievement of communal solidarity.

It would be idle to argue that cross-community relations, integrated education and EMU are ideas new to Northern Ireland. Moreover, the vocabulary of 'two traditions' has been common to liberal unionists in Northern Ireland and Irish nationalists within and outside its boundaries for much of the 1980s. Equally, the attempt to tackle religious discrimination in employment is hardly a novel undertaking. Yet, the active promotion of these policies within the context of an at times bumpy but developing Anglo-Irish process is suggestive of an imaginative approach.

Promoting the post-modern?

The concept of 'alienation', current in Northern Ireland until very recently, has been displaced by an official readiness to promote the value of diverse and mutually enriching traditions. Instead of antagonistic blocs set in concrete, inhabitants are encouraged to think in terms of cultural pluralism within a community possessed of a common heritage. In a sense, there is perhaps something post-modern about this approach, at least in the terms by which the politics of Northern Ireland is invariably conducted.

The classic consociational model, whether expounded in voluntaristic or coercive terms, is rooted in the proposition that within segmented societies a political settlement is governed by the immutable relations which exist between or among distinctive and distrustful populations, each jealous of its respective identity. This reflects a modernist consciousness, accepting as it does that political cleavages which developed in the pre-democratic era are frozen with the advent of modern democratic procedures. Such traditional alignments thereby pattern a country's party system, which subsequently remains highly durable if not entirely impervious to change.

In underwriting the pursuit of power-sharing and the requirement of its widespread acceptance within Northern Ireland, the Anglo-Irish Agreement appears at one level to be fully consistent with the modernist assumptions upon which consociational thinking is based. It accepts as a given what one might term 'either/or-ism': one is either a Catholic, and thus a nationalist/republican; or a Protestant and hence a unionist/loyalist. Yet recent policy initiatives in the fields of education and employment appear to confront those same assumptions. They indicate less the top-down approach characteristic of the classic consociational model and more a bottom-up strategy which, if it is not a contradiction in terms, may be styled 'inverted consociationalism'. Instead of seeking to manufacture a fragile elite consensus which spans an inextricably divided society, they seem to represent attempts to erode the modernist and monolithic blocs within which the region's social segments are cast.

The vocabulary of this imputed strategy is instructive. Insistence upon a 'shared cultural heritage' and coexistent 'mutually enriching traditions' bespeak pluralistic not monolithic thinking. To that extent the Anglo-Irish process can be construed as a vehicle for the articulation of post-modern ideas: after all, to be a pluralist in Northern Ireland is to espouse post-modernist ideas, whereas to take refuge in what seem to be its eternal verities is to accept uncritically the weight of modernist orthodoxy.

Such post-modern thinking, if that is what it is, presents a radical challenge to the ultras in the region, from whichever social segment they are drawn. It invites them to engage in an introspective examination of their respective identities, an exercise that may reveal sundry coexisting varieties of Irishness. In such circumstances the impulse to hold what they have, or aspire to, is compelling: it is also easier than unleashing existential doubts about self and place. To admit of the doubt that such self-examination would generate is to unleash profound uncertainties about the future. For that reason the successful diffusion of post-modernist thinking is likely to proceed at a glacial pace.

Conclusion

No one imagines that there is a quick fix to the syndrome of problems afflicting Northern Ireland. The Anglo-Irish Agreement is, among other things, an antidote to short-termism. It is an imaginative framework within which the process of securing peace, stability and reconciliation can be advanced. Should it be superseded by some other arrangement the need to promote what I have termed 'inverted consociationalism' is unlikely to recede – not least because it is not tied to a predetermined constitutional end.

This is not to gloss over the profound differences in identity and aspiration that exist in Northern Ireland, nor is it to diminish the need to reform aspects of the criminal justice system, policing and economic policy. Equally, it is not to underestimate the force of conservative sentiment, from whichever quarter it derives, to resist integrated education. Above all, it would be mistaken to assume that policies which celebrate cultural pluralism will beget political pluralism as a matter of course. While the one may facilitate the other, it is more than plausible that such policies will become worthwhile ends in themselves.

Finally, if current educational and anti-discrimination policies represent a post-modern approach, this does not preclude concurrent discussions aimed at bringing about a conventional form of consociation: to the contrary, such efforts would be mutually supportive. Moreover, Lijphart intends consociationalism ultimately to appear as an interim measure, having made itself redundant by contributing to the development of inter-communal trust and the evolution of more normal political institutions. But these less elevated policies may succeed in prompting expansive, inclusive thinking at the grassroots level instead of the inhibiting and exclusive precepts that underpin competing territorial imperatives. If that is the case, and the motivation, Northern Ireland may yet witness the growth of plural thinking which, in turn, would provide a more secure basis upon which to construct a constitutional settlement.

Acknowledgement

I would like to acknowledge the contribution of my colleague Richard Jay. It was from frequent discussions with him that the idea of an 'inverted consociation' was to emerge. Needless to say, he bears no responsibility for the manner in which it is here deployed.

Notes

1 B. O'Leary, 'The Limits to Coercive Consociationalism in Northern Ireland', *Political Studies*, 37 (1989), 562–88.
2 A. Lijphart, *The Politics of Accommodation: Pluralism and Democracy in the Netherlands*, University of California Press, Berkeley and Los Angeles, 1968; A. Lijphart, 'Consociational Democracy', *World Politics*, 21 (1969), 207–25; A. Lijphart, 'Consociation: the Model and its Application in Divided Societies' in

D. Rea (ed.), *Political Cooperation in Divided Societies: A Series of Papers Relevant to the Conflict in Northern Ireland*, Gill and Macmillan, Dublin, 1982.

3 O'Leary, 'Limits to Coercive Consociationalism'.

4 J. Whyte, 'How Much Discrimination Was There under the Unionist Regime?' in T. Gallagher and J. O'Connell (eds), *Contemporary Irish Studies*, Manchester University Press, Manchester, 1983.

5 *Fair Employment in Northern Ireland* (Cm. 380), HMSO, London, 1988.

6 Standing Advisory Commission on Human Rights, *Religious and Political Discrimination in Northern Ireland* (Cm. 237), HMSO, London, 1987, p. 42. The 1½ : 1 ratio was only one of a total of 123 recommendations contained in the report.

7 See R. Jay and R. A. Wilford, 'The Politics of the Fair Employment Act in Northern Ireland: Internal and External Dimensions', paper presented to the Political Studies Association Annual Conference, University of Durham, 1990.

8 *Continuous Household Survey* No. 2/85, Policy Planning Research Unit, Belfast, June 1985.

9 C. O'Leary, S. Elliott and R. A. Wilford, *The Northern Ireland Assembly 1982–1986: A Constitutional Experiment*, Hurst, London, 1988.

10 *NIA Debs*, vol. 2, no. 50, 30 April 1974, cols 298–312.

11 *NIA Debs*, vol. 2, no. 54, 8 May 1974, cols 629–776.

12 For an overview of inter-schools contact and the integrated education movement in Northern Ireland, see J. Darby and S. Dunn, 'Segregated Schools: The Research Evidence' in R. D. Osborne, R. J. Cormack and R. L. Miller (eds), *Education and Policy in Northern Ireland*, Policy Research Institute, Belfast, pp. 85–98. In the same volume, see also A. Spencer, 'Arguments for an Integrated School System', and G. Loughran, 'The Rationale of Catholic Education'.

13 In addition to religious education, the curriculum of all pupils of compulsory school age will include six areas of study which may comprise more than one subject: English; mathematics; science and technology; environment and society; creative and expressive studies; and language studies (secondary schools only). The six compulsory cross-curricular themes, the first four of which are interwoven throughout primary school, are information technology, EMU, cultural heritage, health education, economic awareness and careers education. See DENI, *Education Reform in Northern Ireland: The Way Forward*, Belfast, 1988, pp. 4–6.

14 *HC Debs*, vol. 163, (1989–90), cols 1092–3.

15 Text of speech, Northern Ireland Information Service, 15 May 1989.

16 Ibid. (emphasis added).

17 Text of speech, Northern Ireland Information Service, 16 January 1989.

18 Text of speech, Northern Ireland Information Service, 27 February 1989.

19 Press release accompanying the publication of the Draft Order, Northern Ireland Information Service, 13 June 1989.

4

The impact of the European Community

Edward Moxon-Browne

Northern Ireland became part of the European Community (EC) in January 1973 when the United Kingdom, together with Denmark and the Republic of Ireland, acceded to membership. The immediate implications of membership were not very different from those applying to the United Kingdom as a whole. The Northern Ireland economy had long had to compete within the broader market of the United Kingdom, and increasingly with the Republic of Ireland as trade barriers between Ireland and Britain were removed. In the longer term, however, it can be argued that Northern Ireland has benefited more from the advantages, and suffered more from the disadvantages, of membership than has the United Kingdom as a whole. Some premonitions of these dispropor-tionate effects had been signalled in a White Paper[1] issued by the Northern Ireland government in 1971. There it was pointed out that while the lowering of tariffs between 'the Six' and the United Kingdom would offer Northern Ireland exporters new opportunities in continental Europe, it was equally true that these same exporters would no longer be protected from Western European competition in the British market which had accounted for about 60 per cent of Northern Ireland exports. Secondly, whereas previously foreign investors might have selected Northern Ireland (because of relatively lower wage costs) as a point of access to UK (and EFTA) markets, this advantage might be partly offset by higher transport costs in a wider customs union. Thirdly, although fairly buoyant prospects were in view for farming under the Common Agricultural Policy (CAP), the relatively greater dependence of Northern Ireland farmers on imported feedstuffs, to say nothing of the relative inefficiency of farms that were, on average, half the size of British ones, meant that even these prospects might be somewhat illusory. In the event, the only special concession granted to the United Kingdom with respect to Northern Ireland was a derogation, for five years, from the EC legislation requiring freedom of movement of labour for EC citizens.[2]

Entry into the EC in 1973 coincided almost exactly with the imposition of direct rule from Westminster. The British Parliament enacted the Northern Ireland (Temporary Provisions) Act in March 1972 which effectively vested in a Secretary of State the powers previously exercised by the Northern Ireland government. Except for an interlude in 1974 when a 'power-sharing' Executive took over some of these functions, this framework of government has remained in place ever since. These two events, direct rule and EC entry, represented almost totally opposite political tendencies: direct rule involved the resumption of political control over Northern Ireland from London, ending half a century of devolved administration, whereas EC entry represented an acknowledgement that forces greater than the nation-state were now significant enough to be absorbed formally into national decision-making. In other words, while direct rule reflected a reassertion of national sovereignty in the traditional sense, membership of the EC reflected a major concession to the more modern view that national sovereignty was effectively finite and ought to be pooled, at least in part, with the sovereignties of neighbouring nation-states. At the peak of its civil unrest (1972 was the worst year for fatalities), Northern Ireland was entering uncharted political waters in two senses: a new relationship with London, and participation in the wider arena of EC membership. In any assessment of the impact of the EC on Northern Ireland, it is worth bearing in mind not only these new political realities, but also the economic reality of the 'oil crisis' of 1973–4, creating an international recession that coincided with the Community's enlargement. In the discussion that follows, it will be convenient to discuss the impact of EC membership on Northern Ireland from three distinct but interrelated perspectives: the political, the economic and the legal.

The political context

The formal links between Northern Ireland and the EC are conducted through Whitehall departments in London, and through the Northern Ireland Office and various Civil Service departments in Belfast. The latter's views are taken into account in London when a common UK position is being adopted for negotiations in Brussels. Northern Ireland Civil Servants are seconded to the Commission in Brussels, and Commission officials visit Northern Ireland and meet with Civil Servants in Belfast. For a population of 1½ million people, Northern Ireland is well served by its links, formal and informal, with Brussels. Northern Ireland is slightly over-represented, with its three MEPs, in the European Parliament and, for most of the time, these three have also been Westminster MPs, providing a useful link with the national legislature. In the European Parliament, the three MEPs have been able to capitalize on the evident sympathy for Northern Ireland, by speaking in unison on mainly economic issues. Three major reports from within the European Parliament

(Martin Report, Haagerup Report, and Maher Report[3]) have provided considerable publicity, but little tangible assistance, for the region's problems. There are, in addition, many informal groups that pursue direct contacts with Brussels, such as the Ulster Farmers Union, which is affiliated to COPA (the EC's own pressure group for farmers); and the region's Consumers' Council, which is connected to BEUC (the EC's consumer organization). The EC's own information office in Belfast provides a local point of contact – there is no other information office in the EC servicing such a small population – for a wide range of individuals and organizations.

Northern Ireland's experience in the EC was widely expected to have a generally beneficial effect on the region's political problems. First, it was assumed that as national frontiers became less important, relations between North and South in Ireland would improve, and differences between the two parts of Ireland become less marked. Second, regular contacts within the Council of Ministers were expected to provide the British and Irish governments with a neutral forum in which to address issues of bilateral concern. Third, increasing contacts between the people of Ireland, North and South, and the inhabitants of Western Europe could reasonably have been expected to lessen tensions in Northern Ireland by juxtaposing its internal quarrels with the problems of more forward-looking societies elsewhere. In particular, the example of Franco-German reconciliation, within the framework of the Community's decision-making institutions, was believed by some to provide a model for reconciliation between the two communities in Northern Ireland.

In the event, none of these hypotheses was borne out by events. Community membership placed London and Dublin on an equal footing at about the same time as Belfast's relationship with London had been downgraded. EC membership, perversely as it turned out, emphasized the border between North and South more clearly than hitherto. The operation of the Common Agricultural Policy, with different 'green' rates on either side of the border, made smuggling a fact of life for the two economies, constituting a serious drain on the EC's resources. In 1979, the Republic of Ireland joined the European Monetary System, but Britain did not; and this led quite soon to a break between the British and Irish currencies after a monetary union that had lasted for 150 years. EC membership has affected the North and South quite differently: and contrasting rates of VAT, excise duties and social security systems have all helped thwart any integrative impact the EC might have had.

Secondly, Anglo-Irish relations have not been particularly smooth as a result of EC membership. They have fluctuated dramatically – often over problems that have little to do with the EC and for which the EC has no easy remedy. Indeed, on some occasions the EC has provided the arena for bitter exchanges between London and Dublin – for example, over the Irish decision to drop sanctions against Argentina during the Falklands war in 1982. None the less, the regular meetings between the two governments under the aegis of the Community have provided opportunities for 'megaphone diplomacy' to be softened, and for discreet dialogue to take its place. Any improvements in Anglo-Irish relations have, however, been matched by growing suspicions on the part of unionists in Northern Ireland that their case is falling on increasingly deaf ears, and that Dublin is making all the running with the British government. While this process has not been all one way – for example, Mrs Thatcher gave a sharp rebuttal to the Report of the New Ireland Forum in 1984, and sympathized with unionist dismay at the Haagerup Report at about the same time – the signing of the Anglo-Irish Agreement in 1985 seemed to reflect the Dublin view of the problem and worse, in unionist eyes, Britain's acceptance of that view.[4]

Thirdly, contact between Northern Ireland and continental Europe did little to place the conflict in a new context. On the contrary, the European arena seems to have provided political protagonists in Northern Ireland with an 'extended platform'[5] on which to fight out an essentially unchanging battle. The three European Parliament elections in Northern Ireland have produced almost identical results; and in all three campaigns European issues were decidedly marginalized by local priorities. The leading candidate in all three elections was a convinced anti-marketeer (Ian Paisley) and his success in European elections has always been interpreted by him as a vindication for his current political hobby-horse, whether it was 'smashing Sinn Fein' in 1984, or 'saying no to the Anglo-Irish Agreement' in 1989. The relative isolation of the two unionist MEPs in the European Parliament, far from moderating their views, seems only to have convinced them further of the need to trumpet their cause.

It has been within the European Parliament, above all, that the links between Northern Ireland and the EC have been best publicized, and where the Northern Ireland 'problem' has been most effectively aired. The SDLP leader, John Hume, has successfully taken advantage of his membership in the Socialist Group in the Parliament to construct broad-based support for various initiatives affecting Northern Ireland. Moreover, he has successfully exploited much of the nascent sympathy in continental Europe for his own belief that any constructive political dialogue on Northern Ireland can be carried out only in an Anglo-Irish context. Equally effectively, the leader of the DUP, Ian Paisley, has used the European Parliament to publicize the unionist cause by means of orchestrated 'incidents' that attract media attention. At the opening of the first directly elected Parliament in 1979, Paisley interrupted the proceedings to protest at the fact that the Union Jack was flying upside down outside the Parliament building. The following day he interrupted the Irish Prime Minister, Jack Lynch, as he was addressing the Parliament in his role as President of the Council, calling him a murderer, and saying that the 'blood of Ulster's dead' was on his hands. In October 1988, Paisley screamed abuse at the Pope as he addressed the Parliament, and had to be hustled out of the chamber. In these incidents, and others like them, Paisley skilfully exploited the presence of cameras in the chamber to transmit powerful political images back to his constituents in Northern Ireland.

Despite the strongly contrasting political outlooks of John Hume and Ian Paisley, it is important to emphasize that they have not always been at loggerheads in the Parliament. Pinpointing the economic problems of Northern Ireland as a peripheral region of the Community, the Martin Report (published in 1981) was supported by all three MEPs from Northern Ireland.[6] All three publicized the crisis in the region's textile industry; all three lobbied for help for agriculture; and all three were behind the 'integrated operations' for Belfast and protested at delays in their implementation.

More contentious issues, with a more obvious political content, have usually divided the SDLP leader (and MEPs from the Republic) from the two unionist MEPs. In 1981, a debate on conditions in the Maze prison was instigated by two MEPs from the Republic, producing a resolution which though highly critical of British policy in the North, was sufficiently amended by British Conservatives to be supported by 107 votes to 68. A more embarrassing reverse for the British government came in 1984 when the Parliament supported a ban on the use of plastic bullets by 110 votes to 43.

Although the Parliament has always been aware of the risks of discussing the internal affairs of any member state, and especially an issue as sensitive as the situation in Northern Ireland, a decision was taken by the Political Affairs Committee of the Parliament in 1983 to lauch an investigation with a Danish MEP, Niels Haagerup, as rapporteur. The ensuing investigation and Report were to have lasting political consequences.[7] The Report demonstrated how difficult it was to separate economic and social matters from the purely political; it highlighted differences between Conservatives at Westminster and Conservatives in the European Parliament; it created tensions between the Northern Ireland Office and Downing Street; and, above all, it epitomized the very different outlooks between the SDLP and the unionists on the relevance of the 'European dimension' to the situation in Northern Ireland. The Haagerup Report had been largely an initiative of John Hume's, whereas the two unionist MEPs took the view that the Parliament had no competence to investigate an issue that was essentially internal to the United Kingdom. In the broader international context, the Report revealed how isolated the unionist cause had become, and it was widely interpreted as a victory for Hume's strategy of using international opinion as a lever to effect change in British policy towards Northern Ireland. It is no accident that the Anglo-Irish Agreement, signed in 1985, incorporated many assumptions already made explicit in the Haagerup Report the previous year.

In the debate on the Report, the battle lines were clearly drawn. One MEP from the Republic blamed Britain for having created the problem sixty years previously, and for having supported sectarian institutions ever since in a political entity that had clearly failed.[8] British Conservative MEPs were torn between their approval of much of what the Report said, and their disapproval of Northern Ireland being discussed at all in the Parliament. In the end, they abstained on the Report. The biggest clash came between Hume and Paisley.

Hume (in the Socialist Group) argued for a reappraisal of attitudes from nationalists and unionists and asked whether it was too much to expect Ireland to emulate the example of Europeans who, having twice been locked in conflict in this century, had risen above it and come together. In response, Paisley condemned the Report as 'riddled with falsehoods' and 'an ill-informed piece of republican propaganda'; and asserted that the recognition by Dublin of the North's right to remain in the United Kingdom would be the best prescription for peace. The isolation of the unionist viewpoint was reflected in the final vote on the Report: 124 votes for and 3 against, with 63 abstentions.

Following the signing of the Anglo-Irish Agreement in November 1985, the Parliament passed a resolution welcoming it. This sentiment was translated into financial support when a sum of 15 million ECUs was donated by the EC to the International Fund for Ireland in March 1989. Parliament's support for the Agreement helped legitimize Britain's policy in Northern Ireland, and made it less likely that either the British or Irish governments would renege on their commitment to it. The Agreement effectively crystallized the convergence of British and Irish policy on Northern Ireland: from being purely an internal matter for the United Kingdom, the interest of the Republic had now been recognized. The provisions of the Agreement built on the assumptions and recommendations of the Haagerup Report: there was scope for cross-border co-operation; there was to be greater recognition of the two traditions in Northern Ireland, and greater efforts at mutual understanding (for example, in education). Power-sharing, of some kind, remained the goal of the British government; and it was clearly hoped that the Agreement might be largely transcended by a political partnership between the unionists and the SDLP. This, also, had been foreshadowed in the conclusions to the Haagerup Report, where allusions are made to 'political reform involving both unionist and nationalist parties' and a 'system of participation in government of both communities'. The European Community has provided an arena in which Dublin and London have come closer together, although it is doubtful if nationalists and unionists within Northern Ireland have followed suit. Unionists have been right to fear the 'Europeanization' of their predicament, just as nationalists have sought to encourage it. The SDLP has appreciated that Europe's own post-war experience of reconciliation, coupled with a widespread belief that 'geography and politics should run together', would rebound in favour of the party's own diagnosis of the problem.

The economic balance-sheet

While it is possible to calculate with some degree of accuracy the financial flows between Northern Ireland and the EC, there are other more elusive economic indicators that should be part of any attempt to draw up a balance-sheet of Community membership. Among these latter are the price-support mechanisms of the CAP, and the extent to which participation in a customs union of 324 million people has enhanced Northern Ireland's export performance.

Northern Ireland's share of the UK contribution to the EC budget is roughly equivalent to the share of UK tax revenue attributed to Northern Ireland. This has ranged between around 1.5 per cent and 2.8 per cent, which can be usefully compared with the region's share of the UK population (2.7 per cent) or its share of national GDP (2 per cent). Northern Ireland's receipts from the three 'regional' funds of the EC (the European Regional Development Fund (ERDF) for infrastructure, the European Social Fund (ESF) for unemployment, and the European Agricultural Guidance and Guarantee Fund (FEOGA) for agriculture) have increased steadily since 1973, reaching about £86 million in 1986 but falling some way short of the province's contribution to the EC budget. Thus the shortfall experienced by the UK as a whole as far as its balance of contributions to and receipts from the EC budget are concerned, is replicated in Northern Ireland.[9] However, if an amount is added to Northern Ireland's receipts to cover the price support mechanisms of the CAP, it is possible to argue that Northern Ireland makes a net profit on its financial relationship with the EC.[10]

It is, however, through the Regional and Social Funds of the EC that Northern Ireland receives the most publicized economic benefits, though as we shall see, there are problems in estimating exactly how generous this aid has been. The main emphasis of the Regional Fund has been on infrastructure projects designed to facilitate industrial development and improve communications. Thus roads, harbours, airports, power supplies and advance factories have been beneficiaries of ERDF grants in Northern Ireland. The Social Fund has been used almost entirely to complement training schemes organized by the Department of Economic Development, with a heavy bias towards the young, the long-term unemployed and women. One problem that has vitiated the perceived effectiveness of grants under both the ESF and the ERDF has been that of 'additionality': the extent to which grants from the EC are actually additional to what the government would otherwise have spent on a particular project. The issue is important because the Commission intends its money to make schemes possible that would not otherwise have materialized. It is, in fact, very difficult to prove that EC grants actually extend the scale or the scope of the government's public expenditure. What we can say with some certainty is that the government, in setting its public expenditure commitments for Northern Ireland, takes into account the amounts by which its net contribution to the EC budget is reduced by grants received from the ERDF and the ESF.

One serious attempt to enhance the effectiveness of EC aid to Northern Ireland was the Integrated Operations[11] proposal, formally launched in 1980. Under this proposal, it was suggested that the various funds of the EC might be harnessed most effectively in one programme to target the special needs of a specific urban area: Belfast and Naples were selected as the pilot projects under this new initiative. Co-operation between government authorities and the EC proceeded much more quickly in Naples than in Belfast, one of the most thorny issues being the wish to include housing as part of the Belfast urban renewal strategy – something which was not acceptable to other member states lest it create an awkward precedent. In the event, the amounts of money involved were less than had been anticipated partly because unwarranted expectations had been aroused by the ambiguity of the original proposal. The reference to a 'crock of gold' in Brussels, waiting to be plundered, turned out to be an optimistic rolling together of existing funds, not the setting aside of new funds for the Belfast plan.

In the run-up to 1992, the regional policy of the EC has been reorganized to concentrate resources more effectively on the more deprived areas (in what is now a twelve-member Community) with a view to mitigating the worst effects of centre–periphery divergence arising from the completion of the single market. With the same aim in view, the funds allocated to regional development will have been doubled by the time the single market is completed. In the context of the twelve-member Community, Northern Ireland's economic problems appear relatively less serious. Partly because of the 'southern' enlargement in 1986, and partly because of a more refined method of calculating the 'deprivation index', Northern Ireland, as a region, now ranks thirty-third (among 160 regions) instead of second (among 131 regions). The various funds will now be more closely co-ordinated; and their objectives have been defined more precisely under five categories. The first of these, 'the development and structural adjustment of the less prosperous regions', makes Northern Ireland eligible for aid under the newly restructured funds, but only because a special exception was made to include the region on account of its political problems. Normally, an 'Objective 1 region' must have a GDP per capita of less than 75 per cent of the EC average. The Commission will have a greater say in the disbursement of funds than has been the case hitherto, and Northern Ireland can be moderately optimistic about attracting EC funding in the future, albeit on a more selective basis. However, this optimism has to be tempered by the knowledge that many regions in Spain and Portugal have more serious economic problems than Northern Ireland, and that the immense restructuring of Eastern Europe's economies will be a major drain on the EC budget in the 1990s.

Agriculture is one of the most important economic activities in Northern Ireland, and one which has been directly affected by the CAP of the EC. The agricultural sector in Northern Ireland employs proportionately three times as many people as in the rest of the United Kingdom, and as a proportion of GDP is more than twice as important. The average size of a farm in Northern Ireland is about half that for the United Kingdom as a whole. Cattle and milk production account for about two-thirds of agricultural output. The cost of supporting dairy prices in the EC led to the introduction of production quotas in 1984 and, given the dominant position of milk in Northern Ireland agriculture, could have led to a downturn in production. However, the higher retail prices of dairy products and the possibility of transferring unused quotas from Scotland to Northern Ireland have enabled Ulster's dairy farmers to maintain a fairly buoyant output in terms of value. Nevertheless, there has been a slow decline in the number of dairy cows and, in the longer run, a downturn in the value of milk production can be expected. In contrast to the mildly favourable prospects for the dairy industry, the pig industry has declined sharply as a result of price supports for cereals (as feedstuffs). In 1973 pigs accounted for about a fifth of the total agricultural output in terms of value; but by the 1980s this was down to about a tenth. Another objective of the CAP, the rationalization of farm size, has affected Northern Ireland. The number of farms fell by about 14 per cent by 1980, and during the 1980s there has been a slight rise in the number of larger farms.[12]

As the most disadvantaged region in the United Kingdom, and the one with the highest level of unemployment, it has always been government policy to offer a range of aids to industry to ensure both the viability of firms and the preservation of employment. Under the 'competition policy' of the EC, all aids to industry have to be cleared by the Commission to ensure that they do not distort competition between similar firms in different parts of the Community. The two main job-promotion agencies in Northern Ireland, the Industrial Development Board (IDB) and the Local Enterprise Development Unit (LEDU), will be able to continue their work in the run-up to 1992 because the Commission recognizes that regional incentives that do not distort competition with other parts of the Community are vital if the 'core–periphery' effects of the single market are to be counter-balanced. When approving aid to a particular industry in Northern Ireland, the Commission has to be sure that: the aid will not cause production to expand; the aid will be temporary; and that the aid will not preserve an industry at a level of viability that is unrealistic in the context of the Community as a whole. Northern Ireland's traditional industries – shipbuilding, textiles and man-made fibres – have each been affected by the Commission's policy. In the case of textiles and man-made fibres, low-priced competition from outside the EC made open-ended support of those industries in Northern Ireland pointless. In the case of shipbuilding, and in recognition of its central importance as a source of employment in the local economy, the Commission has allowed government subventions to Harland and Wolff, but only up to an agreed level.

The effects of the completion of the single market at the end of 1992 are potentially detrimental for a peripheral region such as Northern Ireland. To the extent that the single market favours large firms, capitalizes on rapid transport networks, and focuses on high-income consumer markets, the outlook looks rather bleak for Northern Ireland. One has to be a rather sanguine supporter of the 'trickle-down' school (that is, a believer in the inexorable spread of wealth as it is created) to imagine that regions like Northern Ireland will do well from the single market. The demands of the

Iberian peninsula, and the need to transform the economies of Eastern Europe, reflect a shift of the Community's centre of gravity away from the Atlantic periphery towards the east and the south. The capacity of the EC itself to change the socio-economic outlook in Northern Ireland has always been rather modest compared with that of the British government: the latter's annual expenditure has always been well over ten times the combined income from various EC sources. In crude financial terms, therefore, the achievement has been less than spectacular. In other economic respects, Northern Ireland's membership of the EC opens up opportunities for specific sectors to do well: marketing skills, transport costs, price and quality will prove to be the crucial variables if Northern Ireland firms are to exploit successfully the challenges offered by the market of 324 million consumers.

The legal implications of EC membership

Of all the implications that EC membership has for Northern Ireland, it may be the legal ones that prove to be the most decisive in the long term. EC law is separate from the national legal systems of the twelve member states but also closely intertwined with all of them. This relationship has been likened to the 'tide' of European law flowing up the 'estuaries' of national laws, and gradually encroaching on the areas previously covered by national law. The important point is that the two systems coexist and where they conflict it is EC law that takes precedence. The primacy of EC law has long been asserted by the Court of Justice, and gradually conceded by the member states. In a judgment in 1978, the Court stated unambiguously:

> Every national court must, in a case within its jurisdiction, apply Community law in its entirety and protect rights which the latter confers on individuals and must accordingly set aside any provision of national law which may conflict with it, whether prior or subsequent to the Community rule.[13]

EC law is directly applicable in the sense that it is not always necessary for a national parliament to incorporate EC law into its domestic statutes. In the case of the United Kingdom, EC legislation applies by virtue of the European Communities Act 1972. National courts take on the role of enforcing Community law on behalf of the EC. The national court faced with a relevant point of EC law may (and often must) refer the question to the EC Court of Justice in Luxembourg. The interpretation of the Court of Justice is final, and the Court ensures that EC law is applied in a uniform way throughout the Community. Consequently, individuals have effective recourse to a higher level of legal protection if the point at issue touches on EC law: the judge must refer the case to Luxembourg, and the eventual finding may deem inapplicable a national law under which the person was brought to court in the first place.

These so-called 'preliminary rulings' are the largest category of cases to come before the Court, and the number increases annually. These rulings serve three useful purposes: they ensure that national courts make sound judgments; they promote the uniform application of EC law throughout the EC; and they provide a means whereby an individual can gain redress against the effects of a national law if it can be shown that the national law is incompatible with EC legislation.

Exactly such an issue arose in 1977 when a pig farmer in County Armagh in Northern Ireland was stopped by the police while transporting seventy-five pigs and was unable to show a certificate giving him permission to do so. Since the 1930s the pig-farming industry in Northern Ireland had been under the control of the Pigs Marketing Board, a body designed to control prices and the trade in pigs. The specific piece of legislation that the farmer was alleged to have infringed was the Movement of Pigs Regulations (NI) 1972 which prohibited the transport of all pigs other than to one of the Board's purchasing centres for which a destination certificate was required. In court the farmer argued that the laws supporting this role of the Board were incompatible with basic articles of the Rome Treaty and with regulations passed for the implementation of these articles. The resident magistrate in the case, seeing that a point of EC law was at issue, referred the case to Luxembourg, and the Court there ruled that marketing boards organized on a regional or national basis and vested with compulsory powers are to be considered incompatible with Articles 30 and 34 of the Rome Treaty and EC Regulation 2759/75 concerned with the organization of the common market in pigmeat. Although the Pigs Marketing Board argued, in its own defence, that it was playing an important role in supporting farm incomes in an area of chronic social and economic disadvantage, that the market in pigmeat was particularly vulnerable in Northern Ireland, and that one of the Board's objectives was to prevent smuggling, the European Court dismissed the case against the farmer as 'ill-founded' and ruled that the relevant national legislation was incompatible with EC law. The case was the first occasion on which a court in Northern Ireland had referred an issue to the Court of Justice in Luxembourg. It illustrated in a clear-cut way the extent to which individuals could rely on an EC legal ruling to vindicate their own position in a national court.

Another occasion on which the existence of EC law made all the difference to an individual arose in 1984 when the Industrial Tribunal in Belfast referred a case to the European Court of Justice in Luxembourg concerning a Mrs Johnston whose contract, along with those of all female full-time police reservists, had not been renewed four years previously. The Chief Constable had argued that there were sufficient women in the regular police force to fulfil all duties normally covered by female personnel. Mrs Johnston took her case to the Industrial Tribunal (with the support of the Equal Opportunities Commission) on the grounds, first, that by the non-renewal of her contract she had been unlawfully discriminated against, and second, that she had been denied vocational training in the use of firearms. Relying on an article of the Northern Ireland Sex Discrimination Order 1976 that allows considerations of public safety and national security to override the Order's anti-discrimination provisions, the Chief Constable could have expected the case to have been settled in his favour at that point. However, EC Directive 76/207 on gender equality in employment allowed governments to be excused from the implementation of equality in employment only in cases where in the 'nature' or the 'context' of the employment, the 'sex of the worker constitutes a determining factor'. The European Court of Justice ruled that the 'nature' of the employment did not justify discriminatory treatment, but conceded that in some circumstances the 'context' of some police activities might, in fact, justify differential treatment on grounds of gender, but that this was a matter for the domestic court to judge. In the event, the case was settled out of court with Mrs Johnston, and thirty other women, receiving in total about £250,000 in compensation. The case had not only brought tangible benefits, albeit after six years' delay, to the individuals concerned, but also marked out the narrow bounds within which EC governments could deviate from the principle of equal treatment in the employment field.

As Northern Ireland constitutes a separate jurisdiction within the United Kingdom, it is for Northern Ireland judges to apply EC law where appropriate, and to seek preliminary rulings from Luxembourg when required to do so; and equally it is for the Northern Ireland legal profession to be aware of the EC dimension when advising clients or pursuing cases in the courts. In a veiled reference, perhaps, to those who cling to the outworn notions of absolute national sovereignty in Anglo-Irish relations, J. Temple Lang reminded a Belfast audience that EC law not only involves a restriction on the sovereignty of individual nation-states, but also that 'every Member State now has influence over the affairs and policies of all the Member States. In the economic and social spheres national boundaries and national powers are very much less important than they used to be'.[14]

Conclusion

Although our analysis has concentrated on the separate political, economic and legal aspects of the Community's impact on Northern Ireland, it is worth remembering that the three perspectives are, in fact, closely intertwined. The legal framework created by the Rome Treaty and the pre-eminent position of EC law within the member states effectively dilute orthodox notions of national sovereignty by ensuring that legal norms are increasingly applied across the EC without respect for national frontiers: thus the political and the legal are closely enmeshed. It is, however, no less the case that economic forces, within the context of the single market after 1992, entail commercial decisions in one country being increasingly influenced by, and in turn influencing, commercial decisions in another: thus the political and the economic are also bound together in a situation where no government can remain immune to economic developments in other member states. Finally, the legal and the economic are linked in so far as the mutual recognition of standards, the EC's competition policy, or the gradual encroachments of environmental and social security legislation dictate the pace, the scope and the direction of economic expansion in the 1990s.

Notes

1 *Northern Ireland and the European Communities* (Cmd. 563), HMSO, Belfast, 1971.
2 The Safeguarding of Employment Act 1947 had instituted a system of permits for those seeking employment in Northern Ireland. This legislation was allowed to continue in force for a period of five years. The early years of Northern Ireland's membership of the European Community are discussed in M. Kolinsky (ed.), *Divided Loyalties: British Regional Assertion and European Integration*, Manchester University Press, Manchester, 1978, pp. 23–43.
3 See Mme S. Martin, rapporteur, *Report drawn up on behalf of the Committee on Regional Policy and Regional Planning on Community Regional Policy and Northern Ireland.* European Parliamentary Working Documents, 1981, Doc. 1–177/81; N. J. Haagerup, rapporteur, *Report drawn up on behalf of the Political Affairs Committee on the Situation in Northern Ireland.* Euro. Parl. Working Documents, 1984, Doc. 1–1526/83; T. J. Maher, rapporteur, *Report drawn up on behalf of the Committee on Regional Policy and Regional Planning on an Integrated Rural Development Programme for the Less Favoured Areas in Northern Ireland.* Euro. Parl. Working Documents, 1986, Doc. A2–105/86.
4 See E. Moxon-Browne, 'Northern Ireland and the European Community: An Extended Platform' *Études Irlandaises* (1991).
5 Ibid.
6 Martin, *Community Regional Policy and Northern Ireland,* Doc. 1–177/81.
7 Haagerup, *Situation in Northern Ireland,* Doc. 1–1526/83.
8 European Parliamentary Debates, vol. 312, 1984–5, pp. 160–75.
9 See J. V. Simpson (ed.), *Northern Ireland and the European Community,* Commission of the European Communities, Belfast, 1988, p. 14.
10 See A. Aughey, P. Hainsworth and M. J. Trimble, *Northern Ireland in the European Community: An Economic and Political Analysis,* Policy Research Institute, Belfast, 1989, p. 146.
11 For a fuller discussion of the Integrated Operations proposal, see M. McGurnaghan, 'Integrated Operations and Urban Renewal: the Belfast experience 1981–85' in Simpson, *Northern Ireland and the EC,* pp. 65–77.
12 See M. Trimble, 'The Northern Ireland Agricultural and Sea Fishing Industries' in Simpson, *Northern Ireland and the EC,* pp. 115–35.
13 *Simmenthal* v *Commission* [1979] ECR 777 (case 92/78).
14 See J. Temple Lang, 'European Community Constitutional Law: The Division of Powers Between the Community and Member States' *Northern Ireland Legal Quarterly,* 39, 1988, p. 234.

5

Administering policy in Northern Ireland

John Loughlin

Since 1969, Northern Ireland has become one of the most studied regions of Western Europe. There has been a plethora of histories of the 'troubles' by journalists and academics, political analyses of the problem as a whole as well as its parts, and treatises on the economic roots of the problem. However, in all of this literature, there has been a relative neglect of public policy and administration.

Birrell and Murie's *Policy and Government in Northern Ireland*[1] still remains a standard, albeit somewhat dated, text on the system of public administration. Connolly and Loughlin's *Public Policy in Northern Ireland*[2] is a first step toward filling the gap in the area of public policy. Some former senior Civil Servants, such as Shea[3] and Oliver,[4] have usefully contributed their memoirs to the literature. However, it remains the case that, to use Easton's famous model of politics, we have been so fascinated by the political inputs to the system and particularly by their breakdown that we have neglected to look inside the black box of the system itself and its outputs, that is, policies. Yet it is very important to look inside the black box and to explore the relationship between politics, policy and administration.

The reforms in Northern Ireland since the late 1960s have attempted to separate these three aspects of government in the province. The implicit notion underlying this approach has been the idea that the formulation and implementation of policy would be more efficient and effective if removed from the bitter sectarian conflict that constitutes Northern Ireland politics. It is true that this technocratic as opposed to political approach to administering policy underlies administrative reform in other countries such as the USA, France and indeed Great Britain. It received, however, a special impetus in Northern Ireland as a result of the serious political violence which broke out in 1968–9 and which has put into question the existence of the state itself.

This chapter will examine the relationship between these three aspects of government – politics, policy and administration – in Northern Ireland. In particular, it will attempt to ascertain the extent to which the separation of 'politics' from 'administration' and 'policy' has been successful and what its effects have been on the sectarian conflict. Before examining the Northern Ireland case in some detail, however, it would be useful to say something about the theoretical underpinning of what is called the 'policy approach' to politics and how this has modified traditional political science approaches.

The policy approach to understanding politics

Before the Second World War, political science was primarily concerned with what might be called the 'inputs' into the political system: the nature of the electorate, political parties, elections, parliamentary formations, coalition formation and the functioning of Cabinets and prime ministers. It was assumed that policies were formulated by governments, ratified by parliaments and administered by the various branches of the executive: the civil service, local government and various kinds of statutory body. Such a schema fitted well into the liberal-democratic theory of government where the legislative, executive and judicial branches of government were clearly separated and where the legislative arm legislated while the executive arm executed its decisions. This might be termed the 'instrumentalist' view of public administration – the latter is simply an 'instrument' in the hands of the political masters.

The 'instrumentalist' understanding of public administration began to change in the early 1950s when there was a reformulation of the way in which political scientists viewed public administration and public policy and the way in which they regarded the relationship between politics and administration. Basically through the works of authors such as Herbert Simon[5] and Charles Lindblom[6], political scientists began to become aware of the importance of decision-making and organizational structures in public administration. Indeed, public administration itself began to assume an importance as an object of study in its own right, albeit still within the field of political science. This was related to increasing interest in the study of 'policy'.[7] Political scientists were interested no longer simply in what government was but now also in what it did in practice. According to Dye, the policy approach is concerned with 'what governments do, why they do it and what difference it makes'.[8]

At first, it was assumed that 'policies' could be clearly identified both by legislators and bureaucrats and could be implemented in the form in which they were formulated. It was not until the 1960s that scholars began to pay serious attention to problems of implementation. This followed the failure of the great liberal programmes to eradicate poverty and racial disadvantage in the USA, formulated in the optimistic period of the early 1960s but appearing, according to Ham and Hill,[9] to have collapsed by the end of the decade.

Political scientists, especially those who had supported these programmes, began to ask what had gone wrong. These authors assumed that the problem lay, not with the policies, but with their implementation. Pressman and Wildavsky[10] initiated a debate which led to the development of implementation theory. This in its turn might be seen as a debate between rival schools: basically those, such as Pressman and Wildavsky, who advocate a 'top-down' approach and others, such as Ham and Hill, who advocate a 'bottom-up' approach. The 'top-down' school assumed that 'policy' is a given entity and that failure occurs because of ambiguity, outside interference, or too many links in the chain of command from the top to the bottom. Some authors try to construct an ideal-type model of 'perfect administration' containing the features of an administrative system in which the 'implementation deficit' (the gap between the intention of the policy-makers and the actual implementation result) would be non-existent.[11] The 'top-down' approach implies a technocratic approach to decision-making and attempts to keep 'politics', especially party politics, at arm's length. The 'bottom-up' approach, on the other hand, stresses what it sees as the essentially ambiguous nature of policies and of the role of politics in the policy process. This is an exercise in pluralist bargaining and compromise where policy is developed in an incrementalist manner. Furthermore, implementation in its turn becomes part of the formulation process by a process of feedback. Hence, it is impossible to delineate clearly either what is meant by the term 'policy' or even what is the substantive content of any particular policy area. Politics is seen as an exercise in vagueness and ambiguity. We shall see below in our analysis of the Northern Ireland case that the assumptions of the technocratic approach underlay the reforms of administration in the province.

Where do these approaches stand in relation to political science? We have seen that both public administration theory and public policy theory developed out of mainstream political science. Basically, the shift that has taken place is from public administration conceived in the instrumentalist manner outlined to one where it is seen as dynamic, process-orientated and semi-autonomous. What matters here is not the formal structures of the organization as defined on paper but the 'real' relationships of power and influence that may not exactly coincide with such paper definitions. From the perspective of political science, the important point is that administrators are as much involved in decision-making as elected politicians. Indeed, some authors would claim that the former are even more powerful than the latter. Whatever judgement one might make about this, it is probably generally agreed by contemporary political scientists that the relationship between politics and administration is a close one and that senior administrators do exert a powerful influence. More recent studies of implementation also point to the influence of lower-level administrators sometimes known as 'street-level bureaucrats'.

Policy studies, called by various names – policy sciences, policy analysis, the policy approach[12] – could be seen as a branch of political science but also as having modified traditional approaches to the discipline. Basically, the policy approach has reinforced the shift away from the 'constitutional-legal' approach to the more dynamic and output-orientated one outlined above which is concerned with processes rather than structures. Not only are elected politicians involved in policy-making but also an array of unelected individuals, organizations and groups. Sometimes these groupings are referred to as 'policy communities' and 'policy networks'.[13] They have a sociological rather than a legal existence and cluster around particular policy arenas such as agriculture, education and health. In any case, what is important is to look behind the formal sets of relationships that one expects from a 'constitutional' understanding of the political system to those more 'hidden' dimensions that may be revealed by techniques of sociological analysis.

There is a tendency in this school to underestimate the importance of the state and to blur the distinction between public-sector and private-sector organizations. These are classified simply as 'organizations'. However, in recent times, there has been an attempt to bring the state back in.[14] A public-sector organization like a government department is not simply an organization like a computer firm. While they have certain features in common, each possesses characteristics not found in the other. These considerations are particularly relevant when we examine in some detail the case of Northern Ireland, which has such an important public sector and whose 'constitutional' position is central to the nature of its politics. First, it is necessary to examine the relationship between politics and administration within Northern Ireland.

Politics and administration in Northern Ireland

The present system of public administration in Northern Ireland was set up following the Government of Ireland Act 1920 to assist the newly devolved government and Parliament of Northern Ireland to carry out its task of governing the six-county province. The Northern Ireland Civil Service (NICS), like its southern counterpart, the Irish Civil Service, was a successor to the all-Ireland administration whose centre had been in Dublin Castle. Some of its senior members had served in the Irish Civil Service, others were imported from the Home Civil Service (HCS), colloquially known as the 'Imperial' Civil Service, in Whitehall. However, the conventions, traditions and operating procedures were mostly based on the Whitehall model. The Northern Ireland government and Parliament resembled a mini-Westminster while the Northern Ireland Cabinet ministers oversaw the six ministries following the same conventions of ministerial responsibility as existed in Westminster and Whitehall. Local government in Northern Ireland had its roots in the UK local government reforms of the 1880s, and this remained largely unchanged in the new regime except for some redrawing of boundaries which benefited the Unionist Party at the local level.

Northern Ireland might, therefore, be regarded as a kind of miniature United Kingdom in its political and administrative structures. Despite the rather extravagant and over-blown nature of the system for a population of about 1½ million, the UK government seems to have devised it this way as a means of ensuring that the Northern Ireland problem did not impinge on politics in Great Britain. There was a convention, established in 1923, that no Westminster MP could raise in the House of Commons any issue which was the direct responsibility of a Stormont minister. This was to remain the case until the 1960s, when it was breached by Gerry Fitt, Westminster MP for West Belfast.

Although the politico-administrative system in Northern Ireland was modelled on that in Great Britain, the nature of politics in the two parts of the United Kingdom was quite different. In Great Britain, as in other industrialized countries, the basic political cleavage was based on socio-economic issues reflecting the interests of opposing social classes. After the decline of the Liberal Party in the early part of the century, the Conservatives mostly represented the middle and upper classes and business interests; Labour mostly represented the working classes and the trade union movement. Clearly some workers did vote Tory and some middle-class people did vote Labour. Furthermore, the British Parliamentary system was characterized by the alternation in power of two great parties, a system encouraged by the first-past-the-post system which tended to squeeze out smaller parties. In Northern Ireland, however, the basic political cleavage related to a conflict between two political *blocs* concerning the future of Northern Ireland itself, sometimes known as the constitutional question: would Northern Ireland remain a part of the United Kingdom, as advocated by the unionist bloc, or would it join with the Republic of Ireland, as advocated by the nationalist bloc? This cleavage overlapped with other cleavages but especially with the religious cleavage: most Catholics were nationalists, most non-Catholics (called for convenience Protestants, although many Anglicans and Quakers deny that term as applying to themselves) were unionists. Northern Ireland, comprising just six of the nine counties of the historic province of Ulster, was designed to ensure that its majority would consist permanently of unionists and, indeed, between 1921 and direct rule in 1972, only the Unionist Party formed the government of Northern Ireland. In other words, there was no alternation in power between the two great political blocs.

This basic political cleavage and the political domination of unionists had consequences for the system of public administration. It would be an exaggeration to say that this was simply a tool in the hands of the unionist masters. Yet, because Civil Servants only ever had to obey one political party, they tended, particularly at the senior level, to adopt the values and attitudes of that party. Several factors served to reinforce this tendency. First, Northern Ireland, despite its extravagant politico-administrative structures, was, both demographically and geographically, a very small society compared to Great Britain. The usual comparison made was with a medium-size local authority in Britain such as Yorkshire or Humberside. This smaller scale meant that ministers and senior Civil Servants were able to establish a much closer relationship than existed in Great Britain. Second, politics in Northern Ireland was in practice a part-time job even for ministers. This meant that much of the decision-making was left in the hands of the Civil Servants who were very quickly able to master any problems which arose. However, the Civil Servants were broadly in sympathy with the political values of the ministers so their approach was broadly unionist. Third, recruitment to the upper reaches of the Civil Service was almost exclusively restricted to those 'loyal' to the regime – either Northern Irish Protestants or English people. Catholics, suspected by most unionists of being disloyal, seemed to have been systematically excluded, although there is a debate about the extent of this and the reasons for it.[15] To this extent, then, the local political cleavage affected the system of public administration and, therefore, the nature of policy-making in Northern Ireland.

It would be a mistake, however, to see Northern Ireland Civil Servants simply as tools of the Unionist Party. Two qualifications must be made to this. First, the NICS, especially after the Second World War, tended to follow the lead of its Whitehall counterpart in most policy areas. This was the period of the establishment of the Welfare State and then of regional economic planning, both the inspiration of the British Labour Party. The Northern Ireland Unionist Party, being a branch of the Conservative Party, was not sympathetic to either of these developments. However, it did not actively oppose them either and, indeed, adopted a 'step-by-step' policy which ensured that Northern Ireland kept parity with the rest of the United Kingdom.[16] But it does seem that the Civil Servants were more enthusiastic about the reforms and indeed may have taken the initiative with regard to important issues such as economic development. In other words, they displayed an independence of their political masters which had definite consequences for the social and economic life of the region. The second point to be made is that administration was carried out with about as much or as little efficiency and effectiveness as was the case in Great Britain and in many policy areas the constitutional question did not impinge on this. This was particularly true of areas such as the delivery of health and personal social services, where sectarian bias was difficult to achieve because underlying the rationale of the welfare state was the desire to promote equality of opportunity across the entire United Kingdom. This meant that there would be parity of services whatever the degree of wealth or poverty of the particular area.

Sectarian bias in policy was more evident in local government in Northern Ireland. This affected both employment by local authorities and the delivery of services for which local government was responsible. The most important of these was housing, which became a major bone of contention between the two communities and indeed was one of the principal issues which sparked off the civil rights protests in the 1960s. Most of the seventy-two local authorities were controlled by unionists and it is true to say that, as a result, most of the discrimination was practised against Catholics.[17] However, some discrimination did occur against Protestants in some of the minority of local authorities controlled by nationalists. Finally, it should be pointed out that discrimination by local authorities was not a generalized phenomenon but took place in just a minority of authorities mostly situated west of the Bann. However, taken together all of these small-scale acts of discrimination, coupled with the widespread discrimination in the private sector, were sufficient to enrage and alienate the nationalist community who felt they had little stake in the politico-administrative system. Furthermore, Stormont government ministers, including Prime Ministers such as Lord Brookeborough, not only did little to stop the discrimination, but seemed actively to encourage it. This did little to reinforce the confidence of nationalists in the regime. In the end, the system broke down when the latter withdrew their consent completely.

Administrative reform in Northern Ireland

By the 1960s, it was clear that major reforms of the administrative system were needed in Northern Ireland. This was especially true of local government which, originally devised in the nineteenth century, was unsuited to the conditions of the second half of the twentieth. This was also true of Great Britain, as the Wheatley Commission for Scotland and the Redcliffe-Maud Commission for England and Wales had pointed out. Indeed, the Wheatley Report for Scotland was thought to be particularly relevant for Northern Ireland and influenced official thinking here. This was clearly evident in the Macrory Report,[18] which explicitly acknowledges its debt to Wheatley rather than to Redcliffe-Maud.

Basically it was recognized that the existing structure of local government was incapable of delivering the services for which it was responsible in an efficient and effective manner. There were too many local authorities, many of whom were too small and lacking in personnel, expertise and financial resources to carry out any but the most basic tasks. Furthermore, as in Great Britain, nineteenth-century local government was based on a distinction between rural and urban areas which was irrelevant in an age of urbanization and where personal transport had reduced the distance between town and country. In other words, the initial impetus for reforming the administrative system in Northern Ireland followed not a political but an administrative logic. The Macrory Report, partly following the recommendations of previous government reports and partly innovating, recommended that the large number of local authorities be reduced to twenty-six and a considerable number of their functions be removed to either central Stormont departments or to centralized *ad hoc* or area boards. Government departments were given responsibility for town and country planning, roads, water and sewerage; centralized boards took over housing, economic development and fire services; area boards became responsible for health and personal social services, education and library facilities. This followed the distinction, made by Macrory, of regional and district tiers of government. It was assumed that the regional parliament and government at Stormont would remain to act as an overseer of the administration and as a forum of democratic accountability.

However, what might be called the 'technocratic impetus' to reform soon became overshadowed by the political situation. The civil unrest related to the civil rights agitation for better conditions for Catholics and the reaction against this by extremist Protestants soon influenced the reform programme. While the Stormont government had been willing to introduce a number of reforms of the local government system, these were not as radical as the reforms that were largely forced on them by the British government which from the late 1960s began to take more interest in Northern Ireland than hitherto. The crucial area was housing. In the initial reform proposals it was envisaged that responsibility for this would remain with local government. However, in 1969, even before the Macrory Commission was under way, the Northern Ireland government and the British government announced that a centralized agency responsible for the provision of housing would be set up.[19] This was deliberately to remove housing from the political arena and to ensure that housing was allocated on a fairer basis. Because house-building entails several other services such as sewerage, road-building, and electricity provision, Macrory recognized that the provision of these would also need to be centralized at Stormont. The Northern Ireland Housing Executive (NIHE) was established in 1971. The NIHE drew up a points system related to criteria of need rather than the religion of the applicant. In the end, local government lost most of its powers and ended up with responsibility for a small number of rather insignificant services.[20]

Another political development that affected the Macrory reforms was the suspension of the Stormont Parliament and government in March 1972 when the Northern Ireland government of Brian Faulkner refused to accept that Westminster should take responsibility for security following the killings by British paratroopers of thirteen civil rights demonstrators in Derry shortly before. This inaugurated a period of direct rule through the Northern Ireland Office (NIO), whose head is the Secretary of State for Northern Ireland. Since the Secretary of State is chosen from the party ruling at Westminster and people in Northern Ireland have no opportunity of voting for the main British parties, the people are effectively unable to hold accountable through the ballot-box those with political responsibility for the major administrative services which affect their lives. Since Macrory had originally envisaged that such account-ability would be exercised through the regional parliament at Stormont, this lack is sometimes called the 'Macrory gap'.

Lacking a regional forum and being powerless at the Westminster level, the local parties have used local government as a means of expressing the political conflict that divided them. This means in effect that local councillors have preoccupied themselves with matters that theoretically lie outside the scope of the responsibilities of local government. For example, local government has been used by the unionist parties to protest against Sinn Fein, the political wing of the IRA, and against the Anglo-Irish Agreement. Sinn Fein, in its turn, is clearly delighted with the disruption that is caused by these protests since it brings into disrepute the political system itself.

It might be said about the reform of the Northern Ireland politico-administrative system that while the administrative reforms are largely in place, the political dimension is still in abeyance. Indeed, as has been seen in Chapter 2, it has been central to British government policy since 1973 that there would be a devolved government in Northern Ireland but only on condition that there be power-sharing between the communities. One of the tasks of the Secretary of State for Northern Ireland is to try to devise such a devolved system with the agreement of the political representatives of the two communities, or at least with those politicians not associated with paramilitary groups. So far, a solution has eluded successive Secretaries of State. William Whitelaw (the incumbent from March 1972 to December 1973) did succeed in bringing about the power-sharing Executive of 1974 but this was soon crushed by the loyalist Ulster Workers' Council (UWC) strike. Other Secretaries of State have pursued a solution with greater or less vigour. The least interested in a political solution was Roy Mason of the Labour Party (Secretary of State from September 1976 to May 1979). Perhaps the most tenacious is the current (mid-1991) Secretary, Peter Brooke, who, after over a year of pursuing 'talks about talks' has succeeded, to everyone's surprise including perhaps his own, in getting the main parties on the unionist and nationalist sides to agree to participate in further talks. These will be about the three sets of relationships affecting both islands: within Northern Ireland, between Northern Ireland and the Irish Republic, between the Irish Republic and the United Kingdom. Between William Whitelaw and Peter Brooke, Northern Ireland has had the power-sharing Executive, the Constitutional Convention, the Northern Ireland Assembly, and, most importantly, the Anglo-Irish Agreement (since 1985). The last 'initiative' allows the Republic of Ireland an influence in certain policy areas in Northern Ireland which has boosted the position of consti-tutional nationalists and forced the unionists into agreeing to the Brooke talks. In other words, the Anglo-Irish Agreement has changed the configuration of Northern Ireland politics and provided the basis for going forward to (possibly) a more definitive solution.

The politico-administrative system that has evolved under direct rule has had important consequences from the point of view of policy-making. The most significant is that local politics and local administration have been largely separated. There is no regional political forum and locally elected politicians enter either Westminster or local government. Since there are only seventeen MPs at Westminster their influence is minimal. At most they can introduce questions at Prime Minister's Question Time or perhaps sit on a Parliamentary committee. However, since most legislation concerning Northern Ireland consists of Orders in Council, there is no opportunity to comment on it in detail as happens with the enactment of Bills.[21] Local councillors, on the other hand, are just as powerless. Since the local authorities were stripped of most of their responsibilities in the 1973 reforms and housing was taken from them in 1971, there is little of importance that they can oversee. The different statutory agencies – health and social services, education and library boards – do allow for a proportion of their members to be drawn from the local authorities; however, this is not a large enough number to be able to exercise a decisive influence over the activities of these bodies. This means that local administrators cannot be held accountable to the politicians elected by the local population. Instead, they are accountable to the ministers of the NIO who are elected by electors mostly in Great Britain.

This powerlessness on the part of local politicians means that local administrators have developed a style of their own. Being largely free of the influence of the local politicians, of whom they are rather contemptuous, they tend to see themselves as being above the local conflict. This is true even of local government officers, who are more under the influence of the politicians than is the case with Northern Ireland Civil Servants. This technocratic approach is even the source of a certain amount of pride on their part. On the other hand, the diminution of the status of politicians has sometimes led to a lack of responsiveness to the public on the part of administrators.

Northern Ireland and the United Kingdom

Despite the peculiarities of its politico-administrative system and the differences in its political cleavages with Great Britain, Northern Ireland still forms part of the United Kingdom. It might be expected, therefore, that 'policy' here would simply reflect 'policy' as formulated in London. At this point it might be useful to recall from the policy science literature that the concept of 'policy' itself is not very easy to define. The classical liberal-democratic theory of politics and approaches such as the rationality-based models of authors like Simon[22] assumed that there was a clearly defined entity called a 'policy' in a particular area, usually defined in legislation. However, it is increasingly recognized that policy itself is much more complex and involves not simply formulation but also the implementation of decisions which may in turn feed back into the system to be reformulated. One author defined policy as a 'stance' taken by government toward a particular problem or set of problems. Thus privatization could be seen as a general stance on the part of the

Conservative government while the concrete realities of its implementation might be quite complex.[23]

Understood in this way, policy in Northern Ireland has indeed tended to follow policy in Great Britain.[24] As has been mentioned earlier, the Stormont government tried after the Second World War to ensure parity by following a 'step-by-step' approach. Some of the substantive policies, such as social welfare policy, may not have been congenial to the conservative Unionist governments. However, the latter did see the advantages in political terms of marking their distance from the Irish Republic, whose social welfare system was much inferior to the British (only recently has the gap narrowed considerably). As well as that, too great a difference between Northern Ireland and Great Britain would have weakened their own support base among the Protestant population in Northern Ireland. This tendency to follow policy in Great Britain has been intensified under direct rule. The Secretary of State for Northern Ireland is already a member of the British Cabinet and would largely share the collective understanding of the Cabinet, even if this post was sometimes reserved for those who disagreed with the Prime Minister over policy, as was the case with James Prior, exiled to Northern Ireland by Mrs Thatcher. At the same time, Prior would not have found himself in fundamental disagreement with all Conservative policy, otherwise he could not have remained a minister and a member of the party. The convergence with British policy is also encouraged by the nature of the NIO.[25] This is an office that straddles both the Whitehall and Stormont Civil Services and which attempts to provide an overall coherence to policy in Northern Ireland. Because of this the Northern Ireland departments are much less isolated from each other than is the case with their Whitehall counterparts. This means that they tend to follow even more closely what happens in Great Britain. Finally, it has long been the custom for Stormont departments to 'shadow' their counterparts in Whitehall. This is particularly true of agriculture and health and social services.

However, it would be wrong to see the Northern Ireland departments as simply adopting slavishly what is formulated in Great Britain. Indeed, some Secretaries of State under Mrs Thatcher used the opportunity to pursue an approach to policy that was considerably 'wetter' than would have been possible in Great Britain. This could be justified by appealing to the 'special circumstances' of Northern Ireland. It might be truer to say that Northern Ireland accepts the general policy stance of Westminster governments but implements it in a way appropriate to the circumstances of Northern Ireland. This adoption might be represented as a continuum going from a high degree of convergence to a high degree of divergence. Health and social services follow quite closely the system in Great Britain, even if the administrative structure is rather different. Education has traditionally been very distinctive in Northern Ireland, which escaped the 'comprehensivization' of education that occurred in Great Britain in the 1960s, although the Mawhinney reforms (for example, bringing in testing at various ages and a common curriculum) of the 1980s have attempted to bring about a greater convergence. The most distinctive area of policy is in the area of security, obviously because of the civil unrest that is a permanent feature of life in Northern Ireland. The roles of the police and the Army are very different in Northern Ireland from Great Britain. Interestingly, prison policy in Northern Ireland is much more liberal and humane than that across the water, where it still seems caught in the Victorian system. Finally, the Thatcher reforms of the British administrative system have been applied to Northern Ireland, but not always at the same pace and in the same way. The Financial Management Initiative (FMI) was introduced in Northern Ireland. But it was at first thought that Ibbs's 'Next Steps' initiative would not apply to the region.[26] Ibbs was appointed as successor to Lord Rayner to continue the reform of the Civil Service initiated by Mrs Thatcher. He proposed that agencies would be created to carry out some of the tasks of the Civil Service, thus reducing the number of Civil Servants. However, it was later decided to introduce a version of this initiative to Northern Ireland. By April 1991, three agencies were set up: Training and Employment Services, Social Security Operations, and the Central Rating Agency.

Policy is made and implemented not simply through the constitutionally recognized administrative structures of departments but also more informally through what are known as 'policy communities' and 'policy networks'. These also exist within Northern Ireland. What distinguishes Northern Ireland from Great Britain, at least during the Thatcher years, is that trade unions have been involved in such communities to a much greater degree in Northern Ireland.[27]

The Anglo-Irish Agreement

The Anglo-Irish Agreement (AIA) aims to promote peace and stability in Northern Ireland, the reconciliation of the two traditions (the term used for the two political blocs) and the defeat of terrorism. This has been analysed comprehensively in other literature.[28] It suffices to say here that the Agreement allows the Irish government to become involved in certain policy areas monitoring political, legal, security and other issues of concern to the nationalist minority. An Intergovernmental Conference (IGC) bringing together British and Irish ministers was established with a permanent secretariat, staffed by Civil Servants from both countries, at Maryfield near Belfast. There are regular summits between the Secretary of State and the Irish ministers to discuss issues in Northern Ireland. The Irish government has not hesitated to use the IGC to pursue policy issues which it felt to be important. The IGC might be seen as a unique institution which, although it cannot *take* decisions, does exercise an important influence over policy. In essence, it allows the government of another state to become involved in the affairs of its neighbours. What is interesting here from the perspective of the relation between politics, policy and administration is that what seems to be a *de facto* system of joint sovereignty is in operation, although theoretically sovereignty remains exclusively with Westminster. This might be seen as a new policy community dealing with issues affecting the nationalist minority and involving ministers and Civil Servants from two states.

The European dimension

One of the factors that facilitated the signing of the AIA was the fact that both the United Kingdom and the Irish Republic were members of the European Community (EC). Part of the thinking was that the traditional notion of national sovereignty had become less important since many decision-making powers were passing to Brussels in any case. The United Kingdom, therefore, could allow the Republic to participate to some extent in the policy process. However, as seen in Chapter 4, membership of the EC is affecting Northern Ireland on a wider level than simply the AIA. Many areas of policy, for example, are now decided by the European Commission rather than by Westminster/Whitehall or by Stormont.[29] This leads to more tiers of administration and less accountability on the part of the public.

However, Northern Ireland's interests in the EC are at present represented by London, although attempts are being made to allow it to establish an independent voice as is the case with other regions. It is frequently pointed out that because Northern Ireland has an important agricultural sector, its interests do not coincide with those of the United Kingdom as a whole whose agricultural sector is small and of a different nature from that in Northern Ireland. In fact, it has more in common with the Irish Republic, which has used its sovereign state status to achieve more from the EC than Northern Ireland ever could as a peripheral region of the United Kingdom. However, this question, too, is bound up with the local political conflict. Nationalists would be quite happy to see Northern Ireland link up with the Republic in the pursuit of its interests in Europe. For unionists, this is anathema.

Conclusion

To some extent the aim of the reformers to separate politics from administration and policy in Northern Ireland has been successful, even if we mean by this sectarian or party politics. Administrators no longer have the close relationship with unionism that existed before 1969. Futhermore, administrative reforms have made the administration more streamlined and enable it to function more effectively and efficiently. Most people are happy with the centralization of certain services and with the reduction of the powers of local government.

However, politics still continues to influence the system. It is clear that the setting up of the Intergovernmental Conference under the AIA was a political rather than an administrative act, and was directly related to the local political conflict. However, there is no evidence that the IGC affects the running of the Northern Ireland departments or the other administrative agencies in Northern Ireland. It is concerned with what might be called 'high politics', that is, issues connected to the constitutional question, than with 'low politics', that is 'bread and butter' issues. Apart from the AIA, there is a general feeling of unhappiness at the lack of accountability on the part of administrators to the general public because of the 'Macrory gap'. Unionists feel this more strongly than nationalists, although even the latter would support a locally devolved system provided it was based on power-sharing. It is this lack of accountability that explains the distance of many administrators in Northern Ireland, who often take decisions without proper consultation with local people. Whether the forthcoming talks between the constitutional political parties will improve this situation remains to be seen.

From the point of view of our initial theoretical discussion, it might be said that, in the Northern Ireland case at any rate, 'constitutional-legal' issues and institutions cannot simply be dissolved into 'policy communities' or similar amorphous entities. This is a consequence partly of the importance of the 'constitutional' question and partly also of the close watch kept over the system of administration by the general public of both communities, who are fearful lest 'their side' is disadvantaged (and in this sense there is a kind of accountability, although this is not as formal as Parliamentary scrutiny). For example, the NIHE is held in some suspicion by loyalists, while the NICS is still regarded with suspicion by nationalists because its upper echelons are still almost exclusively Protestant. However, the institutional dimension is also important because the reforms have largely been organizational reforms, with the supposition that other kinds of societal change would follow in their wake. To some extent this has happened and policy in Northern Ireland could be seen as bureaucrat-led rather than politician-led. Finally, the study of Northern Ireland confirms the wide definition of policy as a 'stance' rather than as something that can be clearly defined as a discrete entity. Generally speaking, 'policy' in this sense is defined at Westminster/Whitehall and applied more or less faithfully depending on the policy arena in question. However, even those areas applied most faithfully will have Northern Ireland variations.

Notes

1 D. Birrell and A. Murie, *Policy and Government in Northern Ireland*, Gill and Macmillan, Dublin, 1980.
2 M. Connolly and S. Loughlin, *Public Policy in Northern Ireland: Adoption or Adaptation*, Policy Research Institute, Belfast, 1990.

3 P. Shea, *Voices and the Sound of Drums*, Blackstaff Press, Belfast, 1980.
4 J. Oliver, *Working at Stormont*, Institute of Public Administration, Dublin, 1978.
5 H. Simon, *Administrative Behaviour*, Macmillan, London, 1947; 2nd edn, 1957.
6 C. Lindblom, 'The Science of "Muddling Through"', *Public Administration Review*, 19 (1959), 79–88.
7 C. Ham and M. Hill, *The Policy Process in the Modern Capitalist State*, Wheatsheaf, Brighton, 1984.
8 T. Dye, *Policy Analysis*, University of Alabama Press, Tuscaloosa, 1976.
9 Ham and Hill, *Policy Process*.
10 J. Pressman and A. Wildavsky, *Implementation*, University of California Press, Berkeley, 1973.
11 B. Hogwood and L. Gunn, *Policy Analysis for the Real World*, Oxford University Press, Oxford, 1984.
12 See Ham and Hill, *Policy Process*; Hogwood and Gunn, *Policy Analysis for the Real World*; and M. Burch and B. Wood, *Public Policy in Britain* (2nd edn), Basil Blackwell, Oxford, 1989.
13 See R. A. W. Rhodes, 'Power-Dependence, Policy Communities and Intergovernmental Relations', *Public Administration Bulletin*, 49 (1985), 4–31.
14 Ham and Hill, *Policy Process*.
15 J. Whyte, 'How Much Discrimination Was There under the Unionist Regime, 1921–1968?' in T. Gallagher and J. O'Connell (eds), *Contemporary Irish Studies*, Manchester University Press, Manchester, 1983.
16 Birrell and Murie, *Policy and Government*.
17 See Whyte, 'How Much Discrimination?'
18 *Review Body on Local Government in Northern Ireland* (Cmd. 546), HMSO, Belfast, 1970.
19 *Text of a Communiqué issued following discussions between the Secretary of State for the Home Department and the Northern Ireland Government in Belfast on October 9 and 10, 1969* (Cmnd. 4178), HMSO, London, 1969.
20 C. Knox, 'Local Government in Northern Ireland' in Connolly and Loughlin, *Public Policy*.
21 B. Hadfield, 'Legislating for Northern Ireland at Westminster' in Connolly and Loughlin, *Public Policy*.
22 Simon, *Administrative Behaviour*.
23 S. Baker, 'Privatization Policy in Northern Ireland' in Connolly and Loughlin, *Public Policy*.
24 See Connolly and Loughlin, *Public Policy*.
25 P. Bell, 'Direct Rule in Northern Ireland', in R. Rose (ed.), *Ministers and Ministries*, Clarendon Press, Oxford, 1987.
26 C. Knox and M. McHugh, 'Management in Government – the "Next Steps" in Northern Ireland', *Administration*, 38 (1991), 251–70.
27 A. Erridge and T. Cradden, 'Employers and Trade Unions in the Development of Public Policy in Northern Ireland', in Connolly and Loughlin, *Public Policy*.
28 M. Connolly and J. Loughlin, 'Reflections on the Anglo-Irish Agreement', *Government and Opposition*, 21 (1986) 146–60; A. Kenny, *The Road to Hillsborough: The Shaping of the Anglo-Irish Agreement*, Pergamon Press, Oxford, 1986.

29 A. Aughey, P. Hainsworth and M. Trimble, *Northern Ireland and the European Community: an Economic and Political Analysis*, Policy Research Institute, Belfast, 1989.

6

Voting systems and political parties in Northern Ireland

Sydney Elliott

The devolved institutions created in 1921 added a new level of elections between those for Parliament and those for local authorities. During the seventy years since 1921 two different methods of election have been used. Elections to Parliament at Westminster have always used the simple plurality system in single-member districts (the first-past-the-post system). Elections to the Stormont Parliament in 1921 and 1925 used the single transferable vote (STV) method of proportional representation (PR) but reverted to the Westminster system from 1929 to 1969. The STV method was reintroduced for the new devolved Assembly in 1973, the Constitutional Convention in 1975 and the Assembly of 1982. At local government level the experiment with PR in 1920 was reversed in 1922 and the simple majority system was restored until 1972. The restructured and reformed system of district councils after 1973 returned to STV in multi-member units. The elections to the European Parliament since 1979 have used STV in a single constituency with three members. PR has survived for eighteen years, in part because after 1972 control of elections became a function reserved by Westminster but possibly also because its experimental reintroduction still awaits official evaluation.

The electoral provisions of the Government of Ireland Act 1920 were the result of four home rule proposals over thirty-four years and debate about safeguards for minorities. Under the 1920 Act, so far as Northern Ireland was concerned, representation at Westminster continued but with thirteen instead of thirty members and no power to amend electoral laws relating to Westminster elections. The Northern Ireland House of Commons had fifty-two members for sixteen borough, thirty-two county and four university seats. Members were elected by STV, using the Westminster constituencies, for a five-year term. The Senate was elected by the Northern Ireland House of Commons by STV for a period of eight years, with half retiring every four years. All electoral laws then applying in the United Kingdom also applied to

Northern Ireland. The electoral system was guaranteed under the 1920 Act for a period of three years after which it could be altered by the Northern Ireland Parliament. The local government electoral system was not mentioned by the Act; it derived from the Local Government (Ireland) Act 1898 and the Local Government (Ireland) Act 1919 which introduced STV for local elections. Finally, the 1920 Act prohibited laws which interfered with religious equality. This system represented what was considered appropriate for local needs and reflected the current debate on electoral systems in the United Kingdom.

The basic problem facing Northern Ireland in 1921 was to bring dissident opinion, nationalist, unionist and other, into the life of the new political entity. Enloe outlines three strategies for states lacking unity due to ethnic factors,[1] namely allocation of resources, autonomy for border areas and use of the electoral system. In Northern Ireland, the third of these strategies had the most potential. In general, if the electoral system assisted the formation of coalitions or promoted cross-cutting cleavages it could pull groups into the political system. By giving minorities representation, PR could specifically reduce tension over electoral boundaries and the feeling of injustice where plurality methods were used.

The penalty for failure was outlined by Rabushka and Shepsle.[2] Their paradigm of politics in plural societies set out the dynamics of ethnic competition and stressed the significance of electoral machination in a progression towards violence. They stated that the temptation to manipulate was overwhelming in two types of circumstances: first, where the majority felt politically insecure due to the size of one of the minorities; and second, where there was a dominant majority and minorities were significant only in the event of splits in the majority or in the use of violence. In both these circumstances small communities were less willing to co-operate and more likely to insist on communal representation and other protections against majoritarianism.

The electoral system contains several elements capable of manipulation for partisan advantage. The first element is the retention of outdated or fancy franchises and the disfranchisement of opponents. The second is the over-representation of rural or urban constituencies by boundary neglect or, intentionally, by gerrymandering through the manipulation of electoral boundaries. The third is the manipulation of voting rules and methods of representation: dominant groups prefer majoritarianism while minorities prefer proportionalism; dominant groups prefer representation by territory but minorities prefer communal representation.

Franchise

Northern Ireland inherited the same franchise as applied throughout the United Kingdom in 1920. Under the Representation of the People Act 1918 there was universal male adult suffrage on the basis of residence. Apart from the university vote, the only other franchise retained was for occupancy of business premises worth £10 per annum. The local government franchise was granted to all owners or tenants but not to all residents. There was a residence qualification of six months in the constituency, contiguous borough or county. Servicemen had a less restrictive residence qualification, and could vote at nineteen, while conscientious objectors were disfranchised for five years. Women over thirty were enfranchised if they were local government electors or the wives of local government electors. Plural voting was permitted only on different types of qualification and no one could vote more than twice.

This franchise was used in Northern Ireland at the Westminster elections of 1922, 1923 and 1924. It was also used for Stormont elections in 1921 and 1925 and for the local government elections of 1920, 1923–4 and annually or triennially thereafter. It was altered for Westminster elections by the Representation of the People (Equal Franchise) Act 1928. The Bill had two substantive provisions: the first two clauses granted the Parliamentary and local government franchise on the same terms to women as to men; the fourth clause enabled women to vote on their husband's business premises qualification.

The equivalent Bill in Northern Ireland was the Representation of the People Act (NI) 1928. The principle of equalizing the franchise was welcomed unanimously. Opposition centred round the introduction of a three-year residence qualification[3] and a limited liability company franchise in local government elections. Both proposals were carried against Nationalist and Labour opposition. The main provision increased the electorate in Northern Ireland by 24.9 per cent: the male electorate increased by 3.3 per cent and the female electorate by 55.6 per cent. Women were a majority of the electorate (51.4 per cent) and were in the majority in every county borough and county except Fermanagh and Tyrone.

The franchise remained the same until the wartime preparations for peace. The Vivian Committee recommendations on registration were embodied in two Acts at Westminster and one at Stormont, the Parliament (Elections and Meeting) Act (NI) 1944.[4] The Speaker's Conference of 1944 recommended several important changes, including a Boundary Commission to redistribute seats and the assimilation of the Parliamentary and local government franchises. The latter became law in the Representation of the People Act 1945. However, Northern Ireland decided against assimilation and retained the ratepayer franchise in local government, making only a few adjustments to meet hardships created by wartime conditions. Finally, the Representation of the People Act 1948 abolished the business and university vote, extended postal vote facilities and abolished the residence qualification.[5] Northern Ireland did not follow the lead for Stormont elections on the business vote and university vote.

In summary, therefore, after the electoral reforms at Westminster between 1944 and 1949, the Unionist government chose to retain the business vote and university vote for Stormont elections and the ratepayer suffrage and the

Table 6.1 Adults, local government electors and religion, 1961

	Adult population	Electorate as percentage of adult population	Roman Catholic percentage of population
Belfast	264,686	75.0	27.5
Antrim	167,629	75.4	24.4
Armagh	70,627	73.7	47.3
Down	167,592	74.9	28.6
Fermanagh	31,075	67.6	53.2
Londonderry	94,316	71.1	50.6
Tyrone	78,184	69.9	54.8
Total	874,109	73.8	34.9

company vote in local government. Speeches revealed that the government believed the choice provided the best possible electoral system for Northern Ireland. The question was whether the decisions had any partisan impact singly or cumulatively.[6] The most frequently debated of these issues was the ratepayer franchise.

The retention of the ratepayer suffrage after 1946 in Northern Ireland meant that by 1961 only 73.8 per cent of the adult population had the local government vote. In 1967 some 220,000 Westminster electors in Northern Ireland could not vote in local government elections. In addition, by refusing assimilation of the Parliamentary and local government franchises and creating some exceptions for servicemen and those affected by wartime housing shortages, there were seven different categories of voter on the local government register. Nationalists argued constantly after 1946 that the ratepayer suffrage affected them adversely, that it was responsible for Unionist control of Tyrone and Fermanagh and that the Dáil had assimilated the Parliamentary and local franchise in 1935. The literature assumes that it was a significant disadvantage to nationalists.

Some scattered but specific local evidence suggests that this may not have been correct.[7] Consider also Table 6.1. First, there was an evenness in the distribution of local government electors which had little connection with the percentage of Roman Catholic population. The difference for Tyrone and Fermanagh appeared only between 1951 and 1961. Second, most of the adults without the vote were from areas with a proportionally large non-Catholic population. Third, Belfast was the largest single unit and had 28.9 per cent of all adults without the vote in 1961. Fourth, the lower figures for Tyrone and Fermanagh may be due to the rural nature of the population, because Londonderry County Borough, 67.1 per cent of whose population was Roman

Catholic, had 75.3 per cent of its adults on the register, and was second only to County Antrim.

The stable party situation in local government, the frequency of uncontested elections and the secrecy about unofficial party registration figures make it difficult to be more precise. However, there are other means of getting closer to an answer. First, it is possible to examine the increase in the electorate between 1967 and 1970 after the principle of assimilation was accepted in 1969. The figures are complicated by population movement, natural increase and the decision to lower the voting age from twenty-one to eighteen, but some generalizations can be made. In local authorities with a Roman Catholic majority of adults in 1971 the electorate increased by 5–10 per cent more than other areas in the same locality. However, there were some urban areas with non-Roman Catholic majorities where the increase far exceeded that in Roman Catholic areas.

Second, the effect of the franchise change might be deduced from the change in party control in the 1973 local government elections. The elections were for a new system of district councils and new electoral areas impartially determined, with a new method of election favourable to minorities, STV, and the new franchise. These changes were expected to alter completely the party control of local authorities: the SDLP expected to win at least six of the twenty-six district councils. However, with a turnout of 68 per cent the results showed that unionists had a majority in twelve districts and loyalists controlled one; unionists constituted the largest party in nine other districts and the SDLP the largest in three, including Londonderry, with one in which no party was predominant. The face of local government had changed but not the party face.

Electoral boundaries and vote counting

The Government of Ireland Act did not create an independent body responsible for the conduct of elections or the supervision of electoral boundaries. The Northern Ireland Parliament had power to regulate its own elections; but it could not increase the number of members and in any redistribution it was bound to pay due regard to the population of constituencies. For local government elections, county boroughs and boroughs could recommend their own ward structure. The county council electoral divisions had to be as nearly equal in population as convenient, with regard to changes since the last census and the pursuits of the urban and rural population. The Local Government Act (NI) 1922 added rateable valuation to the factors to be considered. In addition, the redistribution of Parliamentary seats in 1917 provided a body of practical guidance on procedure.

The adequacy of these provisions was tested throughout the period. Disputes over electoral boundaries were the main feature of the electoral debate between the Unionist government and opposition parties. They emphasized the different expectations over territorial versus communal representation. The detailed nature of the disputes precludes anything other than a cursory review of the main types and periods of dispute.

The single-member Stormont constituencies formed in 1929

When it became clear that the Unionist government would abolish PR before the end of the second Parliament, opposition parties demanded a Commission to redistribute seats. Nationalists feared that the opportunity would be taken to reduce their members from ten to six; Labour members asserted that failure to establish a Commission would be proof of an intent to gerrymander. However, the request was rejected in 1927 and when the Bill was introduced in 1929 the Prime Minister Viscount Craigavon (James Craig) stressed his personal responsibility for it.

During the debate there were some claims for communal rather than territorial representation; some Nationalists were willing to accept the termination of PR in return for the guarantee of sixteen seats or representation on the basis of religion. Nationalists claimed that the redistribution scheme gerrymandered Antrim and Fermanagh by taking away a seat from them in Antrim and giving Unionists two seats in Fermanagh. Craigavon replied that it was impossible to create a Nationalist seat of sufficient size in Antrim and that the joint representation of Fermanagh and Tyrone would continue the same as under two PR elections in 1921 and 1925.[8]

Nationalist fears were not realized in the 1929 election, and they won eleven seats. During the third reading Joseph Devlin, leader of the Nationalist Party, had stated that it was the duty of the government to ensure that the minority would not be worse off under the new scheme. In effect this had been accomplished with some rough justice in Fermanagh and Antrim. If there was gerrymandering in 1929 it was of an honest variety.

From a technical point of view, no constituency lay outside the normal range of plus or minus one-third of the population quota for the forty-eight territorial constituencies or the range within the multi-member constituency from which they were derived. Only two technical issues seem to have occurred – whether to give Fermanagh two or three seats and the West Belfast area four or five seats. Both issues were resolved by favouring the easier course and retaining intact the registration areas of 1920.

Ward changes in Omagh, Londonderry and Armagh

In the mid-1930s inquiries were held in Omagh UDC and Londonderry County Borough as a result of ratepayers' associations seeking improved representation. The ratepayers' associations were thinly disguised and were in effect Unionist. Although their ward plans were rejected in both instances, the effect of subsequent ministry action favoured the spirit of the proposals. The proposals for Omagh resulted in a change of party control to Unionist and in Londonderry the three-ward structure ensured a permanent Unionist majority when it would have disappeared in a few years under the five-ward system.[9] In addition, Armagh UDC was dissolved for maladministration in 1934, and when it was returned to council control it was with a boundary extension and a new five-ward structure which reflected the new Unionist majority in the city.

The failure to establish Boundary Commissions after 1945

After the Second World War, Northern Ireland did not follow Britain in making provision for periodic boundary commissions for Stormont Parliamentary constituencies. Indeed, the nationalist gerrymander motion became a hardy annual at Stormont. Allegations against Stormont constituencies gradually faded as the smallest constituencies became occupied by opposition party candidates while huge Unionist constituencies built up on the fringes of Belfast. Labour members and some of the Unionists with large constituencies began to demand a Commission early in the 1960s. The principle was accepted in 1966 and an Interim Boundary Commission was created in 1968 to create four new territorial seats to replace the university seats. The Electoral Law Act 1968 created a permanent Boundary Commission for Parliamentary seats but it had not reported before direct rule in 1972.

Allegations against local authority areas persisted. The demand for 'one vote, one value' was part of the civil rights demands enshrined in the shorthand slogan 'one man, one vote'. Boundaries for the new system of District Councils, recommended by the Macrory Report of 1970,[10] and the electoral areas within them, were determined by an independent commission. These single-member units were subsequently grouped into multi-member units when PR was reintroduced in 1973. The Local Government Act (NI) 1972 provided for a Local Government Boundary Commission to report every ten years.

To summarize, the number and intensity of disputes over electoral boundaries made it the main area of electoral grievance. Part of the problem concerned the absence of independent procedures but the main period of dispute occurred before the Second World War when independent bodies did not exist in the rest of the United Kingdom. Although there were allegations of widespread gerrymandering, research enables attention to be directed to specific areas: Londonderry County Borough, Omagh UDC, Omagh RDC and possibly County Fermanagh. The two Omagh decisions may have produced wider consequences for control of the county council. However, claims about electoral boundaries are difficult to disentangle, particularly where there was an expectation that territorial representation should produce what only communal representation was capable of achieving. The experience of Fermanagh after 1973 is a cautionary tale. There, despite all the changes, unionists disputed control in the 1970s, lost it in the early 1980s but regained control in 1989 with a one-seat majority over eleven nationalists.

The method of election

The Government of Ireland Act 1920 extended the use of STV in multi-member constituencies from local government elections, under the 1919 Act, to elections for the Northern Ireland Parliament. In the debates it was described as one of the safeguards for minorities and the unionist minority in the South and West of Ireland seemed to be uppermost in debate. However, northern unionists opposed the method and wanted to retain the same system as in Britain. James Craig had opposed PR in evidence to the Royal Commission on Systems of Election in 1910; and during the debates on the Government of Ireland bill Unionists had opposed PR and committed the party to abolishing it at the first opportunity. On the other hand, Nationalists favoured the principle but they had only six members at Westminster and their attention was directed against the principle of two legislatures in Ireland rather than their composition and elections.

The method of election to the Northern Ireland Parliament was guaranteed for a period of three years. However, the 1920 Act did not mention local government and on 31 May 1922 the Local Government (NI) Bill was introduced in the Stormont Parliament to abolish PR in local government elections and return to the previous method and electoral units. The six Nationalist and six Sinn Fein members elected in 1921 were pursuing an abstention policy so that the only opposition to the Bill was from a Unionist Labour member, Thompson Donald. Nationalist-controlled councils issued a resolution of protest but the Bill passed its third reading on 5 July. However, as was mentioned in Chapter 1, the Royal Assent was withheld until 11 September.

Various government statements had encouraged the belief that PR would be abolished for Stormont elections as soon as the three-year statutory prohibition ended in June 1924. However, no action was taken and the 1925 election was also fought using PR. After the election, the Prime Minister came under pressure from the Unionist Party to abolish PR and the Party had lost seats to the Labour Party and other candidates.

The principle of PR was extensively debated in 1927 on a Labour Party motion. Labour regarded abolition of PR as aimed at all minorities, while Nationalists considered that they were the prime targets. In a lengthy and detailed speech the Prime Minister said that he believed in the two-party system and the old method of elections would produce 'men who are for the Union on the one hand or are against it and want to go into a Dublin Parliament on the other'.[11] The debate hinged less on the merits of PR than on a disposition to treat the minority well through seat redistribution.

PR was abolished by the House of Commons (Method of Voting and Redistribution of Seats) Act (NI) 1929. During the debates the opposition parties expressed diverse views about whom the Bill was directed against. There was less debate on the merits of PR than in 1927 and a greater concern about the consequences of redistributing the seats from the multi-member constituencies. The Bill became law on 16 April 1929 and the 'cross' vote for single-member districts was restored for the forty-eight territorial seats. In the 1929 Northern Ireland Parliament elections thirty-seven Unionists, eleven Nationalists, three Independent Unionists and one Northern Ireland Labour Party member were elected. All the parties previously represented retained representation: Unionists and Nationalists gained over the 1925 results and Labour lost two seats. Apart from an increase in the number of unopposed returns in 1929 there seemed little to choose between the two methods of election. However, the steady increase in the number of independent and unofficial Unionist candidates during the 1930s, culminating in 1938 when more than a quarter of the candidates came from that section, meant that the abolition of PR was aimed at divisions within Unionism over social and economic policy and administrative performance.

The effect of the change to the simple-majority system and single-member constituencies from 1929 to 1969 can be briefly summarized. The two largest parties, the Unionists and Nationalists, both benefited in their share of contested seats and unopposed returns. The Northern Ireland Labour Party and splinter Unionist candidates were consistently underrepresented. Anti-partition Labour candidates consistently benefited from the system after 1938, but this may have been due to the size of the constituencies contested. All other groups were underrepresented in proportion to their share of the votes.

In the post-war period there were motions for the reintroduction of PR in 1947 and 1951. During the Electoral Law Bill debates of 1962 Nationalists sought PR but without success. It was only after 'one man, one vote' had been conceded in the Electoral Law (No 2) Bill 1969 that the call for PR was seriously renewed, to the discomfiture of the government. Every opportunity was taken to press for PR and the issue was debated in March 1971. However, the withdrawal of the SDLP and Nationalists from the House in July 1971 and the suspension of the Northern Ireland Parliament and government on 30 March 1972 terminated the Parliamentary debate. The principle was conceded by the Secretary of State, William Whitelaw, as the means to gain SDLP participation in the District Council and Assembly elections of 1973.[12] The Secretary of State never gave any substantial reason for the change except to say that it was the method that most parties mentioned to him. Several years later he stated that there were expectations that it might enable voters to build up the centre ground in politics. Against a background of party fragmentation the only expected outcome was that the parties would win representation in proportion to their votes and entrench the new divisions.

The party system

The Unionists

The Ulster Unionist Party was formed from a number of organizations in 1905 to preserve the Union with Great Britain against the pressure for home rule. It resisted the Home Rule Act of 1914 but in the changed circumstances after 1918 had to accept a local devolved Parliament in the Government of Ireland Act 1920. It won every election in the period 1921–69 and formed the government with clear majorities over all other parties. Although in the majority in Northern Ireland, its attitude was defensive locally and towards Westminster parties.

A considerable variety of unofficial unionists contested elections after 1921. They opposed the Unionist Party on social and economic policies and gained regular but limited success. They were consistently underrepresented by the electoral system; for example, in 1938 they polled 29 per cent of the votes but gained only two seats (4 per cent). After the War the extension of the Welfare State to Northern Ireland reduced criticism from that direction and it was instead expressed by the NILP. In the 1950s, however, some independent unionists reappeared but espousing réligious and fundamental constitutional views.

A major split developed in the Unionist umbrella after the Stormont meeting between the Northern Ireland Prime Minister, Terence O'Neill, and the Taoiseach, Séan Lemass, in 1965.[13] O'Neill had not trusted his Cabinet colleagues with knowledge of this first formal visit by the Taoiseach and was accused by some of abandoning traditional Unionism. In the Stormont election of 1969 five Unionist groups offered themselves for election, namely, the pro-O'Neill and anti-O'Neill factions, the Protestant Unionists of Ian Paisley and the usual independent and unofficial unionists. The process of fractionalization continued after the resignation of O'Neill in April 1969 when his successor, James Chichester-Clark, appeared to accept Westminster dictation on matters within the jurisdiction of the Northern Ireland Parliament. In 1970 the expulsion of five Unionists from the party whip and the loss of two by-elections to Protestant Unionist candidates indicated greater disarray than at any previous time.

Two of the expelled Unionists, Desmond Boal and John McQuade, joined with the two Protestant Unionists, Ian Paisley and William McCrea, in September 1971 to form the Democratic Unionist Party.[14] Fundamentally, the party was working-class, held libertarian views and was highly critical of the Unionist Party's social and economic policies. It was also hostile to middle-class control of the Unionist Party and feared a sell-out on constitutional issues. It also opposed the centralization of power since 1945. Another of the expelled Unionists, William Craig, formed the Vanguard organization in February 1972. By March 1973 this had become the Vanguard Unionist Progressive

Party. In the process of formulating a new system of government under direct rule after 1972, the Democratic Unionists advocated integration and the Vanguard Unionists called for the restoration of a strong Northern Ireland Parliament, but also considered a federal UK and even some form of independence in certain circumstances.

The conflict within the main Unionist Party continued under the new leadership of Brian Faulkner. Law and order, power-sharing proposals for a new Assembly and an Irish dimension stirred divisions. The reintroduction of STV institutionalized the splits in the previously monolithic party. In the Assembly elections of 1973 there were fifty Unionist members, but twenty-three were pro-Faulkner, twelve anti-Faulkner, eight Democratic Unionists and seven Vanguard Unionists. For the first time since 1921 the Ulster Unionist Party did not have a majority of the seats. The formation of the power-sharing Executive – comprising the pro-Faulkner Unionists, the Alliance Party and the Social Democratic and Labour Party – and the Sunningdale Agreement widened the divisions within the Unionist Party. After the Ulster Unionist Council rejected the Council of Ireland on 4 January, Faulkner resigned as party leader on 7 January with the intention of forming a new party around the twenty pledged Unionists in the Assembly. The party, the Unionist Party of Northern Ireland, was formed in September 1974. Hence the process of fragmentation had produced four unionist parties with different policies.

During the late 1970s some of the newer parties began to decline and unionist support centred on two main parties: the Democratic Unionists became the focus for a loyalist tendency and the Official Unionists for a unionist tendency. The peak of Democratic Unionist support was in 1981 when it polled 26.6 per cent to the Official Unionists' 26.5 per cent at the District Council elections. Thereafter the DUP vote declined and at the end of the 1980s was around 19 per cent compared to 32 per cent for the OUP, except in European elections where the positions were reversed.

The Nationalists

The Nationalist Party was the remnant of the old constitutional Nationalist Party destroyed everywhere else in Ireland by Sinn Fein at the 1918 general election. In the first election to the Northern Ireland Parliament in 1921, six Nationalists and six Sinn Fein members were elected but with a commitment not to take their seats in a partitionist institution. Ten Nationalists were elected in 1925 and two Republicans, but Republican candidates did not appear in 1929 and only fleetingly in 1933 before leaving the field to the Nationalists. The initial Nationalist policy of abstention was breeched in 1925 and had ended in 1928. Although the Nationalists were the single largest opposition party, they consistently refused to accept the role of official opposition and denied the opportunity to others. The Party had the minimum of organization and was in effect a group of local notables who met infrequently and usually only to select a candidate for election. From time to time it attempted to renew itself by forming organizations: the New National League in 1928, the National Union Association in the 1930s, the Anti-partition League of the 1940s and the National Unity Movement of the 1960s. However, despite its regular election successes it was prone to outbreaks of abstentionism in the 1930s. After 1938 the Party ceased to contest urban seats in Belfast, leaving Falls, Central and Dock to Independent Labour, Socialist Republican, Éire Labour, Republican Labour and National Democratic Party candidates. After 1945 the party was also affected by abstentionism, and it stepped aside and gave Sinn Fein candidates a free run in the Westminster elections of 1955 and 1959. It consistently refused the formal role of official opposition until 1965.

In 1964 the Nationalist Party issued its first policy statement for some time and in 1965, after the O'Neill–Lemass meeting, it accepted the role of official opposition. In 1966 the Party held a conference and began to establish a territorial organization. However, after the clashes in Derry on 5 October 1968 it abandoned that role and the elections of 1969 showed that it was in danger of being left behind by political developments. The Party lost three seats to civil rights candidates, including the defeat of the Party leader, Eddie McAteer, by John Hume. The formation of the Alliance Party early in 1970 removed another MP and for a time appeared to threaten the middle-class Catholic support. While the formation of the Social Democratic and Labour Party in August 1970 removed only one further MP, Austin Currie, it was to sound the death-knell of the Party.[15] The remaining Nationalist MPs withdrew from Stormont in July 1971 and took part with other minority parties in the rival Assembly of the Northern Irish People at Dungiven.

The intervening period of government review of future institutions after direct rule in March 1972 was disastrous for the future of the Nationalist Party. It boycotted the border poll in March 1973. In the elections for the twenty-six new District Councils in May, using PR, it promoted only sixteen candidates for the 526 seats, polled 0.6 per cent of the vote and won four seats. In the Assembly elections in June three candidates polled 1.1 per cent and no one was elected for the first time since 1921. Events since 1968 made it a casualty of the troubles and it was replaced by the SDLP.

The Social Democratic and Labour Party

The Social Democratic and Labour Party was formed in August 1970 from six members of the Stormont House of Commons and one Senator.[16] They came from diverse political groups and varying degrees of experience in local politics: two were elected in 1969 as Republican Labour, three as Independents, one as a Nationalist and one from the Northern Ireland Labour Party. The new party described itself as anti-sectarian and promised policies based on 'radical left of centre principles' and the promotion of co-operation, friendship and understanding with the South with the view to reunification by the consent of the majority of the North and South. The constitution of the SDLP was approved at its conference in October 1971. The principles and objects of the Party were defined as organizing and maintaining a socialist party, promoting conference policies, co-operation with the Irish Congress of Trade Unions (ICTU) on joint political and other action, promoting the cause of Irish unity with the consent of the majority of the people in Northern Ireland and co-operating with other Labour and social-democratic parties. In contesting elections its stated aims were the abolition of all forms of religious, political and class discrimination, the public ownership and democratic control of essential industries and services as the common good required, and the use of the power of the state to provide employment by publicly owned industry.

The party walked out of Stormont in July 1971 and reinforced its policy of boycott after the introduction of internment in August 1971. The Party, however, was not without influence for its leader, Gerry Fitt, had extensive contacts at Westminster with Labour politicians. In the discussions to create new institutions for Northern Ireland the Party did not attend the Darlington conference in September 1972 but published its own proposals aimed at creating a new North and a new South.

The Party boycotted the border poll in 1973, but having won PR for the new District Council elections it promoted 166 candidates. The SDLP experienced localized opposition from Unity, Nationalist and Republican Clubs candidates but the electorate confirmed it as the largest minority party with 13.4 per cent of the vote and eighty-three seats out of 526. The SDLP did not win control of any District Council, but it was the largest single group on three councils. In the Assembly election it became the second largest party, with 22.1 per cent of the vote and nineteen of the seventy-eight seats and was the only minority party. In the short-lived power-sharing Executive it held four posts, with a further two in the wider administration of fifteen.

Hopes for a new Assembly were raised by the Constitutional Convention of 1975–6, where the SDLP was the only nationalist party represented. The Party increased its vote share to 23.7 per cent but it won seventeen instead of the nineteen seats in 1973. The SDLP still faced competition, however localized, from Unity candidates and Republican Clubs. After the District Council elections of 1977 when the SDLP won 113 seats with 20.6 per cent of the vote and became the largest party on six councils, it faced new competition from the Irish Independence Party.[17] This party attacked the nationalist credentials of the SDLP and forced it to respond with a 'British withdrawal' motion. Although the IIP had 3.9 per cent of the vote and twenty-one seats, compared to 17.5 per cent and 103 for the SDLP, in 1981, the larger party had proved vulnerable on the nationalist right in the hunger strike elections.

The biggest challenge to the SDLP came when Provisional Sinn Fein decided to contest elections in 1982.[18] In the Assembly elections of 1982 PSF candidates polled 10.1 per cent of the vote and won five seats, while the SDLP polled 18.8 per cent and won fourteen seats. The Sinn Fein vote peaked at the general election of 1983 with 13.4 per cent and the winning of the symbolic West Belfast seat by Gerry Adams. Although the SDLP polled 17.9 per cent and John Hume, the Party leader, won the Foyle seat, another party was winning some 42 per cent of the nationalist vote. In the 1985 District Council election the SDLP had 101 seats against Sinn Fein's platform of fifty-nine expressing a different viewpoint.

Since then the Anglo-Irish Agreement and other measures to assist the SDLP have seen the Sinn Fein vote level out at around 11 per cent while the SDLP progressed to 21 per cent. The Westminster elections of 1987 saw the SDLP win three seats but it failed to win West Belfast from Adams and Sinn Fein retained 11.4 per cent of the vote. By 1989 the District Council elections revealed a widening gap in seats when the SDLP rose to its best ever figure of 121 and Sinn Fein fell to forty-three with 11.2 per cent of the vote. Hence after seven years of electoral competition Sinn Fein still managed to retain approximately one-third of the nationalist vote.

The centre parties

The Northern Ireland Labour Party

The Northern Ireland Labour Party (NILP), formed in 1924 from several labour organizations, was never very successful at the polls.[19] Faced with a working class divided on the border issue, it attempted to balance this division within its own ranks by refusing to take a policy position on the constitutional question until 1949.

The support for the NILP increased sharply in 1945 but by this time rival pro- and anti-partition Labour parties had been set up. Development and organizational work in the 1950s resulted in the election of four MPs to the Stormont Parliament in 1958 where they formed the official opposition.

However, in 1965 the new Unionist leader, Terence O'Neill, campaigned strongly against it and it lost two of its four seats. In addition, it lost the status of official opposition in 1965 when the Nationalist Party assumed that role in an era of improving relations. While the NILP retained two seats in 1969 its share of the vote had fallen to 8.1 per cent, only slightly above the 1949 level. In 1970 the Party applied to become a regional organization of the British Labour Party but was refused.

The NILP was seriously affected by the process of party fragmentation and formation from 1970. The formation of working-class loyalist organizations giving support to the Democratic Unionists and Vanguard Unionists streamed off Protestant voters. The formation of the SDLP provided a new alternative for Catholic voters and enabled the British Labour Party to draw back from the NILP connection as its policy towards Northern Ireland began to change. Finally, the formation of the Alliance Party provided an alternative for the non-sectarian middle-class vote which had long been cultivated by the NILP. The cumulative effects of these influences were seen in the elections of 1973. In the District Council elections of May the NILP polled only 2.6 per cent of the vote and won four seats, failing in areas where it had traditionally been represented. In the Assembly election of June it polled 2.6 per cent of the vote and elected one member. From a position of 98,000 votes (12.6 per cent) in the Westminster election of 1970 the Party had been bypassed by events. Its only District Councillor retired at the 1989 elections.

The Alliance Party

The Alliance Party was formed in April 1970 from the liberal unionist groups which had supported O'Neill in the 1969 Stormont general election.[20] It described itself as an alliance of Protestants and Catholics, moderates committed to supporting the constitutional link with Britain and in favour of the UK government reform programme. The Party gained representation at Stormont when P. O'Neill, a lifelong Unionist, T. Gormley, a Nationalist, and R. McConnell, a recently elected pro-reform Unionist, joined the Party. The new party proved adept at publicity and creating an organization throughout Northern Ireland.

At the District Council elections in 1973 the Alliance Party contested every council to give voters the widest chance to support the new party. However, the moderate centre proved to be smaller than expected and only sixty-three of the Party's 237 candidates were elected, with a vote share of 13.7 per cent. In the June 1973 Assembly elections eight Alliance members were returned out of thirty-five candidates and a 9.2 per cent vote share. In the subsequent power-sharing Executive the party held one place on the Executive and a further place in the wider administration. In the Convention election of 1975 the Party retained eight seats with 9.8 per cent of the vote.

It remained a narrower bridge than expected. In subsequent District Council elections the Party's best performance was in 1977 when it won seventy seats with 14.4 per cent of the vote. While it has never won a Westminster seat, its best performance was in 1979 with 11.8 per cent of the vote. In the 1982 Assembly elections it won ten seats with 9.3 per cent of the vote. However, its position continued to erode during the 1980s. Although its share of the vote in the 1987 general election improved to 10 per cent, its position in District Councils diminished. In 1981 it blamed polarization for its showing of thirty-eight seats and 8.7 per cent, but in 1985 it fell to thirty-four seats and 7.1 per cent. In 1988 it lost its young leader, John Cushnahan, to Fine Gael. In 1989, under John Alderdice, it gained 39 seats and 6.8 per cent of the vote. The centre ground had proved even narrower than the NILP had experienced earlier.

The method of election and the parties

In three regional elections in 1973, 1975 and 1982, using the STV method in multi-member Westminster constituencies, the nationalist minority parties

Table 6.2 Average distortion in Northern Ireland elections, 1921–82

Method of election	Average number of parties	Average vote/seat deviation per party
PR (5)	12.2	1.65
Plurality (10)	9.4	4.90

retained similar representation. The SDLP was the exclusive representative in 1973 and 1975 with nineteen seats (24.4 per cent) and seventeen seats (21.8 per cent), respectively, out of seventy-eight; in 1982 the SDLP won fourteen seats (18.0 per cent) and Sinn Fein 5 seats (6.4 per cent). With a larger Assembly, with half as many seats again as in the old Stormont Parliament, and PR, minorities ought to have benefited more but their share of the seats remained relatively stable.

The experience of two different methods of election in Northern Ireland provides the basis for a unique comparison. Comparison of the two methods usually focuses on the relationship between the party share of the votes polled and the seats won; this is usually referred to as 'proportionality' or 'distortion'. Electoral distortion is the product of several interactive factors: some arise from the rules of the electoral system, that is, the method of election and constituency size; others result from the political environment in which the system operates. But it is the area into which the most empirical research has been conducted. In his comparative study Rae presented a number of propositions concerning electoral systems in general and some which distinguish plurality from proportional systems. Rae found that the average deviation of vote and seat percentages in thirty-nine plurality elections was 3.96 per cent and 1.63 per cent in seventy-one PR elections.[21] In Northern Ireland the average deviation of vote and seat percentages in ten plurality elections was 4.9 per cent. In five STV elections the average deviation was 1.65 per cent; this was close to Rae's average of 1.63 per cent for PR elections.

The marked difference in distortion for the STV elections of 1921, 1925, 1973, 1975 and 1982 and the plurality elections of other years is evident from Table 6.2.

Rae also found that the largest party gained disproportionately from electoral systems: in proportional systems there was a benefit of 1.24 per cent but in plurality systems a benefit of 8.12 per cent. In Northern Ireland the average bonus to the largest party in five PR elections was 2.5 per cent; in 1975 there was a negative score of −1.0 per cent; the bonus in ten plurality elections was 12.7 per cent.

Rae also calculated that the two largest parties gained by 2.9 per cent in all PR elections and in plurality elections by 5.46 per cent. In Northern Ireland the two largest parties benefited by 12.0 per cent in ten plurality elections but in four STV elections the average was − 0.1 per cent which covered the range − 2.9 to 3.8 per cent. However, the definition of the two largest parties in Northern Ireland has to be qualified. The Unionist Party was invariably the largest single party in votes and seats but the second largest varied and frequently the second largest party in terms of votes was not the second largest in seats. The second largest party in seat share was Nationalist but in 1921 it shared that position with Sinn Fein and in 1973 was replaced by the Social Democratic and Labour Party. However, in terms of vote share the National-ists were the second party only in 1925 and 1949; frequently, the second largest share of the vote was won by independent Unionists or the Northern Ireland Labour Party, but in 1973 the emergence of SDLP regularized the position.

Northern Ireland has a multi-party system operating within a division, formed in the home rule struggles from 1886, on the constitutional link with the United Kingdom. Between 1921 and 1969 parties with forty different labels contested elections and twenty-two were successful. The outbreak of the 'troubles' caused further fragmentation. In the 1973 election to the new Assembly fifteen parties were in competition and eight were successful; in 1975 twelve parties contested and nine were successful; in the 1982 Assembly ten parties contested the seventy-eight seats and seven won representation. For District Council elections it is not unusual for thirty different party descrip-tions to be used. This variety of opinion pre-dated the reintroduction of PR but gains from it.

In examining Northern Ireland experience of elections it is clear that an enormous amount of time was spent considering electoral activities. Electoral competition was very salient in group relations. The abolition of PR, the retention of outdated franchises, and the control over electoral boundaries by the government produced an active series of causes for minorities. Finally, the 'one man, one vote' issue, taken over by the Northern Ireland Civil Rights Association from the NILP and the unions, provided the occasion for a bid for power by the only means available in a majority-dominant system. Retro-spectively, several of the grievances seem to have had less significance than was believed at the time. Cumulatively, they were believed to be significant and that was sufficient in a situation of tension to produce a spark. After 1972 it was not surprising that power over electoral matters was reserved to Westminster.

Notes

1 C. H. Enloe, *Ethnic Conflict and Political Development*, Little, Brown, Boston, 1973, pp. 85–8.
2 A. Rabushka and K. A. Shepsle, *Politics in Plural Societies: A Theory of Democratic Instability*, Merrill, Columbus, Ohio, 1972, pp. 74–92.
3 The Representation of the People Act (NI) 1934 extended the qualification to seven years.

4 *Report of the Committee on Electoral Machinery*, (Cmd. 6408) (Vivian Committee), HMSO, London, 1942.
5 The Representation of the People Act 1949, which permitted citizens of the Republic of Ireland to vote in UK elections, meant that there developed a difference between the register for Stormont and local elections, on the one hand, and Westminster elections, on the other. This was evident when the Stormont equivalent legislation, the Electoral Law Act of 1962, retained the residence qualification.
6 S. Elliott, 'The Electoral System in Northern Ireland since 1920', unpublished PhD thesis, Queen's University, Belfast, 1971, pp. 757–70, 787–94.
7 The *Armagh Observer*, 16 May 1964, cited figures showing that 72.5 per cent of Roman Catholic electors in Armagh could vote in Westminster and local government elections compared to 71.5 per cent of Protestant electors.
8 The new single-member constituencies in 1929 returned three nationalists and two unionists in Tyrone and two unionists and one nationalist in Fermanagh. The eight member Fermanagh-Tyrone constituency in 1921 and 1925 elected four unionists and four nationalists using PR.
9 This provided a *cause célèbre* for campaigns such as the Mansion House campaign at the end of the 1940s and the Northern Ireland Civil Rights Association campaign of 1967–9. The figures used showed one unionist vote to have the same value as two nationalist votes. They ignored the deprivation of Labour representation.
10 P. Macrory, *The Review Body on Local Government in Northern Ireland* (Cmd. 546), HMSO, Belfast, 1970.
11 *HC Debs (NI)*, vol. 8, 25 October 1927, cols 2275–6.
12 R. J. Lawrence, S. Elliott and M. J. Laver, *The Northern Ireland General Elections of 1973* (Cmnd. 5851), HMSO, London, 1975, pp. 18–20.
13 W. D. Flackes and S. Elliott, *Northern Ireland: A Political Directory 1968–88*, Blackstaff Press, Belfast, 1989, pp. 210, 281.
14 Ibid., p. 110.
15 Ibid., p. 198.
16 Ibid., p. 254.
17 Ibid., pp. 156–7.
18 Ibid., pp. 237–40.
19 Ibid., pp. 203–4.
20 Ibid., p. 62.
21 D. W. Rae, *The Political Consequences of Electoral Laws*, Yale University Press, New Haven, Connecticut, 1971, pp. 70, 87–103.

7

Policing in Northern Ireland

Adrian Guelke

Policing has been a major source of contention within Northern Ireland since the onset of the present 'troubles'. In part, this simply reflects the importance of the maintenance of public order in a deeply divided society beset by political violence. However, at times the issue of policing has become bound up with the even larger question of the legitimacy of political institutions, making policing a central issue in the Northern Ireland conflict itself. This has placed a further burden on policing and on the Royal Ulster Constabulary (RUC) as an institution. Four different phases of policing during the present troubles in Northern Ireland can be identified. The first was the discrediting of the RUC and of the Ulster Special Constabulary (B Specials) in 1968 and 1969. Not merely did they appear unable to quell unrest but through their partiality they were seen as major contributory factors in their own right in the province's slide towards disorder. The second was the civilianization of policing as a result of the recommendations of the Hunt Committee. While civilianization itself was a failure, many of the reforms introduced by Westminster in 1969 and 1970 to this end survived and have had a lasting influence on the institutional framework of policing. The adoption of the policy of police primacy in 1975 and 1976 marked the start of a third phase of policing. The British government's acceptance under Article 7(c) of the Anglo-Irish Agreement of the need for 'a programme of special measures . . . to improve relations between the security forces and the community, with the object in particular of making the security forces more readily accepted by the nationalist community' constituted the beginning of a fourth phase, even though it involved no change in the overall framework of policing policy.

The difficulties that beset the police in the late 1960s had their origin in the formation of the RUC and of the B Specials against the backdrop of Northern Ireland's turbulent birth as a political entity. The formation of the Ulster Special Constabulary actually preceded that of the RUC. It was established in the closing months of 1920 to assist the existing all-Ireland police force, the Royal Irish Constabulary (RIC) in coping with unrest in the newly created province of Northern Ireland. Its creation was the result of Unionist pressure on the British government to legitimize the patrolling and other activities being undertaken by a revived Ulster Volunteer Force (UVF) to counter attacks by the Irish Republican Army (IRA) within the six counties. The new force consisting of A, B, and C Specials (though only the B Specials were retained after 1925) drew most of its recruits, unsurprisingly, from the existing UVF network in Northern Ireland. Just as inevitably, it was to all intents and purposes a wholly Protestant force.

By contrast, the basis on which the RUC was formed held out the prospect that the force would be representative of both communities in Northern Ireland. Originally, the British government had envisaged that the RIC would simply be split in two to serve devolved governments in Dublin and Belfast. However, resistance to Britain's constitutional proposals in the South made that impracticable and as a consequence of the Anglo-Irish Treaty of December 1921 the decision was made to disband the RIC. More or less at the same time, responsibility for law and order in Northern Ireland was transferred to the Unionist government, which set up a committee to draw up recommendations for the formation of a new police force to take the place of the RIC. The committee recommended that the new force should comprise an establishment of 3000 and that a third of the force should be Catholic. It was envisaged that most of these would be drawn from the RIC, reducing Northern Ireland's share of the costs of the RIC's disbandment. However, despite this financial incentive, the commitment to establish a force roughly proportionate in its religious composition to the population of the province was not sustained. Catholic representation in the force was at its peak in 1923 at 21.1 per cent[1]. By the late 1920s the Catholic proportion of the force had fallen to just 17 per cent, while by the start of the troubles it was a little over 10 per cent. None the less, the point is worth underscoring that the RUC has never been a wholly Protestant force in the way that the B Specials were or that the Ulster Defence Regiment (UDR), set up to replace the B Specials, has become.

However, in other respects, the legacy of the early years of Northern Ireland's existence exerted a malign influence on the development of the RUC. Even before the passage of the Constabulary Act establishing the RUC in June 1922, the Civil Authorities (Special Powers) Act became law, giving the Northern Ireland Minister of Home Affairs sweeping emergency powers through the right to issue regulations under the Act. Typical of these were the arbitrary powers of arrest and search accorded to the RUC. The Special Powers Act, as it was colloquially known, was modelled on UK legislation enacted to meet the post-war emergency in Ireland. Its initial justification was that extraordinary measures were needed to deal with the high level of political violence that accompanied partition – there were 295 murders in Northern Ireland in 1922 alone. From the onset, the Act was used virtually exclusively against Catholics, ensuring that the RUC was seen as an instrument of the Unionist government. By the 1930s reliance on the Special Powers Act had become such an ingrained part of policing in Northern Ireland that the legislation was made permanent, obviating the need for the government to justify its renewal. The fact that the Act remained in force through long periods of relative tranquillity in the province was a reflection of the failure of the rule of law to take root in Northern Ireland. Order was seen as resting on Catholic acquiescence in their subordination as a community and the Act as a means to that end. It was an attitude with which both the Unionist government and the RUC were identified by both communities.

That began to change under the reforming leadership of Terence O'Neill, Prime Minister of Northern Ireland from 1963 to 1969. But while the RUC sought to modernize its equipment in line with the prevailing trends of the period, there was no equivalent change in the RUC's perception of its role in relation to the two communities. That was true to an even greater extent of the B Specials, which became a repository of Protestant resentment at the pressures for reform. In the circumstances, it was hardly surprising that repeal of the Special Powers Act and disbandment of the B Specials figured prominently in the demands of the civil rights movement, which sought the creation of a more equal society within Northern Ireland. Disorder grew when the civil rights movement took to the streets, reflecting Catholic disappointment with the fruits of reform from above. The police responded in traditional terms, viewing the civil rights movement simply as yet another manifestation of a long-standing republican conspiracy against Northern Ireland's political institutions. It was a disastrous misjudgement. This was most dramatically demonstrated by the event generally held to mark the onset of the present phase of Northern Ireland's troubles, the clashes between civil rights demonstrators and the police on 5 October 1968 in Londonderry (or Derry, as Catholics call Northern Ireland's second city). The ferocity of police action to prevent the demonstrators from embarking on a march that the Minister of Home Affairs had banned attracted widespread and universally hostile publicity not just within the British Isles but internationally.

The Cameron Commission appointed by the Governor of Northern Ireland to examine the causes of the disturbances was highly critical of police conduct in relation both to the march and to the riots that followed. The Cameron Report castigated the police for 'breakdown of discipline' and acts of 'misconduct' involving 'assault and battery', 'malicious damage to property' and 'the use of provocative sectarian and political slogans'.[2] Developments between the October disturbances and the publication of the Cameron Report in September 1969 had strongly reinforced what was already a widespread perception in Britain that partisan policing was one of the main causes, if not *the* principal cause, of the troubles in Northern Ireland. An example was the involvement of off-duty members of the B Specials in the ambushing of a civil rights march at Burntollet Bridge near Londonderry in January 1969. The failure of the RUC to protect the marchers from the assaults of the loyalist mob also attracted widespread criticism. The annual apprentice boys' parade sparked off further sustained rioting in Londonderry in August 1969. The disturbances spread to other parts of the province, exhausting the resources of the local security forces and resulting in the British government's dispatch of troops to Northern Ireland 'to aid the civil power'. That inevitably entailed the deeper political involvement of Westminster in Northern Ireland's affairs. However, most British politicians regarded with alarm the prospect of the re-entry of the Irish Question into British politics. It was therefore not surprising that the British government should seek to limit its involvement as far as possible.

The one area for which the British government obviously could not evade responsibility, given the deployment of British troops, was the maintenance of law and order. It was inevitable, therefore, that reforming policing would be a focus of British involvement, especially given the extent to which the RUC and the B Specials had been discredited by the events of 1968 and 1969. What proved disastrous was the British government's assumption that such reform obviated the need for fundamental change in the province's political and constitutional dispensation. In effect, this made the local security forces the scapegoat for the province's descent into disorder. At the same time, to many Catholics the British government's desire to restrict the scope of its involvement looked like a programme for putting the pieces back in the box and restoring the status quo ante the arrival of British troops. The result was a radicalization of Catholic opinion, which itself contributed to the failure of the reforms in the security field. In August 1969 the Home Secretary, James Callaghan, sent two mainland police officers (Robert Mark and Douglas Osmond) to examine the condition of the RUC. Their critical report prompted the appointment of a committee under Lord Hunt to give urgent advice on the organization of the police in Northern Ireland.

The Hunt Report was published in October 1969. It argued that the police's dual role (performing 'all those duties normally associated in the public mind with police forces elsewhere in the United Kingdom', while also undertaking 'security duties of a military nature'[3]) should be ended. Its main recommendations were the disbanding of the B Specials; the creation of a part-time reserve force to take over the policing role carried out by the B Specials; the disarming of the RUC; the establishment of a Police Authority to provide a buffer between the Unionist government and the RUC; and the repeal of much of the Special Powers Act. What this amounted to was a programme to civilianize policing in Northern Ireland in line with practices elsewhere in the UK. While the Hunt Report's main recommendations were accepted by the Unionist government, its publication was greeted by serious rioting in Protestant districts of Belfast, during which the first police fatality of the troubles occurred. The violence reflected loyalist fears that the real purpose of the British government's reform of policing was to deprive

Protestants of the means of maintaining their position of dominance as a community.

However, there was a positive response to the reforms within the RUC itself. In particular, the emphasis on the force's autonomy from political pressures and on professionalization to insulate the police as a whole from social pressures was warmly welcomed and established deep roots within the RUC. Autonomy and professionalization were seen as the means by which the force could recover its reputation by shedding its image as a sectarian and partisan force. However, civilianization itself proved less durable. While it initially enhanced the acceptability of the force in Catholic areas, this did not survive the escalation of political violence in 1971. Early in the year police officers were rearmed for their own protection after police fatalities in shooting incidents. But it was the introduction of internment in August 1971 that destroyed any possibility that the model of policing on the UK mainland could be successfully transplanted to Northern Ireland. Internment produced an explosion of violence, reflecting the hostility of the Catholic community to its introduction. Despite its subsidiary role to the Army in the security field, the RUC was directly damaged by internment. Its competence was called into question as a result of the poor intelligence it provided to the Army for the round-up of suspects, while members of the RUC's Special Branch, working alongside Army officers, were caught up in the scandal over the use of (officially authorized) interrogation techniques that involved the physical maltreatment of suspects.

The imposition of direct rule from Westminster in March 1972 represented an important change in the political context of policing, with the British government assuming full responsibility for security matters. However, the role of the police was little affected by the change as it still remained subordinate to the Army in the security field. However, the refusal of any elements of the RUC to be drawn into unionist opposition to the imposition of direct rule enhanced the force's reputation in the eyes of the British government and encouraged the belief that reliance could be placed on the reformed force to stand above Northern Ireland's sectarian divisions. The British government's priority at this time was to bring about a political settlement. This was achieved with the establishment of the power-sharing Executive in January 1974. However, this constitutional experiment collapsed within five months after a general strike by Protestant workers. The strike exposed the shortcomings of the existing security arrangements. The Army's preoccupation with the problem of republican terrorism meant that Army officers gave a low priority to dealing with lesser threats to public order such as the erection of barricades by loyalist paramilitaries to prevent people going to work, while the RUC remained reluctant to take action that might be seen as a violation of its guidelines to maintain a low profile. The difficulties of the security forces during the strike were compounded by poor communications and a lack of trust between the Army and the police.

Table 7.1 Size of RUC and RUC Reserve 1970–89

Year	RUC	RUC Reserve
1970	3809	578
1971	4086	1284
1972	4257	2134
1973	4391	2514
1974	4565	3860
1975	4902	4819
1976	5253	4697
1977	5692	4686
1978	6110	4604
1979	6614	4513
1980	6935	4752
1981	7334	4870
1982	7718	4840
1983	8003	4493
1984	8127	4439
1985	8259	4508
1986	8234	4414
1987	8236	4646
1988	8231	4654
1989	8264	4625

Source: *Northern Ireland Digest of Statistics* and *Chief Constable's Annual Reports.*

After the collapse of the power-sharing Executive, a further attempt was made by the British government to achieve a political settlement through the election of a constitutional convention in 1975. The failure of this initiative prompted a wide-ranging review of British policy. In the absence of any prospect of agreement among Northern Ireland's parties on devolution on terms acceptable to the British government, it was recognized that a more durable basis for the maintenance of law and order needed to be found with less reliance on emergency measures. The result was a radically changed approach to security. The key elements of the new strategy were a policy of police primacy in security matters, Ulsterization of the security forces, and the criminalization of political violence. Detention without trial was ended, though so also was the provision of special category status for those convicted for terrorist offences. The new strategy entailed expansion in the size of the RUC and extensive re-equipping of the force for its new role (see Tables 7.1 and 7.2). The acceptance by the British government that direct rule would form the basis for the government of the province for the foreseeable future formed the political backdrop to the new security strategy. Direct rule was no longer

Table 7.2 Net expenditure of the Police Authority of
Northern Ireland, 1970–71 to 1989–90 (£ million)

Year	Expenditure
1970–71*	7.8
1971–72	15.8
1972–73	19.2
1973–74	25.2
1974–75	36.2
1975–76	48.9
1976–77	62.2
1977–78	76.8
1978–79	92.7
1979–80	124.7
1980–81	159.0
1981–82	201.5
1982–83	217.9
1983–84	236.0
1984–85	257.5
1985–86	278.1
1986–87	318.5
1987–88	364.9
1988–89	383.5
1989–90	420.7

* Eight-month period.
Source: Police Authority of Northern Ireland.

seen as a short-term expedient but as the least unacceptable option for ruling Northern Ireland's two communities.

The new approach was intended to take advantage of a widely perceived desire in both communities for a return to normality after the traumatic events of the first half of the decade. The most obvious manifestation of this desire was the mass support given to the demonstrations organized by the Peace People, formed in 1976 to demand an end to political violence. The failure of a loyalist general strike against security policy in 1977 was seen as a further vindication of the new approach. The RUC relished its role during the strike. The clearing of barricades and the effective action to prevent intimidation by loyalist paramilitaries were in marked contrast to the police's passivity during the 1974 strike and enhanced the RUC's reputation as a force that would enforce the law impartially. These successes ensured that the new approach took root. Despite subsequent setbacks, the basic framework for security policy that was established in 1975 and 1976 has remained unchanged ever since, notwithstanding changes in other areas of policy.

Many of the problems that were to beset the RUC in the years after 1976

Table 7.3 Deaths in Northern Ireland arising out of the security situation
1969–89

Year	RUC	RUC Reserve	Army	UDR	Civilians*	Total
1969	1	–	–	–	12	13
1970	2	–	–	–	23	25
1971	11	–	43	5	115	174
1972	14	3	103	26	321	467
1973	10	3	58	8	171	250
1974	12	3	28	7	166	216
1975	7	4	14	6	216	247
1976	13	10	14	15	245	297
1977	8	6	15	14	69	112
1978	4	6	14	7	50	81
1979	9	5	38	10	51	113
1980	3	6	8	9	50	76
1981	13	8	10	13	57	101
1982	8	4	21	7	57	97
1983	9	9	5	10	44	77
1984	7	2	9	10	36	64
1985	14	9	2	4	25	54
1986	10	2	4	8	37	61
1987	9	7	3	8	66	93
1988	4	2	21	12	54	93
1989	7	2	12	2	39	62
Totals	175	91	422	181	1904	2773

* Including members of paramilitary organizations.
Source: *Chief Constable's Annual Report 1989*, Belfast, 1990.

stemmed from the same cause, the failure to anticipate the durability of the
Provisional IRA's campaign. While there was a marked drop in the number of
fatalities as a result of political violence after 1976 (see Table 7.3), much of the
fall was due to a virtual end to the campaign of random sectarian assassinations carried out by loyalist paramilitaries. The continuation of the Pro-
visionals' campaign had far-reaching implications for policing. Police primacy
in these circumstances inevitably entailed the partial remilitarization of the
RUC. This in turn presented an obstacle to the achievement of the consent and
the flow of information the police needed to secure convictions through the
courts, as the objective of criminalizing political violence required. The gap in
the system was filled by confessions obtained by the police during lengthy
periods of interrogation. However, from an early stage, there were disturbing
allegations about the physical maltreatment of suspects to obtain confessions,

particularly in the Castlereagh holding centre in Belfast. By mid-1978 these amounted to a scandal that deeply damaged the reputation of both the RUC and the British government not only domestically but also internationally. In particular, in August 1979 the US State Department suspended the sale of weapons to the RUC in accordance with the Carter administration's policy of not supplying arms to countries or organizations that violated human rights. The decision was a reflection of the strength of the Irish-American lobby and of Britain's vulnerability internationally over the issue of Northern Ireland. Even more importantly, the Castlereagh scandal was a factor in sustaining nationalist suspicion of the RUC, reflected in the highly qualified support given to the police by the Social Democratic and Labour Party (SDLP).

Further cause for nationalist alienation from the security forces arose out of the crisis in the prisons. This was another consequence of the policy of criminalization. Resistance by republican prisoners to the ending of special category status had escalated to the point of a hunger strike by the closing months of 1980. After this ended in confusion and recriminations between the authorities and the prisoners, a further hunger strike was embarked on by protesting prisoners. This time the protest was staggered to have the maximum effect. Ten prisoners died during the course of the strike. This cause attracted widespread support among Catholics, undermining the whole *raison d'être* behind the policy of criminalization. Between 1 March 1981 when the hunger strike began and 3 October when it was called off there were a total of 1205 demonstrations in support of the prisoners. In that period, seven people were killed by plastic bullets fired by the security forces to quell disturbances. In the course of the year as a whole almost 30,000 plastic bullets were fired by the security forces. While the hunger strike crisis had an adverse impact on the RUC's relations with the Catholic community, it had little direct effect on security policy. Its main impact was on the political context of security policy as the British government responded belatedly to the political fallout of the crisis.

The deaths in street disturbances during 1981 ran counter to the general trend in the political violence afflicting the province. This was towards covert violence directed at specific targets. In the case of the Provisional IRA this meant members of the security forces. Deaths of members of the security forces as a proportion of total deaths rose and with the policy of police primacy, an increasing proportion of these were members of the RUC or RUC Reserve (see Table 7.3). The reaction of the security forces was to step up surveillance and other means of gathering intelligence. Organizationally, the RUC responded by setting up special units trained in counter-insurgency, such as E4A, a surveillance unit attached to the Special Branch. These units quickly became embroiled in controversy. A series of incidents in the closing months of 1982 involving a number of these units was to inflict lasting damage on the reputation of the RUC. In November 1982 three members of the Provisional IRA were shot dead by a police unit at a checkpoint outside Lurgan. In the same month, Michael Tighe, a youth without paramilitary connections, was killed at a police stakeout of an arms find in County Armagh, while in December two members of a republican paramilitary organization, the Irish National Liberation Army (INLA), were shot dead when police officers stopped their car on the outskirts of the city of Armagh. The incidents led to press speculation that they were the first fruits of a deliberate toughening of security policy, a perspective supported by the briefings that journalists received from official sources.

In fact, there was a wide measure of agreement among unionists and nationalists that the incidents did indeed mark a change of policy. However, while unionists welcomed what they saw as a change for the better, nationalists strongly attacked the change as a 'shoot-to-kill' policy. The incidents occurred at a time when the British government was in political difficulty because of the breakthrough that Sinn Fein had achieved in the elections to the new Northern Ireland Assembly in October 1982 and because of the boycott of the Assembly by the SDLP in protest at the absence of an Irish dimension to the government's rolling devolution initiative. With the Official Unionist Party's threat to boycott the Assembly over the issue of security, there was a real danger that the government's whole initiative would founder ignominiously, since the Assembly was its centrepiece. The Assembly survived this particular threat and, indeed, became a platform for unionists to express their continuing dissatisfaction with the government and others over security policy. For example, in the Assembly in February 1983, the Democratic Unionist member, David Calvert, bitterly attacked the SDLP and the Catholic hierarchy, declaring 'if it had not been for their pressure perhaps the Government would have continued with a policy of exterminating the IRA'.[4] By this time, it was clear that the government had abandoned any such ideas. The prosecution of a police officer on a charge of murder arising out of the third of the incidents seemed to set the seal on official repudiation of the whole notion of a 'shoot-to-kill' policy.

However, the issue came back to haunt the government. At the trial of Constable John Robinson in 1984, the details came out of the context in which the two INLA men had been shot dead. In particular, they had not been shot dead because they had driven into a random checkpoint, as claimed, but as a result of a lengthy surveillance operation during which RUC officers had actually crossed the Irish border in order to continue tracking their suspects. Furthermore, Robinson, who was acquitted, revealed that he had been instructed to tell lies by senior police officers in order to maintain the confidentiality of special operations. The revelations were particularly embarrassing to the British government because of the importance it attached at the time to relations with the Irish government. After the Conservatives had come to power in 1979, the Secretary of State for Northern Ireland, Humphrey Atkins, had launched a fresh political initiative, partly in response to US pressure. In fact, a general weakness of direct rule as a long-term policy had been its vulnerability to international criticism. After the failure of the Atkins initiative, the government had concluded that attempting to cajole the Northern Ireland parties into an internal settlement was a fruitless enterprise. It adopted a different track, one of seeking the support of the Irish government for its policies in Northern Ireland. The Anglo-Irish process was launched in December 1980, helping the government to ride out the hunger strike crisis internationally. The process went through ups and downs. At the time of the 1982 shootings, it was close to its nadir as a result of the British government's fury at the stance taken by the Irish government over the Falklands war. However, by 1984 the government regarded the Anglo-Irish process as a crucial element in its efforts to stem the electoral rise of Sinn Fein following the hunger strike crisis.

To defuse controversy over Robinson's revelations, the British government appointed the Deputy Chief Constable of Manchester, John Stalker, to conduct an inquiry into the 1982 incidents. Two years later in May 1986, Stalker was suspended from the inquiry, ostensibly because of allegations concerning his conduct as a police officer in Manchester. The weakness of the allegations against Stalker, who appeared to be about to implicate senior RUC officers in authorizing or covering up covert operations outside the law, prompted widespread speculation that his suspension had been engineered to abort the inquiry. By this time, the political background had changed once again. On 15 November 1985 the British and Irish governments signed the Anglo-Irish Agreement, giving institutional form to the Anglo-Irish process in an international treaty. The Agreement recognized the Republic's right to be consulted about policies pursued by the British government in Northern Ireland. In political terms it represented a major effort by both governments to shore up the position of the SDLP against the challenge from Sinn Fein. Its detailed provisions contained substantial concessions to the viewpoint of constitutional nationalism. In particular, the need to make the security forces more acceptable to the nationalist community was explicitly recognized, along with a number of specific suggestions about how this might be achieved.

In so far as the provisions of the Agreement could be interpreted as the basis for an input into policing by the Irish government, it represented a serious challenge to a core value of the reformed RUC, autonomy from political interference. Reconciling the Agreement with the force's autonomy required a clear distinction between operational matters and issues of policy. Over such questions as whether police officers would in future accompany UDR patrols, as the British government appeared to promise at the time of the Anglo-Irish Agreement, it proved a very difficult line to draw. In the particular case of the UDR patrols, the government's promise was flatly contradicted by the Chief Constable of the RUC. The RUC's sensitivity over the Agreement's implications for policing was also demonstrated by the hostility it showed to attempts to attribute reforms of policing to the Agreement. At the same time, unionists made the RUC the main target of their hostility to the Agreement, in the belief that if the force began to disintegrate under the pressures from within and without, the government would have no alternative but to repudiate the Agreement. Against this background, Stalker's zeal in pursuit of the truth about the 1982 shootings must have seemed potentially the final straw for the force.

The unionist protests against the Agreement placed enormous strains on the police. The force was strongly criticized by nationalist politicians and by the Alliance Party over its failure to take more effective action to curb intimidation during the one-day general strike called by unionists as a protest against the Agreement. But police restraint during the strike on 3 March 1986 did little to temper loyalist attacks on the police, which were not confined to verbal criticism. The month following the strike was marked by a series of attacks on the residences of police officers in Protestant neighbourhoods in the course of which over thirty police families were driven from their homes. The fact that the RUC did not succumb to these pressures considerably enhanced its reputation among nationalists. In addition, in the wake of the Agreement a number of changes to police powers and procedures were introduced with a view to increasing the confidence of Catholics in the RUC. For example, under the Public Order (Northern Ireland) Order of 2 April 1987, the organizers of parades were required to give the police seven days' notice of their intentions. The Order provided the police with an effective lever for imposing route changes on march organizers and was used, in particular, to stop members of the Orange Order from parading through Catholic neighbourhoods where their presence was unwelcome, though nationalist politicians continued to be dissatisfied because some of the routes the police allowed still traversed Catholic areas. In 1987 a code of conduct for police officers, entitled 'Professional Policing Ethics', was introduced, while in February 1988 an Independent Commission for Police Complaints with increased powers to supervise the investigation of complaints replaced the Police Complaints Board established in 1977.

However, the changes fell short of the programme of special measures for improving public confidence in policing suggested in Article 7 of the Anglo-Irish Agreement. In particular, the suggestions for 'training in community relations' and 'action to increase the proportion of members of the minority in the Royal Ulster Constabulary' do not appear to have been followed up, though 'greater recruitment from all sections of the community' was listed among priorities for the force in a strategy document issued by the Chief Constable in February 1990. A recent estimate is that fewer than 10 per cent of police officers are Catholics.[5] Further, as the change to the complaints system was in line with reform introduced in England and Wales, it seems likely that it would have occurred anyway, independently of the existence of the Anglo-Irish Agreement. Even more clearly, the changes to police procedures as a result of the Police and Criminal Evidence (Northern Ireland) Order of 1989, which came into force in 1990, were a case of Northern Ireland broadly following practice in England and Wales.

While there has been less criticism of the police by constitutional nationalists since the Agreement, the SDLP has continued to maintain its stance of only qualified support for the RUC. The festering Stalker affair was one factor in continuing nationalist distrust of the force. The Chief Constable of West Yorkshire, Colin Sampson, was appointed to take over the inquiry into the 1982 shootings following Stalker's suspension. Stalker himself was reinstated as Deputy Chief Constable of Manchester in August 1986 after the inquiry into his behaviour as a police officer in Manchester failed, as expected, to turn up any evidence of serious misconduct on his part. After Sampson completed his inquiry into the 1982 shootings, his report was forwarded to the Director of Public Prosecutions in Northern Ireland for a decision on whether there should be criminal proceedings against the police officers implicated in unlawful action. There the matter rested until 25 January 1988, when the British Attorney-General announced that in spite of evidence that a number of police officers had sought to pervert the course of justice, they would not be prosecuted. He gave considerations of national security as the reason for his decision. His announcement provoked a storm of protest, with the Irish government expressing its dismay at the decision and the European Parliament calling for it to be reconsidered. The matter did not end there. On 17 February 1988, the Secretary of State for Northern Ireland announced the setting up of two disciplinary inquiries arising out of Sampson's report. In June the Police Authority cleared three senior police officers, including the Chief Constable, Sir John Hermon, of any disciplinary case to answer, a decision carried by a margin of a single vote. Two officers who had been suspended from duty as a result of the Stalker/Sampson inquiry resigned from the force, while twenty other officers faced disciplinary proceedings. These ended in March 1989 in reprimands or cautions for all but one of the officers.[6] Finally, the retirement of Sir John Hermon as Chief Constable at the end of May 1989 meant that at last there was a reasonable prospect that the 1982 shootings would no longer cast a cloud over the reputation of the force.

In the event, Hermon's successor, Hugh Annesley, soon faced a new problem arising out of the actions of loyalist paramilitaries that was potentially almost as damaging to the RUC as the Stalker affair had been. This was the flaunting by the paramilitaries of their access to classified security information about republican suspects. Copies of documents the paramilitaries had managed to get hold of were leaked over a period to the press. While the principal motive of the paramilitaries was to dispel the impression that they were engaged in a campaign of random sectarian assassinations, the most damaging implications from the government's perspective was the existence of collusion between elements of the security forces and loyalist paramilitaries. In September 1989, the Deputy Chief Constable of Cambridgeshire, John Stevens, was appointed to investigate the matter. Shortly after his appointment there was a further damaging leak of security information from an organization calling itself 'The Inner Circle'. It purported to be composed of serving and former members of the RUC and to have links with the loyalist paramilitary organization, Ulster Resistance. The stated aims of 'The Inner Circle' were to eradicate republican terrorism and to bring down the Anglo-Irish Agreement. The latter aim reflected an appreciation of the damage which leaks did to security co-operation with the South and hence to Anglo-Irish relations.

However, the implication of a conspiracy at the heart of the RUC was not borne out by the outcome of the Stevens inquiry. A summary of the report was published in May 1990. Stevens concluded that the passing of information was confined to 'a small number of individuals and is neither widespread nor institutionalized'. He recommended tighter control over the distribution of intelligence documents and more rigorous screening of UDR recruits. The second recommendation was a clear indication that the UDR rather than the RUC had been the source of most of the leaks of documents. Indeed, the inquiry prompted strong criticism of the UDR and a renewal of demands for its disbandment, with unfavourable comparisons being drawn between the record of the regiment and that of the RUC. The inquiry resulted in a total of thirty-eight people being charged with criminal offences. Those charged included a soldier from the regular Army, eight members of the UDR, and members of loyalist paramilitary organizations. The action taken helped limit the damage that had been done to confidence in the security forces by the immense publicity the leaking of intelligence documents had attracted.

Controversy over the conduct of the security forces took place against the backdrop of the ongoing Provisional IRA campaign against past and present members of the forces and even those who simply conducted business with them. As a proportion of security force casualties, the losses suffered by the RUC continued to be high, as the inevitable consequence of the policy of police primacy. What this meant in human terms can be illustrated by police fatalities during 1990, which statistically were broadly in line with the trend of previous years, at a level that in fact has changed little since virtually the start of the troubles (see Table 7.3). In March a Reserve constable was shot dead at his home in Armagh. In June a retired RUC reservist and his wife died after a car-bomb attack, while two constables were shot dead in Belfast city centre. In July three police officers died in a bomb attack near Armagh. A nun was killed in the same incident. In September, a detective constable was kidnapped at a paramilitary roadblock and then murdered. In October, a RUC dog-handler died as a result of the injuries he received in another shooting attack in Belfast city centre, while in November two off-duty police officers were among four people shot dead while wildfowling. The Provisional IRA admitted responsibility for all of these attacks, while claiming that the deaths of civilians, such as that of the nun, had been 'mistakes'.

While it is possible to argue that the RUC has paid a very high price for controversies, such as the Stalker affair, which have damaged its relations with the minority in Northern Ireland, it would be wrong to conclude that they have been the last obstacle to the full acceptance of the reformed RUC, even by constitutional nationalists. The SDLP has always taken the position that there can only be full acceptance of the police in the context of a political settlement endorsed by the minority. The Anglo-Irish Agreement is seen only as a step in that direction. At the same time, the SDLP's attitude towards the RUC itself has been a factor in unionist hostility towards the Party, which has adversely affected the prospects for political accommodation across the sectarian divide. In short, the problem of policing Northern Ireland is deeply enmeshed with the political situation. Another aspect of this, of course, is the Provisional IRA's campaign of violence. Reaction to security force excesses has been a factor in support for the Provisional IRA, but by no means does it provide anything like an adequate explanation of the persistence of its campaign. The reasons for that lie elsewhere, particularly in nationalist rejection of the legitimacy of Northern Ireland as a political entity and the strength of support for the nationalist cause among the Catholic minority.

But if the causes of Northern Ireland's lack of political consensus very plainly are not the responsibility of the police, much of the burden for coping with the consequences have fallen, none the less, on the RUC. This has been compounded by the manner in which the government has sought to limit the damage done to Britain's international image by the conflict in Northern Ireland. By playing down the depth of antagonism between the communities that lies at the root of the conflict and by emphasizing that political violence is contained for the most part through the ordinary enforcement of the law, the government has sought to convey the impression to the outside world that the problem Britain faces in Northern Ireland is one of terrorism. But while the stress on terrorism and its international ramifications – such as the supplies of Semtex that the Provisional IRA has received from Libya – provides a convenient basis for a defence of British policy in Northern Ireland to a global audience, it provides little scope for justifying emergency measures or the employment of armed forces other than the police. The consequence has been the training and equipping of units of the police for a counter-insurgency role that goes far beyond the requirements of normal policing and which would hardly be required if the nature of the problem was as the government presented it. A further difficulty is that while units of both the Army and police do indeed continue to be used in a counter-insurgency role, the legal basis for the conduct of covert warfare by such units does not exist.

The result has been the stretching of the interpretation of such notions as self-defence so that extraordinary operations in an extraordinary situation can be fitted within the scope of ordinary law enforcement. In practice, the burden of reconciling covert warfare with the rule of law has fallen on the security forces rather than the government, and it has been their credibility rather than that of the government that has suffered when this has proved difficult. This has been the case even when, as in 1982, it is security *policy* that has been at issue. In a wider context, the role of the RUC has been crucial for the government. The existence of a reformed police force able, through its commitment to professionalism, to stand above the province's sectarian divisions, despite being drawn predominantly from one community, has played an important role in sustaining the effectiveness of direct rule. Without it, it would have been extremely difficult for the government in Northern Ireland to have maintained its own independence from sectarian pressures to the extent that it has, except at a very high cost. That is a measure of the importance of policing in Northern Ireland.

Notes

1 M. Farrell, *Arming the Protestants: The Formation of the Ulster Special Constabulary and the Royal Ulster Constabulary 1920–1927*, Brandon, Dingle, 1983, p. 267.
2 *Disturbances in Northern Ireland: Report of the Commission appointed by the Governor of Northern Ireland* (Cameron Report) (Cmd. 532) HMSO, Belfast, 1969, p. 73.
3 *Report of the Advisory Committee on Police in Northern Ireland* (Hunt Report) (Cmd. 535), HMSO, Belfast, 1969, p. 13.
4 *NIA Debs*, vol. 5, 1983, p. 462.
5 T. Hadden and K. Boyle, *The Anglo-Irish Agreement: Commentary, Text and Official Review*, Sweet and Maxwell, London, 1989, p. 37.
6 C. Ryder, *The RUC: A Force Under Fire*, Mandarin, London, 1990, p. 353.

8

The role and powers of the Army in Northern Ireland

Clive Walker

Recent events in the Persian Gulf suggest that it is premature to believe that an era of global peace has dawned. However, it is equally clear that a new world order has resulted in fundamental realignments in defence postures and strategies. Yet, the transformation is far from total and, so far as the military situation in Northern Ireland is concerned, may be reminiscent of the following description given by Winston Churchill in 1922:

> Then came the Great War. . . . Every institution, almost, in the world was strained. Great Empires have been overturned. The whole map of Europe has been changed. The position of countries has been violently altered. The mode of thought of men, the whole outlook on affairs, the grouping of parties, all have encountered violent and tremendous changes in the deluge of the war, but as the deluge subsides and the waters fall we see the dreary steeples of Fermanagh and Tyrone emerging once again. The integrity of their quarrel is one of the few institutions that have been unaltered in the cataclysm which has swept the world.[1]

Despite the fact that the British Army's deployment in Northern Ireland has been, and remains, commonplace, its role and powers are remarkably makeshift. Consequently, it is the contention of this chapter that more permanent and considered arrangements which reflect the Army's legitimate position should now be established.

The problems associated with the present unsatisfactory regime – uncertainty, misguided expectations and excessive intervention – may be detected at all levels, from constitutional arrangements to legal powers. Before these details are studied, Army involvement in Northern Ireland will first be related.

Table 8.1 Number of service personnel in Northern Ireland

Year	Total British regiments	Total UDR	Total overall
1969 (June)	2,700	–	2,700
1970 (Jan.)	6,300	1,800 (April)	8,100
1971	7,800	4,000	11,800
1972	14,300	8,500	22,800
1972 (July)	21,800	–	30,300
1973 (Jan.)	16,900	9,100	26,000
1974	16,200	7,700	23,900
1975	15,000	7,700	22,700
1976	15,100	7,700	22,800
1977	14,300	7,600	21,900
1978	14,400	7,800	22,200
1979	13,600	7,600	21,200
1980	11,900	7,400	19,300
1981	11,600	7,500	19,100
1982	10,900	7,100	18,000
1983	10,200	7,000	17,200
1984	10,000	6,800	16,800
1985	9,700	6,400	16,100
1986	10,500	6,600	17,100
1987	11,400	6,500	17,900
1988	11,200	6,400	17,600
1989	11,200	6,300	17,500
1990	–	6,200	–

Sources: Defence Estimates; D. Barzilay, *The British Army in Ulster*, Century Services, Belfast, 1973–81.

History of Army involvement

The Army's presence in Northern Ireland can be catalogued across four distinct periods. The first, and shortest, covers the period from 1920 to 1922, when the Army undertook operations throughout the whole of Ireland mainly against the IRA but also in connection with sectarian attacks in Belfast. However, military activities were circumscribed following the Anglo-Irish Treaty in 1921, and it was subsequently made clear to the Stormont government that the prime responsibility for security was to shift to the police. Consequently, the role of the Army during the second period, from 1922 until 1969, was very much secondary to that of the RUC. Soldiers occasionally assisted in the suppression of disorder, most extensively in 1935 and 1957, but by the end of 1968 military strength stood at just over 2,000.

The watershed came in 1969, when widespread civil unrest exhausted the capabilities of the RUC and Ulster Special Constabulary (the B Specials). Thereafter, the Army became a major element of the security apparatus in Northern Ireland, as Table 8.1 illustrates.

As might be expected, intervention on this scale had profound effects on security policies and on other law-enforcement agencies. There also ensued major political repercussions which in 1972 precipitated direct rule from Westminster. In regard to policies, account had to be taken of the aggressive training of soldiers and their lack of policing experience and community involvement. The inevitable effects included a more confrontational security stance, reflected in a sharp escalation in the number of shootings by, and of, soldiers. Furthermore, the inability of soldiers to detect crime in a forensically acceptable manner prompted a resort to internment without trial as the main plank of security policy. This manner of disposal of suspects caused further reverberations, especially by encouraging the collection of low-level intelligence through detentions and searches.

Next, the reliance upon the Army highlighted the inadequacies of forces based in Northern Ireland, so reform followed in its wake. Following the Hunt Report,[2] the regular police were to be disarmed and made accountable to a police authority, while the B Specials were to be superseded by a RUC Reserve and the Ulster Defence Regiment (UDR). Though the Hunt Report's objective of removing any military or security role from the police has not been secured, its structural recommendations have been duly implemented. Thus, the UDR has been established but exhibits two features which set it apart from other UK reserve forces. First, as at 1 January 1990, 2947 (47 per cent) out of a total of 6208 staff were full-time. Second, recruits are predominantly drawn from Northern Ireland, and deployment is by statute (section 140(2) of the Reserve Forces Act 1980) likewise geographically confined. A further important characteristic is that its membership overwhelmingly derives from the loyalist community (82 per cent in 1970, rising to 98 per cent in 1980), and so it faces accusations from nationalists of being a Protestant militia in the mould of the Specials it replaced.

It has long been realized that military predominance is undesirable. In terms of equipment, training, experience, and procedures, soldiers are illsuited to policing civilians and also lack contact with, and accountability to, the local community. Their legal powers are uncertain, and this may cause confusion and resentment. Furthermore, the presence of the Army may strengthen the claims to combatant status by the paramilitaries. On the other hand, an emphasis on the police coincides with the state's anti-terrorist strategy by emphasizing its policies of criminalization, normalization and Ulsterization. These objectives could not be immediately pursued after 1969, since the RUC was believed to be incapable of fulfilling the role expected of it. However, a Ministerial Committee on Law and Order in 1976 recognized that the time was by then ripe for a diminution in the role of the Army. Consequently, the RUC has been expanded to about 8250 officers (plus 4600 reservists), while the

Army has contracted to about 11,000. Ulsterization has also been achieved by lengthier tours of duty by soldiers and by reducing the number or roulement (temporary) units.

Once again, the fundamental realignment of the security forces in the direction of police primacy has had an important impact on security policies. The experience and training of the police have allowed (with the generous assistance of special powers) suspects to be placed before much modified courts, so internment has been allowed to lapse. The Army has reverted to a secondary role, and its activities now mainly comprise border and street patrols, road checks, guard and escort duties, assistance to the police in search and arrest operations, and undercover work.

The official expectation is that political violence in Northern Ireland can be contained but not eradicated by the security forces.[3] In light of this sobering assessment, the Army's continuing presence and impact as the largest security force should be recognized by the legal system albeit within the overall framework of criminalization and police primacy, which will be assumed to be correct and viable policies. Before considering the implications for law, it may be suggested that the present composition of the security forces is itself inappropriate to this framework. Thus, it has been recommended that UDR personnel be transferred to the RUC or its Reserve and that the RUC be further expanded.

Constitutional arrangements governing Army involvement

The deployment of the Army in Northern Ireland seems to be grounded on the prerogative powers both to decide the disposition of the armed forces and to suppress disorder. This legal basis has the advantages of comprehensiveness and flexibility, but its drawbacks include uncertainty and a lack of accountability to Parliament. The actual employment of troops in aid of the civil power is treated as a matter of common law, since 'any citizen is bound to come to the aid of the civil power when the civil power requires his assistance to enforce law and order'.[4] Given this universal duty, it is not necessary for a military commander to seek permission before intervention, especially in 'grave and sudden emergencies'.[5] Indeed, it may be an offence at common law for soldiers (and civil authorities) to fail to come to the police's assistance whether called upon to do so or even, if soldiers can be said to hold public offices, in the absence of an express request.

In practice, appropriate chains of military command have long been recognized which make it unlikely that 'military aid to the civil power' (as it is officially known) will be rendered without the full approval of both the local police and the civil authorities. The first stage is that the civil administration in the disturbed area will request military help. The request should emanate from the local police chief rather than, as in days of yore, a magistrate and should be addressed not to the nearest barracks but to the Home Office. The Home Secretary will in turn consult with the Ministry of Defence, and orders may then be issued by the Headquarters of UK Land Forces to a suitable commander in the locality. The military officer should take instructions as to the problem to be tackled from the local police if time allows but should form an independent judgement both as to whether any intervention is necessary and, if so, how the task is to be accomplished.

The extent to which this blueprint has been applied in Northern Ireland since 1920 has varied considerably. Between 1920 and 1922, the Army by necessity took a leading role alongside the Specials, since the Royal Irish Constabulary was a demoralized and depleted force shortly to be disbanded. However, the utilization of soldiers between 1922 and 1969 more accurately reflected the accepted model of military aid to the civil power. Thereafter, the crisis of 1969 precipitated some startling rearrangements.[6] First, it was made clear to the Stormont government in 1966 and April 1969 that the General Officer Commanding in Northern Ireland would only respond to requests for assistance after consultation with the Ministry of Defence in London. This limitation was duly observed when the Police Commissioner in Belfast made a direct plea to the local military on 3 August 1969. That request was not acted upon, but a call for intervention by the RUC Inspector-General (retitled, after 1969, the 'Chief Constable') to the Northern Ireland Home Affairs Minister was passed on to Downing Street, and Army assistance followed in Londonderry on 14 August and in Belfast the next day. Further evidence of British mistrust both of the RUC and the Stormont government and consequent departures from the normal procedures resulted from the British insistence on military primacy in security matters. Accordingly, the General Officer Commanding was formally invested with overall responsibility by the 'Downing Street Declaration' on 29 August, though it was later conceded that there should be regular police–Army consultations.[7] The result was to create a new model for military participation which certainly did not depend upon specific invocations by local officials and in some areas wholly replaced them. The police maintained constabulary independence in their own operations, but these could only be undertaken within parameters set by the military.

One can hardly complain that Parliament failed to monitor these changes. Conflict in Northern Ireland was a major political issue at that time which was debated in various contexts. Nevertheless, it is uncertain whether this military takeover was lawful, and it also created the danger of the uncontrolled adoption of dubious military tactics (such as shooting to kill, collusion with loyalist gangs and psychological warfare) and friction with the police.

To some extent, the constitutional relationships reverted to normal in 1977, when, as described previously, police primacy was promulgated by a Joint Directive in 1977. Yet a complaint should still be registered concerning the manner of achievement of this policy – a secret ministerial committee, the findings of which were never published but the outcome of which was presented to Parliament as a *fait accompli*. It is also notable that the changes came about through the direction of central, rather than local, officials.

What constitutional reforms might prevent future governments from playing fast and loose with the legal arrangements concerning military intervention? The only precedent for the statutory regulation of military action is the Emergency Powers Acts 1920–64 (in Northern Ireland, the Emergency Powers Act (Northern Ireland) 1926), which together offer a far from satisfactory model. In regard to 'military aid to the civil ministries' under the 1920 and 1926 Acts (commonly involving the use of troops in response to industrial strikes), Parliamentary approval must be given for invocation by Royal Proclamation, but there is little opportunity for scrutiny of the detailed regulations which follow thereafter. Even worse, 'military aid to the civil community' under the 1964 Act (which can include industrial unrest but also extends to disaster relief) can be authorized by the Defence Council without reference to Parliament. These shortcomings notwithstanding, the Emergency Powers Acts offer a useful reminder of the need for statutory control over military intervention in times of civil unrest. Therefore, further 'sectoral' legislation should be devised.

A new 'Military Aid to the Civil Power Act' might secure a number of advantages over existing arrangements. First, the Act could ensure that Parliamentary approval is given for any deployment and that the reasons for it are initially and periodically scrutinized. The debate might have to be retrospective in an emergency but could still provide an important occasion for the transmission of official information and the airing of grievances. Scrutiny should be aided by the referral of the matter to an independent review body linked to a Parliamentary Select Committee and for periodical factual reports by the government. Second, the proposed legislation could settle some of the procedural uncertainties which bedevil the common law, such as the criteria for military intervention, whether any local distress signal is necessary and, if so, from whom, and to whom the call should be addressed. Third, the relationships between soldiers, police and other civil authorities could be clarified. In particular, should it be possible for the police to direct military actions (or vice versa), or might soldiers at least be placed under a legal duty to consult with the civil authorities? Fourth, the proposed legislation could settle the special powers, if any, which are to be available to soldiers and what extra sanctions might exist in the event of their wrongful exercise. Finally, special, temporary mechanisms of accountability might be interposed between citizens and soldiers while the latter perform a quasi-policing role.

Recent legislation in Canada and New Zealand offers some interesting precedents for statutory regulation. The most ambitious plan is provided by the Canadian Emergencies Act 1988, which envisages disturbances of variable severity, including in Part II a 'Public Order Emergency . . . that arises from threats to the security of Canada that is so serious as to be a national emergency' (section 16). The Act contains some stringent measures of accountability. The Governor-General must reasonably believe an emergency exists and necessitates special measures, and provincial governments are to be consulted (sections 17, 25). Moreover, any declaration must be approved initially and every thirty days by Parliament (which must be summoned if not sitting) (section 18). In turn, its deliberations will be aided by a Parliamentary Review Committee and an official inquiry which must be held into the circumstances of the declaration of emergency (sections 58–63). Rather less satisfactory are the very wide regulation-making powers which arise after a declaration (section 19) and which undermine the purpose of legislative scrutiny.

New Zealand's Defence Act 1990 (which must be read together with the International Terrorism (Emergency Powers) Act 1987) offers another illustration as to how military power can be controlled. Section 5 of the Act allows the raising and maintenance of armed forces for specified purposes, including the 'provision of assistance to the civil power . . . in time of emergency', and section 9(1) goes on to authorize the use of the armed forces in those circumstances. Regrettably, the express statutory powers are then substantially undermined by the reserve provision in section 6(2) (designed to avert judicial review), by which 'Nothing in . . . section 5 of this Act shall affect any power vested in the Governor-General apart from this Act'. The 1990 Act is also less than sure-footed in its regulation of emergencies which have arisen. On the one hand, it does usefully specify that the process must be initiated by the chief of police (section 9(4)), and the special powers then made available are specified. Thus, the police are allowed to issue directions to soldiers (section 9(5)), and, in the case of international terrorism emergencies, both forces are granted a list of extra legal powers (1987 Act, sections 10, 12). On the other hand, accountability to the House of Representatives is limited to informing it of any authorization under section 9(1) and requiring its approval for any extended deployment beyond fourteen days. However, the Act does not require the House to be summoned if not sitting (whereupon any extension can be authorized by the Governor-General), no official reports are demanded and no special committee ever constituted.

It might be argued that permanent, clear statutory authority will encourage 'more frequent, unsolicited military adventurism'.[8] This real danger must be countered by the incorporation of explicit criteria governing military intervention and effective scrutiny of the application of those criteria by experts and Parliament. The evidence from Canada and New Zealand suggests that the task is difficult but not impossible. In any event, almost any statutory scheme is likely to be an improvement on the untrammelled authority which currently vests in the state under common law and prerogative.

Legal powers of soldiers in Northern Ireland

The legal powers wielded by soldiers in Northern Ireland may be categorized under three headings: those possessed as citizens; those arising under the prerogative; and those specially granted by statute. It is intended in this section to describe the three categories and to assess them in principle. The critical principles have to a great extent already been adduced. The overriding consideration is the given strategy of police primacy, which suggests that military involvement should be confined to situations where it is wholly impracticable to expect the police to cope alone and, even then, should occur subject to police direction and presence. This first ideal is in fact being pursued in Northern Ireland, though it is not yet enshrined in statutory form. Another critical criterion arises from the lack of policing training and experience of soldiers and their expectations of straightforward orders; these circumstances mean that any special powers must be clear and simple.

Powers held as citizens

It is stressed by the *Manual of Military Law* that soldiers can exercise any legal powers held by ordinary citizens,[9] and the most relevant are those concerned with arrest, the prevention of crime and disorder, self-defence and the use of force in pursuit of these objects. In practice, it is the use of force which has proved most controversial. The ground-rule is section 3(1) of the Criminal Law Act (Northern Ireland) 1967, which demands that the force applied to prevent crime or effect an arrest be 'reasonable in the circumstances'. The application of section 3 and associated issues has been at the centre of most of the 331 killings by the security forces since 1969, resulting from which two soldiers from British regiments and twenty-three from the UDR have been convicted of homicide.

The most fundamental attack on section 3 is that it sets an unfairly indulgent standard. For example, Article 2 of the European Convention on Human Rights demands that lethal force, if used, be 'absolutely necessary' and so strictly proportionate to the evil. There is strong academic and judicial support for the view that section 3 demands not only that a reasonable person would think that the force used was justified to avert the potential evil (proportionality) but also that force was unavoidable to achieve the objective (necessity). However, it was accepted in *Stewart* v *UK*[10] that 'absolute' is a less flexible standard than 'reasonable'. Consequently, Article 2 and section 3 may differ, though any discrepancy is small.

The next vociferous criticism is that section 3 is vague and uninformative to citizens and soldiers alike, and this uncertainty has not been resolved by subsequent legal or administrative interpretations. The leading legal ruling emphasized that what amount of force is reasonable in the circumstances is always a matter of fact, and so there can be no 'test case' under section 3.[11] Since that opinion, the application of deadly force in archetypal situations – failure to stop for questioning, driving through vehicle checkpoints and armed confrontations – has been somewhat clarified as successive cases have been processed by the courts. Nevertheless, the results contain complications and contradictions, and other uncertainties remain, especially the relationship between section 3 and self-defence.

Aside from the faltering steps towards legal clarification, 'Instructions by the Director of Operations for Opening Fire in Northern Ireland' (the 'yellow card') have been issued to soldiers.[12] These internal restraints are unsatisfactory for two reasons. First, they are secret documents, which means that they cannot operate as a guide for citizens. Second, the card is extra-legal and so may increase uncertainty in so far as adherence cannot be taken for granted, nor is departure from it legally decisive.

The application of force has proved equally problematical with regard to the firing of rubber and plastic baton rounds, which have inflicted seventeen deaths up to October 1989 and the use of which far exceeds that of lead rounds. Any firing falls again to be justified under section 3 or as self-defence; administrative guidance is also available but does not provide legal certainty.

Three reforms may be necessary in order to reflect the fraught situation of soldiers without at the same time ignoring the interests of their victims.[13] The first would be to amend section 3 so as to give more guidance as to when lethal force or plastic baton rounds might legitimately be applied. The second would be to adopt the Australian doctrine of excessive defence, by which manslaughter may be the charge when the circumstances justified the application of force but not to the extent to which it actually occurred. The third would be to allow a defence of superior orders, provided the orders were not manifestly unreasonable and provided that planners could be made liable in civil and criminal law.

Finally, as well as clarifications to the rules governing the use of force, the legal aftermath should also be reformed. In particular, inquests are too narrowly focused to satisfy the public interest, and *ad hoc* investigations (such as the Widgery Report on 'Bloody Sunday'[14] and the Stalker inquiry[15]) have also proved most unsatisfactory. Thus, a more permanent system of judicial inquiries should be constituted in addition to coroners.

Prerogative authority

The existence of a broad prerogative authority to maintain the peace was confirmed in *R v Secretary of State for the Home Department, ex parte Northumbria Police Authority*: 'the Crown does have a prerogative power to keep the peace, which is bound up with its undoubted right to see that crime is prevented and justice administered'.[16] The implication is that central government may deploy and equip soldiers to combat disorder, and, in this way, the Army may act as a rival police force even outside times of emergency. As for what may be accomplished in action under the prerogative (rather than, say, under section 3 above), its main advantage would seem to be to authorize wide-scale operations which are not undertaken in response to specific disorder. An example might be the imposition of a curfew, as applied in West

Belfast on 3–5 July, 1970, internment without trial or even a declaration of martial law. However, any such exercises are now to be avoided as wholly usurping police primacy and treading into areas of great legal uncertainty.

Special statutory powers

It is legitimate both in international law and under the constitutions of many states to derogate from normal rights in times of emergency by granting special powers to the security forces. To expect them to operate normal powers in extraordinary conditions risks the 'tolerance of covert counter-terrorism' and 'obfuscation'.[17] Nevertheless, any derogation and consequent special powers should be as limited as possible so as to avoid undermining the strategies of criminalization and police primacy and so that official ideology, such as the rule of law and personal freedom, can remain intact. Consequently, it would be inappropriate simply to grant soldiers whatever powers have been showered on the police. The Westminster Parliament has never gone that far, but much of its output has been misdirected. As described earlier, Army involvement should be confined to situations where it is not reasonable for the police alone to act, especially because they lack specialist skills or equipment or the personnel to cover large areas or process large numbers of people. Any special powers should reflect these circumstances only, but the reality in Northern Ireland is rather different, as shall now be shown.[18]

As regards arrest powers, section 14 of the Northern Ireland (Emergency Provisions) Act 1978 (as amended) states as follows:

(1) A member of Her Majesty's forces on duty may arrest without warrant, and detain for not more than four hours, a person whom he has reasonable grounds to suspect is committing, has committed or is about to commit any offence.

The history and interpretation of section 14 have been related in other works;[19] the purpose here is solely to argue that section 14 is now inappropriate for three reasons. The first is that its application has declined to the point of redundancy, as evidenced by Table 8.2.[20] Secondly, section 14 may be superfluous in view of the provisions in relation to arrestable offences granted to ordinary citizens (including soldiers) by Article 26 of the Police and Criminal Evidence Order (Northern Ireland) 1989. Though these powers are not as extensive as those granted to the police, such limits are consistent with the official strategy of police primacy. A third factor against section 14 is that it may breach Articles 5(1)(c) and 5(2) of the European Convention on Human Rights because the purpose of arrest is often intelligence-gathering rather than prosecution and because no reasons need be proffered for an arrest. The fact that section 14 cannot comply with international minimum standards undermines the overall policy of criminalization.

Table 8.2 Arrests under special powers in
Northern Ireland

Year	Police arrests	Army arrests (% of total)
1975		4141
1976	Not	8321
1977	available	5878
1978		3692
1979	2197	2572 (54)
1980	1941	1629 (46)
1981	3050	1993 (40)
1982	2730	1288 (32)
1983	2397	476 (17)
1984	2234	241 (10)
1985	1926	142 (7)
1986	2216	71 (3)
1987	1846	105 (5)
1988	1718	64 (4)
1989	1585	85 (5)

Source: Northern Ireland Office.

There may be stronger arguments favouring the retention of the detention
power in section 18 of the Emergency Provisions Act:

Any member of Her Majesty's forces on duty . . . may stop and question
any person for the purpose of ascertaining:

(a) that person's identity and movements;
(b) what he knows concerning any recent explosion or any other [recent
    terrorist] incident . . .
(c) any one or more of the matters referred to in paragraphs (a) and (b)
    above.

Although a power to stop and question as in section 18 is inevitably widely
drawn and dangerous to liberty (and probably breaches Article 5(1) of the
European Convention), there is no readily available alternative power, and
individual rights are less severely affected than on arrest. Thus, section 18
might be justifiable in situations where a significant proportion of detainees
might possess valuable information which they would not voluntarily impart.
Three such scenarios exist in Northern Ireland: persons in the vicinity of the
border other than on approved crossings; persons at the scene of a terrorist
attack; and persons entering vulnerable areas, such as shopping centres. In so
far as section 18 applies in wider contexts, it should be curtailed as amounting
to little more than institutionalized harassment. If a detention power is

Table 8.3 Use of search powers under section 15

Year	Premises searched by Army			Premises searched by police
	Occupied	Unoccupied	Total	
1971	Not available		17,262	
1972			36,617	
1973	14,429	60,127	74,556	
1974	19,576	52,338	71,914	
1975	3,907	26,185	30,092	
1976	10,749	24,190	34,939	
1977	9,264	11,460	20,724	
1978	6,309	9,153	15,462	
1979	4,740	1,212	5,952	
1980	2,960	1,146	4,106	
1981	2,420	1,648	4,068	
1982	2,979	1,066	4,045	
1983	693	800	1,493	
1984	769	513	1,282	
1985	104	184	288	11,852*
1986	137	207	344	1,818
1987	393	232	625	2,474
1988	751	566	1,317	4,136
1989	726	384	1,110	3,027

* Total to end of 1985.
Source: Northern Ireland Office.

retained, it should be conferred on soldiers as well as the police, since it may have to be exercised at times on a wide scale or without notice.

Turning to searches, four distinct powers are granted to soldiers in relation to munitions, transmitters and scanning receivers by section 15 of the Emergency Provisions Act. Those permitting entry into places other than dwelling-houses without warrant, authorization or suspicion (section 15(1)) and the stopping and searching of persons in public places (section 15(3)(a)) may be regarded in a similar light to section 18, at least if confined to the three contexts previously outlined. However, the powers to search dwellings (section 15(2)) on reasonable suspicion and subject to authorization by an officer, together with the searching of persons in private premises (section 15(3)(b)), may be akin to the arrest power in section 14. These forms of search do severely intrude into reasonable expectations of privacy and liberty, while statistical evidence suggests that the incidence of such military searches is now very modest (see Table 8.3). It follows that soldiers should equally have no powers under section 17 to enter dwellings in order to find persons being

Table 8.4 Survey of Army/UDR – District Council relationships

District Council liaison committee (if any)	Whether security matters* discussed in liaison committee	Whether security matters* discussed in full council	Whether security matters* discussed elsewhere in council	Importance of security matters*	Invitations to Army/UDR to attend/make submissions	Invitations by Army/UDR to attend/make submissions	Expression of views on structural relationship	Expression of views on operations
Antrim: Police Liaison Committee	No	Occasionally	No	–	No	Yes: ceremonial occasions	No	No
Ards: Police Liaison Committee	–	–	–	–	–	–	–	–
Armagh	No committee	Rarely	No	–	No	No	No	No
Belfast: Police Liaison and Local Committee	Yes	Occasionally	Yes: General Purposes and Finance Committee	Great	Army: Yes; UDR: no	Army: not known; UDR: no	No, but UDR granted Freedom of City in 1980	Yes
Coleraine: Police Liaison Committee	Occasionally	No	No	Minor	No	Army: no; UDR: yes (ceremonials)	No	No

Derry: Public and Police Liaison Committee	Yes	Rarely	No	–	Army: yes; UDR: no	–	–	–
Down: Police Liaison Committee	No	No	No	–	–	–	–	–
Dungannon: Local Security Committee	Yes	Rarely	No	Minor	Army: yes; UDR: no	No	No	No
Fermanagh: Police and Community Liaison Committee	Yes	Occasionally	No	Great	No	Yes	Yes	Yes
Lisburn: Police Liaison Committee	No	Rarely	No	Great	No	–	No	Yes
Moyle: Police Liaison Committee	No	Occasionally	No	Great	No	No	No	No
Newtownabbey: Police Liaison Committee	No	Rarely	No	Important	No	No	No	No
Omagh	No committee	Occasionally	No	Little	No	No	No	No
Strabane: Police and Public Liaison Committee	Yes	Frequently	Yes: Finance and General Purposes Committee	Important	No	No	No	Yes

* 'Security matters' are defined as the work of the RUC, Army and UDR in combating proscribed paramilitary groups.

unlawfully detained. In this way the Army should be confined to a support role in the searching of dwellings.

Remaining special military powers are either in a state of abeyance (the fate of the power to disperse assemblies under section 24) or might be described as unavoidably ancillary to other operations (especially the powers to infringe property rights under section 19). Conversely, a modest number of additions may be made to the present catalogue, including powers to check identity when exercising other powers and incidental powers to regulate traffic.

Mechanisms of local accountability

The arguments favouring control over the military extend not only to the deployment of troops but also to their exercise of powers. When the Army's intervention does not fit the paradigm of a short sharp intervention and involves extensive contact with civilians, local accountability should in principle apply to soldiers, just as it applies to constables. It might be argued in reply that three distinctions exist between police and Army which warrant a lesser degree of local control over the latter. The first is that local authorities are not liable to finance military costs, and so there is dissonance between taxation and representation. However, liability to taxes is not now recognized as the sole ground for democratic control, and involvement in the community is arguably more fundamental. A second possible distinction is that the Army is not meant to reflect the locality in terms of recruits or policies; its presence is imposed from outside rather than springing from community wishes. However, these characteristics do not detract from the fact that the Army is performing a quasi-policing role, in support of, rather than supplanting, the civil authorities. Thirdly, ministerial accountability does exist for the operations of the Army but is notoriously patchy. Furthermore, local accountability may serve purposes other than the redress of grievances, such as the reduction of alienation.

In view of the strictly hierarchical structure of the Army, with its power-base in London, accountability on the police model cannot exactly be replicated. However, three measures of local governance might be considered.

Local liaison committees

The idea of a forum at District Council level to discuss policing and military issues has long been fostered in Northern Ireland. Despite the absence of any legal authority for their interest, many local authorities have taken initiatives, as a survey conducted in May 1987 shows (see Table 8.4).[21]

Efforts have recently been made to revitalize the police committee system, but no comparable attention seems to have been expended on military–community relations, despite the fact that liaison fills an obvious vacuum.

Consequently, the police committee model should basically be applied to the Army, save that an additional province-wide 'Liaison Grand Committee' could perform some of the functions of the counterpart Police Authority. In particular, a Grand Committee could monitor the work of local boards (whose chairs could comprise its membership) and raise matters of overall concern.

Lay visitors

In contrast to the intermittent enthusiasm displayed towards liaison committees, the notion of lay visitors has not yet taken firm root in Northern Ireland. Nevertheless, lay visitors could offer an important safeguard for the detainee and reassurance for the community and institutional links with it. The idea has been recently championed by the Northern Ireland Police Authority and already successfully operates in England in regard to terrorist suspects. Lay visitors are equally of value in respect of detainees in Army hands, and a rota should be devised to cover the Army's 'screening centres' where even a short period of detention can generate a vast amount of hostility.

Complaints

The manner of dealing with police complaints in Northern Ireland continues to excite great controversy. The system has been overhauled no fewer than three times – in 1970, 1977 and 1987 – and an Independent Commission for Police Complaints has latterly been founded with wide powers to direct and supervise investigations and to oversee procedures thereafter. Whatever deficiencies may persist in this system, the rules for dealing with complaints against soldiers are abysmal by comparison, despite long-standing calls for improvement. The current system is as follows.[22]

It is important to distinguish at the outset between complaints relevant to a complaints system and those properly dealt with elsewhere. The latter category includes allegations of crimes (which are investigated by the RUC assisted by the Royal Military Police), claims in civil law for compensation or damages (which are handled by a Civil Representative from the Northern Ireland Office in the case of alleged property loss or by the Ministry of Defence in the case of alleged personal injury) and the questioning of general operational issues or policy (which may be referred to Army HQ, the Northern Ireland Office, Parliament, or the Anglo-Irish Agreement machinery). The residual category, which comprises the workload of the complaints system, concerns allegations of misconduct not amounting to a crime or serious civil law wrong – such as incivility, abuse, harassment, improper or insensitive behaviour.

Prior to 1988, a complaints system of sorts existed but was rather uncoordinated. Disgruntled individuals were advised to make non-criminal, minor complaints either to the relevant Army unit or to the local Civil Representative of the Northern Ireland Office. Thereafter, depending upon the nature and seriousness of the complaint, the matter was passed on to the Royal Military Police or the HQ of Brigade or the UDR. Following an internal study and with the aim mainly of reducing delays, this system was overhauled in 1988. The new procedures are as follows.

A 'formal' complaint may be submitted either in person or via a District Councillor, Member of Parliament, solicitor, or the Anglo-Irish Secretariat and should be directed to the local Army unit or to a Civil Representative (who will in any event notify the local Army unit). Investigations will be undertaken either by the unit itself or, if serious, by the Royal Military Police. A report will be forwarded to HQ if possible within three to four weeks, though delays will occur if the unit's tour of duty has ended. The complainant may be asked to provide a statement as to the facts and allegations and may be visited by a Civil Representative or unit officer to clarify matters, but no formal hearings are held to which the person is invited or has the opportunity to confront the relevant soldiers. The outcome of the process is that HQ composes a written reply, including notification of the decision, to the complainant, who may also be visited by a Civil Representative, especially if the complaint is upheld. If a complaint is sustained, the remedy will be an apology and possibly also disciplinary action under the Army Act 1955. If the complaint is wholly unsubstantiated, that seems to be the end of the affair, and soldiers do not seem to have adopted the occasional police practice of suing for libel, even though Army HQ alleges that many complaints are malicious:

> There is clear evidence that PIRA/Sinn Fein has been orchestrating a campaign of complaints against the Security Forces for the last two years or so. About one third of all complaints are received from persons who are either PIRA, INLA or Sinn Fein or associates thereof. It is our experience that when stopped by military patrols, members of PIRA or Sinn Fein frequently attempt to provoke incidents which can be exploited for propaganda purposes. When such individuals make complaints, they frequently submit them through intermediaries, such as local priests and solicitors, or pass them to the local press first, in order to give them credibility among nationalists. Investigations generally show that the majority – not all – are either fabrications or distortions of events. In such cases where the Army is sure of the facts the reply takes the form of a firm rebuttal of the allegations.[23]

The new system appears to work satisfactorily from the Army's viewpoint. In the period from January to August 1989 there was a total of 184 complaints made.[24] Of these resolved, sixteen were substantiated, fifty-four were not substantiated, eighty-six were expressly denied and with regard to four complaints it was found that there was fault on both sides. Contentment is also drawn from the observation that few complainants write to express dissatis-faction with their treatment under the system – perhaps half a dozen per year.

In a sense, it is highly commendable that the Army should have expended time and effort on complaints procedures in the absence of any statutory obligation. Yet it is in the Army's own interests that it should pay attention to complaints – so that sources of friction between soldiers and individuals are removed and so that it may demonstrate to the wider community its desire to act with justice. In that light, the present system may be failing in its objectives: many of the same criticisms are levelled against it as are directed against the police complaints system. For example, the procedures are secretive and insular in that they do not allow for participation by the complainant or even reports as to what has been transacted. Next, the system of investigation of complaints lacks any independent element; allegations about soldiers are mainly investigated by other soldiers rather than by outsiders, and there is no provision for lay oversight as to whether the inquiry has been pursued vigorously or comprehensively. Thus, the fact that few complaints have been upheld may be viewed by the complainants and their communities as a sign of weakness of the investigation or of prejudice within the system (perhaps as evidenced by the hostile attitude displayed in the quotation above) rather than of the probity of military activities. Such perceptions may equally account for the relatively modest number of complaints made in the first place. The overall total may also be affected by the fact that some allegations are apparently settled informally at a local level. The criteria for taking complaints out of the formal system, the procedures according to which they must then be considered, and the possible outcomes are not specified. This informal alternative may further marginalize the worth of the complaints system in the minds of onlookers.

So long as the Army's commitment to Northern Ireland remains substantial, there are strong reasons to establish a complaints system at least as thorough as that applying to the police. Comparability would seem fair to complainants and even to soldiers under investigation now that their legal position is similar to that of police officers (including the availability of legal advice under the Police and Criminal Evidence legislation). In the light of these arguments, the government has latterly conceded the principle of an independent element (of a nature as yet unspecified).[25] However, if the military complaints system is to be strengthened, it should be recognized that soldiers cannot, by virtue of their duty to obey lawful commands under section 34 of the Army Act 1955, exercise an unfettered 'right to silence' in the same way as police officers; therefore, statements prompted by demands from superiors should be expressly privileged.

Conclusion

The experience of Northern Ireland, ever since its foundation in 1920 and especially after 1969, suggests that a sharp division between legal normality and emergency may not be tenable. Consequently, it must belatedly be recognized that the UK faces endemic instability in Northern Ireland which will not be cured by transitory military intervention. Unfortunately, 'the illusion of civil control',[26] which demands that a blind eye be turned towards the sizeable and persistent Army involvement, is maintained. Yet policing in such a divided society engenders various unwelcome tendencies (such as selective law enforcement, political interference and under-representation of the minority community) which warrant tighter formal control than usual rather than laxity. Accordingly, the mission is to move towards a new framework for the military in a way which does not put at risk the very values of democracy and individual rights which its presence is supposed to secure. The task is difficult, as legislators in Canada and New Zealand have recently experienced. However, the persistence of a legal regime in Northern Ireland which is obscure, *ad hoc*, and subject to abuses presages an even less palatable future.

Notes

1 W. L. S. Churchill, *The World Crisis, Vol. 5: The Aftermath*, Butterworths, London, p. 314.
2 *Report of the Advisory Committee on the Police in Northern Ireland* (Hunt Report) (Cmd. 535), HMSO, Belfast, 1969.
3 See 'Defence Intelligence Staff Report' in R. Faligot, *Britain's Military Strategy in Ireland*, Zed Press, London, 1983, Appendix 4, para. 3.
4 *Manual of Military Law*, Pt II (9th edn, 1969), HMSO, London, Section V, para. 2.
5 Queen's Regulations J.11.002 (1976); *R v Secretary of State for the Home Department, ex parte Northumbria Police Authority* [1983] 2 WLR 590 at 613–14.
6 *Report of the Tribunal of Inquiry into Violence and Civil Disturbances in Northern Ireland in 1969* (Cmd. 566) Scarman Report, HMSO, Belfast, 1972.
7 *Text of a Communiqué issued on Aug. 29, 1969 at the conclusion of the visit of the Secretary of State for the Home Department to Northern Ireland* (Cmnd. 4158), HMSO, London, 1969; *Text of a Communiqué issued following discussions between the Secretary of State for the Home Department and the Northern Ireland Government in Belfast on October 9 and 10, 1969* (Cmnd. 4178), HMSO, London, 1969.
8 S. C. Greer, 'Military intervention in civil disturbances', *Public Law* (1983), pp. 573–99.
9 *Manual of Military Law*, Pt II, HMSO, London, Section V, para. 2.
10 *Stewart v UK*, Appl. no. 10044/82, [1985] 7 EHRR 453.
11 *Reference under s. 48A of the Criminal Appeal (Northern Ireland) Act 1968 (No. 1 of 1975)* [1977] AC 105.
12 See K. Asmal, *Shoot to Kill*, Mercier, Dublin, 1985, ch. 6.
13 See G. Hogan and C. Walker, *Political Violence and the Law in Ireland*, Manchester University Press, Manchester, 1989.
14 *Report of the Tribunal Appointed to Inquire into the Events on Sunday, Jan. 30,*

1972, *which led to loss of life in connection with the procession in Londonderry on that day* (Widgery Report) (HC 220, Session 1971–2), HMSO, London, 1972.

15 See J. Stalker, *Stalker*, Harrap, London, 1988.

16 *R v Secretary of State for Home Department*, loc. cit. at 600. Residual powers are saved by section 35 of the Northern Ireland (Emergency Provisions) Act 1978.

17 C. Townshend, 'Putting subterfuge in place of strategy', *The Times*, 9 August 1989, p. 14.

18 These measures (except section 24) are being renewed by the Northern Ireland (Emergency Provisions) Act 1991 with some additional powers.

19 Hogan and Walker, *Political Violence*, pp. 50–8; C. Walker, 'Army special powers on parade', *Northern Ireland Legal Quarterly*, 40 (1989) 105.

20 All statistics on the special powers were supplied by the Northern Ireland Office (NIO).

21 The author thanks those District Councils which co-operated with this research.

22 The author thanks Army HQNI for much of this information; see also NIO, *Guide to the Emergency Powers*, HMSO, London, 1990, Annex E.

23 Letter to author, 9 September 1989.

24 Ibid.

25 *HC Debs*, vol. 187 (1990–1), col. 367.

26 See C. Townshend, *Britain's Civil Wars*, Faber, London, 1986, p. 15.

Postscript

It has been announced that the UDR is to merge with the Royal Irish Rangers to form the 'Royal Irish Regiment'. The amalgamation will have the cosmetic benefits of securing a new start on paper and of augmenting Catholic participation (especially since the Rangers recruit from both sides of the border). A more substantial effect will be stronger ties with regular Army structures, including service abroad. Predictably, force levels are not to be affected. (See *HC Debs*, vol. 195 (1990–1), col. 1038; and *Britain's Army for the 90s* (Cm. 1595), HMSO, London, 1991, para. 20.)

9

Northern Ireland's troubles and the judges

Brice Dickson

Who are the judges?

In Northern Ireland the hierarchy of courts is similar to that in England. At the lowest level are the magistrates courts, with criminal appeals and more serious civil cases being heard by the county courts. Next come the High Court, for civil and public law proceedings, and the Crown Court, for the most serious criminal prosecutions. The Court of Appeal can hear appeals from any of these four courts, but sometimes only if a point of law (not one of pure fact) is in dispute. The High Court, Crown Court and Court of Appeal are collectively known as the Supreme Court of Judicature. Appeals from the Court of Appeal can sometimes lie to the House of Lords in London.

The magistrates courts are staffed by seventeen full-time resident magistrates (RMs), the county courts by eleven full-time county court judges, the Supreme Court by the Lord Chief Justice, three Lords Justices and six High Court judges. There are also thirteen part-time deputy RMs, thirty-four part-time deputy county court judges, four full-time circuit registrars (to assist the county court judges) and eight full-time masters (to assist the High Court judges). All of the fifty full-time magistrates, registrars, judges and masters are male. There has never been a full-time female judge in Northern Ireland and it was only in 1989 that the first female Queen's Counsel (a title given to senior barristers) was appointed.

Since 1935 the magistrates courts have been the preserve of legally qualified RMs, at least during the courts' regular (or 'petty') sessions. Before appointment an RM has to have practised as a solicitor or barrister in Northern Ireland for at least seven years. Few would doubt that the legal competence of RMs has led to a fairer system of summary justice in Northern Ireland than exists in England, where the magistrates, apart from 'stipendiary' magistrates in large cities, are predominantly from a non-legal background. There are, of course, exceptions to this generalization. It is not necessarily the best lawyers who are appointed to the magistracy and in Northern Ireland some of the appointees have been as quirky as any lay person might be.

As RMs deal at some point with *every* criminal prosecution, and with the majority of all civil claims, they are in a crucial position to influence the general public's perceptions of Northern Ireland's legal system. During the late 1960s, when the current troubles were just beginning, the RMs were widely perceived to be pro-Establishment figures who had little sympathy for the civil rights demonstrators appearing before them. Several of them had connections with unionism and were distrusted by nationalists. The Attorney-General of the day, Basil Kelly, who was appointed a Supreme Court judge in 1973, was also accused by non-unionist MPs of showing political bias in ordering prosecutions in the first place.

After threats and attacks on various individuals, the government offered some protection to the magistracy by reducing its involvement in terrorist-related cases. Section 3 of the Northern Ireland (Emergency Provisions) Act 1973 (now section 3 of the 1991 version of this Act, the EPA) provided that persons charged with one of the offences listed in schedule 4 of the Act could be granted bail only by a judge of the Supreme Court. The very concept of a scheduled offence also lessened the magistrates' activities in this area because nearly all of the listed offences, even the ones which are not often serious, were made indictable (that is, triable only in the Crown Court). The magistracy was further insulated by section 2 of the EPA 1975 (now section 2 of the EPA 1991), which provides for 'preliminary enquiries' in preference to the longer and more public 'preliminary investigations' whenever the RM is deciding whether to commit for trial in the Crown Court a person suspected of a scheduled offence. Occasionally the prosecution has altogether bypassed a preliminary hearing in front of an RM by resorting to the antiquated device of a 'voluntary indictment'.[1]

County courts in Northern Ireland have largely escaped the opprobrium sometimes attaching to other courts because their jurisdiction is mainly in civil matters. But county court judges also have experience of presiding in criminal trials of terrorist suspects, because the EPA 1973 required most persons accused of scheduled offences to be tried either at the newly created Belfast City Commission or at the Belfast Recorder's Court (the county court for Belfast) and section 4(3) stated that a county court judge could at any time, at the request of the Lord Chief Justice, sit and act as a judge of the Belfast City Commission. But still the power to grant bail was restricted to full High Court judges. Today section 9 of the EPA 1991 requires all trials on indictment of a scheduled offence to be held at the Crown Court in Belfast, unless the Lord Chancellor directs otherwise, which he has not yet done. In 1989 county court judges spent a total of 698 days sitting in the Crown Court, more than twice the number spent there by High Court judges.[2]

The Belfast City Commission was a juryless court, with one judge deciding all questions of fact and law. It became known as the Diplock court because the proposal to try suspected terrorists in the absence of a jury was put forward by the Commission chaired by Lord Diplock (himself a judge in England) which reported in 1972.[3] Following the reorganization of courts effected by the Judicature (NI) Act 1978, the Belfast City Commission became part of the Crown Court for Belfast. In recent years there has been considerable clamour for the Diplock court to be either abolished or reformed, one suggestion being that, as with the comparable Special Criminal Court in Dublin, it should be staffed by three judges, not just by one. The pros and cons of this proposal have been examined by Baker[4] and Jackson.[5] Although the latter concludes that a strong case can be made for the argument that a three-judge court is likely to produce a better-quality decision of fact than a single-judge court, it is well known that the existing senior judges are against the idea. They fear not only that it would increase their workload (though, of course, more judges could be appointed) but also that it would implicitly cast doubt on convictions obtained under the old system. As the Guildford Four and Birmingham Six cases clearly illustrate, judges are reluctant to admit that miscarriages of justice may have occurred. In 1983 the Lord Chief Justice said that he had heard of no instance of a person being wrongly convicted in Northern Ireland,[6] but the current investigations into the convictions of the Armagh Four may eventually undermine such confident assertions.[7]

It is relatively rare for RMs or county court judges to be promoted to the Supreme Court Bench. Only one of the ten current Supreme Court judges had full-time judicial experience prior to appointment. Since the creation of Northern Ireland in 1920 there have been thirty-one Supreme Court judges, eighteen of whom have been in office during the present troubles. They are appointed by the monarch, on the advice of the Lord Chancellor. In England the Prime Minister has a say in who should be appointed to the Court of Appeal, but this has never been the case in Northern Ireland. It is nevertheless a fact that a large number of the appointees have had unionist connections. Writing of the situation in 1970, Boyle, Hadden and Hillyard state:

> It is incontrovertible that the majority of judicial appointments in Northern Ireland had been made from the ranks of Unionism. Of twenty High Court judges appointed since the independent Northern Ireland courts were established, fifteen had been openly associated with the Unionist Party: of twenty-three County Court appointments, fourteen had been visibly connected with the Unionist administration. At the height of the civil rights campaign in the late 1960s two of the three judges in the Northern Ireland Court of Appeal were ex-Attorney-Generals in Unionist governments; one of the four High Court judges was likewise an ex-Attorney-General, and another the son of an Attorney-General; two of the five County Court judges were ex-Unionist MPs and another the son of a Unionist MP; and among the twelve

Resident Magistrates there was an ex-Unionist MP, an ex-Unionist Senator, a defeated Unionist candidate and a former legal adviser to the Ministry of Home Affairs.[8]

In this connection one of the most illuminating of published comments is that of Sir Edward Jones, a Supreme Court judge from 1968 to 1984 and a cousin of a former Attorney-General and Lord Justice of Appeal, Sir Anthony Babington:

> Politics certainly was a great interest in my life in that I adhered to the Unionist cause and I was prepared to do anything within reason to further that cause . . . I was prepared to further the Unionist cause with all the abilities which were at my disposal, the first of which was my ability, such as it was, as a lawyer and a speaker; and if that path should bring me to legal office and ultimately to the Bench, which was the main objective, so much the better . . .[9]

The most important judicial figure in Northern Ireland is the Lord Chief Justice. When the present troubles began the incumbent was Lord Mac-Dermott, a Northern Ireland High Court judge who in 1947 had been a surprise appointment as a Lord of Appeal in the House of Lords. Four years later he returned to the province as 'the Chief', holding that position for twenty years. He had the reputation of being a fair-minded judge of the highest quality. He was succeeded in 1971 by Sir Robert Lowry, the son of a former High Court judge who had been a Unionist Attorney-General. He, too, was to be at the helm for a lengthy period, until 1989. He was even involved in trying to secure a political solution to Northern Ireland's unrest, for in 1975–6 he chaired the Constitutional Convention and undertook behind-the-scenes negotiations with political parties to try to construct a viable compromise on administrative arrangements.[10] Though his efforts failed, he was praised by all concerned for his even-handedness. Given a peerage in 1979, he was created a Lord of Appeal in 1988. His successor as Lord Chief Justice, Sir Brian Hutton, was senior Crown counsel before becoming a High Court judge in 1979.

It is impossible to say that a particular judge has ever been appointed because he was of a particular religion. To allege this of new appointments today would be especially irresponsible. When *The Economist* made such an allegation in respect of a county court appointee, the judge concerned, William Doyle, later received substantial libel damages. But the Lord Chancellor at that time, Lord Hailsham, did admit that attempts were made to preserve a balance in the judiciary as regards religious affiliation. At present the balance is maintained within the High Court, where three of the six judges are Catholic. But in the Court of Appeal all four of the judges have, since late 1989, been Protestant. Of the eighteen Supreme Court judges in office since 1968, fourteen have been Protestant and four Catholic.

The socio-economic background of the Northern Ireland judges has not been systematically studied in the way that it has in England.[11] Superficially, however, a similar picture emerges. Among the thirty-one Supreme Court judges there have been three father-and-son teams; the fathers of two others were a county court judge and a Queen's Counsel. Of the eighteen who have dealt with the current troubles, nine attended a public school and six took a law degree at Oxford or Cambridge. The average age of the ten in office today is sixty.

The fact that there are only ten Supreme Court judges in office at any one time is itself problematical. It means that on occasions a judge will try a case in which he has already had to decide a bail application (where statements may have been made which are not strictly admissible at the trial stage). It means, too, that if several trials arise out of the one incident, such as the killing of two Army corporals in Andersonstown in 1988, a judge may be asked to assess facts which he has already assessed after hearing different evidence at an earlier trial. Nor must we forget that in a typical year Supreme Court judges spend less than one-third of their time on criminal work, which itself embraces almost as many non-terrorist as terrorist cases.[12]

The role of judges in Northern Ireland

Supreme Court judges in Northern Ireland are a small group with comparable life experiences. Before appointment, all will have practised for many years at the Northern Ireland Bar and will know personally the existing judges and other senior counsel. Their own predilections and foibles will be known to the barristers who plead before them. As a result it is probably commoner in Northern Ireland than in England for lawyers to tailor their court presentations to suit the judge of the day. There is also a certain degree of specialization on the Bench, with, for instance, Carswell J hearing most of today's judicial review applications and Campbell J dealing with most of the Chancery matters. Although there is usually the possibility of an appeal, this system does give scope to a High Court judge to place his own stamp on a particular area of law.

In England it is often said that successful barristers are reluctant to become judges because, even though they are then secured a high salary (currently £77,000) and a good pension, the transfer would nevertheless entail a substantial drop in earnings. But the certainty of a knighthood and the prestige attached to the position usually tip the scales. The desire to serve the public may even carry weight in some cases. In Northern Ireland a High Court judge earns the same as his counterpart in England and, at least since 1988, is automatically offered a knighthood (though one Catholic judge rejected this), but the factor which is likely to weigh most heavily against a top barrister becoming a judge is security. All judges in Northern Ireland, and especially the senior ones, have to lead extremely sheltered lives. Constantly guarded, with their movements kept as secret as possible, their donning of the judicial mantle means a complete change in life style. Wives and children are drastically affected too, sometimes preferring to live in Great Britain to make life easier. Several members of the judiciary have paid the ultimate price for their public service. The first to die was William Saunders RM, in 1973. The following year Martin McBirney RM and Judge Rory Conaghan were killed on the same day. In January 1983 the county court judge who had previously obtained libel damages from *The Economist* was shot dead as he was leaving a church in Belfast. Although he was a Catholic, the IRA issued a statement saying that his religion was irrelevant: he was 'a key figure in Britain's oppressive occupation ... [h]e was a member of the loyalist judiciary'. In April 1987 the most senior of the Court of Appeal judges, Gibson LJ, was killed with his wife when a bomb blew up beside their car just after it had crossed into Northern Ireland on a journey from the Republic. Several other murder bids have been unsuccessful. In 1982, for example, an attempt was made to assassinate Lord Lowry while he was visiting Queen's University. Bombs have frequently been placed under cars belonging to members of a judge's family or set off at a judge's current or former home.

The resilience of the judiciary is much to be admired. Even when sentencing defendants, only very occasionally has judicial restraint been abandoned. The most famous instance is when Gibson LJ remarked in 1984, after the acquittal of three policemen for the murder of three unarmed IRA suspects in 1982, that he wished to commend the RUC officers for their courage and determination in bringing these men to justice, 'in this case to the final court of justice'. The outcry which this comment evoked was such that the judge took the most unusual step of returning to court to make a statement explaining what he had meant. It is likely, however, that the incident made him a marked man in the eyes of the terrorists; he was murdered three years later.

Doubtless because of the other calls on their time, as well as their politically sensitive position, judges in Northern Ireland are not usually requested to undertake the independent inquiries or commissions which judges in England often conduct. With the notable exception of Sir Robert Lowry's involvement in the Constitutional Convention, it is only with respect to what are seen as technical legal matters that their judicial expertise has been called in aid. Lord MacDermott chaired the Working Party which reported in 1971 and led to the creation of the Office of Director of Public Prosecutions.[13] Sir Robert Lowry (together with Brian Hutton QC, as he then was) were part of the British membership of the Anglo-Irish Law Enforcement Commission, which resulted in legislation in both the United Kingdom and the Republic of Ireland enabling persons to be tried in one jurisdiction for crimes allegedly committed in the other, an attempt to bypass the difficulties encountered by extradition procedures.[14]

On the other hand, several English judges have been involved in special inquiries dealing with Northern Irish affairs. Scarman J, as he then was, as well as being a member of the Law Enforcement Commission mentioned above, headed a tribunal of inquiry into violence and civil disturbances in 1969.[15] Lord Widgery, the then Lord Chief Justice of England, led the inquiry into the 'Bloody Sunday' deaths on 30 January 1972.[16] Reports in the 1970s by Lords Parker, Diplock and Gardiner examined appropriate measures to deal with terrorism.[17] In 1979 Judge Bennett published his report of a committee of inquiry into police interrogation procedures,[18] and five years later Sir George Baker, a retired family court judge, reviewed the operation of the EPA 1978.[19]

As there has not been much in these reports to satisfy the nationalists in Northern Ireland (or many civil libertarians), it is little wonder that the reputation of the English judiciary is not high in the province. They are often portrayed as being incorrigibly anti-republican. Within the last two years the Guildford Four, the Maguire Seven, the Winchester Three and the Birmingham Six have all been found to have been unjustly convicted by English juries and the judges are viewed as partly responsible for the original convictions and the delays in overturning them. The judges would doubtless defend themselves by saying that they were simply reacting to the evidence presented to them. Unlike in continental Europe, judges in common-law countries such as Britain and Ireland do not themselves oversee the investigation of crimes. They cannot call witnesses whom the parties themselves do not wish to call or 'descend into the arena' to ask searching questions of witnesses. Nor are they supposed to raise legal arguments which have not already been aired by the parties' lawyers.

The attitude of judges in the House of Lords

The judges in the House of Lords – the Lords of Appeal in Ordinary – are widely perceived as being more pro-Establishment in their rulings than the judiciary in Northern Ireland.[20] An early example is their decision in *McEldowney* v *Forde*,[21] where they held that the Minister of Home Affairs for Northern Ireland had acted lawfully under the Civil Authorities (Special Powers) Act (NI) 1922 when he added 'republican clubs and any like organisation howsoever described' to the list of associations which were unlawful under that Act. The decision turned on whether this action was 'for the preservation of the peace and maintenance of order' and three of the five Law Lords held that it was. One of the dissenters, interestingly, was Lord Diplock, as indeed was Lord MacDermott LCJ in the Northern Ireland Court of Appeal.

In *The Attorney-General for Northern Ireland's Reference (No. 1 of 1975)*,[22] sometimes referred to as the *McElhone* case, the issue was whether it is murder, manslaughter or no crime at all when a member of the security forces shoots to kill or seriously wound – during the course of an attempted escape – a person believed to be a member of a banned organization. MacDermott J (the son of the former Lord Chief Justice) had acquitted the soldier of murder. The Court of Appeal was split two to one on the legal question, with Jones and Gibson LJJ holding that it was a question of fact as to whether the force used was unreasonable in all the circumstances, and only McGonigal LJ stating categorically that it was unlawful to shoot a fleeing member of the IRA who was posing no immediate threat. In the House of Lords all the judges agreed with Jones and Gibson LJJ but went further in saying that a soldier was entitled to take into account a very wide range of matters when deciding whether to open fire. Among these, in the words of Lord Diplock, was 'the likelihood of the escaper, if he got away, participating sooner or later in acts of violence'.

This liberal attitude to the use of force by the army was reinforced three years later when the House decided the *Farrell* case.[23] Here an unarmed man had been shot dead by soldiers operating from a nearby rooftop after he had snatched a night deposit bag from a man outside a bank in Newry. The Law Lords would not allow the man's widow to draw the court's attention to the planning stage of the stakeout when it was assessing whether the soldiers had used 'reasonable force in all the circumstances' (the test laid down in section 3(1) of the Criminal Law Act (NI) 1967). Yet when Mrs Farrell took her claim to Strasbourg under the European Convention on Human Rights the British government was prepared to pay her £37,500 in an out-of-court settlement.[24] Unfortunately, the absence of a court judgment means that the result in this case is not a precedent which binds future courts.

Four other cases in the House of Lords further illustrate the prevailing judicial attitude there towards the problems in Northern Ireland. In *McKee* v *Chief Constable of the RUC*[25] the Northern Ireland Court of Appeal had held (O'Donnell LJ and Kelly J; Jones LJ dissenting) that an arrest under section 11(1) of the EPA 1978 was unlawful because the arresting officer's only suspicion was that the arrestee was a member of the Provisional IRA, not that he was a terrorist (which the subsection requires). The House of Lords unanimously reversed this decision because, they said, the arresting officer was entitled to follow his superior's instructions, which here were to arrest McKee as a 'suspected terrorist'. The extent of the arresting officer's own personal suspicion was irrelevant. In *Murray* v *Ministry of Defence*[26] the House held that soldiers who go to a home to arrest a suspect under section 14 of the 1978 Act do not have to speak any words of arrest until after the home has been searched and the soldiers are ready to leave. In *McKerr* v *Armagh Coroner and others*[27] the House of Lords reversed the decision of a unanimous Court of Appeal in Northern Ireland (Hutton LCJ, O'Donnell and Kelly LJJ) in holding that a coroner could not compel a person who has been charged or is likely to be charged with an offence relating to the death to give evidence at the resulting inquest. Hutton LCJ had relied upon the 'clear and well-established principle of law that, with a few specific and limited exceptions, every person is a competent witness', but Lord Goff, for the House, preferred the view that the Ministry of Home Affairs in Northern Ireland had validly restricted this principle in the Coroners (Practice and Procedure) Rules (NI) 1963. He did not allude to the point that the same restriction does not exist in the equivalent English rules.

A pro-Establishment line was also adopted by the House of Lords in the case where the Home Secretary's broadcasting ban of 1988 was challenged.[28] The Lords found little difficulty in upholding its validity because British law does not permit the exercise of an administrative discretion to be reviewed on the ground that it is a disproportionate reaction to the mischief to which it is addressed and nor does it require the standards of the European Convention on Human Rights to be applied (even if it were clear, which it is not, that they grant greater protection to free speech than British law provides).

One matter on which the House of Lords has fully endorsed the approach of the Northern Ireland Court of Appeal, even in the face of conflicting authority in the English Court of Appeal, is the reviewability of disciplinary decisions taken by prison governors. In *Leech v Parkhurst Prison Deputy Governor*[29] the House followed *In re McKiernan's Application*[30] and held that such decisions were too important to escape judicial review. As we shall see, however, other applications by prisoners in Northern Ireland have not fared so well.

The attitude of the judges within Northern Ireland

It is safe to say that the decisions of the judges operating within Northern Ireland are usually imbued with a greater appreciation of the realities of the situation in the province. The local judges know that Northern Ireland is not an entirely lawless community: apart from terrorist and sexual offences, it is the least crime-ridden region of the United Kingdom. But this does not mean that the judges have in any sense been soft on terrorism. On the contrary, they have developed sentencing tariffs which clearly reflect their revulsion at violent acts carried out by paramilitaries. They have been less than interventionist in controlling emergency arrest powers, rejecting controverted confessions or restricting the use of lethal force by the police and army. On occasions, however, they have displayed a gratifying respect for the rule of law and a realization that even in times of grave community violence basic human rights must be upheld. We must remember, as well, that in many of their tasks they are constrained by the evidence put before them by the RUC and the Director of Public Prosecutions, not to mention the clear wording of statutory provisions which they have no power to override.

In the early case of *In re McElduff*[31] McGonigal J had to interpret the scope of an arrest power conferred by a regulation issued under the Civil Authorities (Special Powers) Acts (NI) 1922–33. The regulation required the arresting police officer to suspect that the arrestee was 'acting or about to act in a manner prejudicial to the preservation of the peace or maintenance of order'. The judge explained that the power amounted to one of preventive detention and was not confined to arrests for the purpose of charge and trial. He therefore held that, as a safeguard to the arrestee, he or she should at the very least be told whether the suspicion in question concerned 'a past act, a present or a future intention, or even a combination of two or all three in the conjunctive'. This relatively civil-libertarian stance presages the same judge's dissent in the *McElhone* case (see above).

Unfortunately, this approach has not been mirrored in judicial interpretations of the arrest power conferred by the Prevention of Terrorism (Temporary Provisions) Act 1974 (PTA). In *Ex parte Martin Henry Lynch*[32] Lord Lowry LCJ held that an arresting officer complied with this law if he or she merely told the person that the arrest was taking place under a named section and that he or she was suspected of being a terrorist. He also said that the police could use a wide arrest power in circumstances where a more specific one was available and he legitimized arrests in quick succession of the same person under the same statutory provision. More generally, citing Lord Greene, Lord Lowry approved the traditional view that a judge's role is basically one of subservience to the will of the executive:

> All that the court can do is to see that the power which it is claimed to exercise is one which falls within the four corners of the powers given by the legislature and to see that these powers are exercised in good faith. Apart from that, the courts have no power at all to inquire into the reasonableness, the policy, the sense, or any other aspect of the transaction.[33]

Given that nearly all arrests relating to the troubles now take place under the identical power in the current PTA 1989 (section 14(1)(b)), the significance of *Ex parte Lynch* is hard to over-estimate. Its impact is all the greater because of the concomitant rule that, just as in the case of army arrests, it is enough if the arresting police officer follows instructions issued by a superior. That this is the judges' preferred statement of law was confirmed by Carswell J.[34] In effect the judges have authorized arrests merely for the purpose of questioning. This would formerly have been viewed by most lawyers as highly undesirable, but today it is a phenomenon which has found favour even in cases not connected with the troubles. In England the House of Lords first condoned the practice in 1984[35] and Parliament has since expressly authorized it in the Police and Criminal Evidence legislation (section 24 of the 1984 Act in England, Article 26 of the 1989 Order in Northern Ireland).

Judicial control over the treatment of arrested persons once they are in custody has been more assertive,[36] the main issue being whether confessions should be excluded from consideration because of the way in which they have been obtained. The EPA 1973, on the recommendation of the Diplock Commission, had expressly altered the existing judge-made rule, applicable throughout England, Wales and Northern Ireland, that confessions should be excluded if they were obtained through 'fear of prejudice or hope of advantage exercised or held out by a person in authority, or by oppression'. Lord Diplock felt that this standard was inappropriate in Northern Ireland, where in *R v Flynn and Leonard*[37] the Lord Chief Justice, following the lead of his predecessor,[38] had interpreted 'oppression' as including any conditions which would tend to compel an interviewee to speak when otherwise he or she might not do so. The new section 6 stated that confessions should be excluded only if (a) on the face of it a case were made out that the accused had been subjected to torture or to inhuman or degrading treatment in order to induce him to make the statement, and (b) the prosecution failed to show that the confession had not been so obtained. The wording of section 6 was borrowed from Article 3 of the European Convention on Human Rights, even though that article imposes an outright ban on such treatment at all times and was never intended to be a European standard on the particular question of admissibility of confessions.

On account of the difference in wording between the original judge-made test and the new statutory test, it is little wonder that McGonigal LJ felt compelled to hold that section 6 tolerated 'a moderate degree of physical maltreatment'.[39] A year later, however, in the first inter-state case to reach the European Court of Human Rights, the United Kingdom was condemned for tolerating interrogation practices such as hooding and deprivation of sleep which breached the standard in Article 3.[40] No doubt partly as a result of this condemnation, the judges in Northern Ireland soon changed their approach. In *R v O'Halloran*[41] the Court of Appeal said that any form of ill-treatment would render a confession inadmissible, although the Lord Chief Justice made it clear that the use of lengthy, persistent and even intensive interrogation was not by itself ill-treatment. Moreover, in *R v Milne*[42] and *R v McGrath*[43] McGonigal LJ and Lord Lowry LCJ reminded lawyers that section 6 excluded confessions only if the ill-treatment was applied *in order to* induce a confession. It was not enough for the confession to have been made *as a result of* the ill-treatment. The judges thereby seemed to leave open the possibility of legitimate pre-interrogation beatings.

While accepting a narrow rule for the inadmissibility of confessions, the judges nevertheless maintained that, even if confessions were admissible, they had a discretion to exclude them if they felt that this was fair in all the circumstances. To assert this position was quite courageous, because it contradicted the apparent intention of Parliament in deliberately excluding such a discretion from the wording of section 6. Although the discretion was rarely exercised especially in cases of forceful questioning or the issuing of threats or promises,[44] the judicial viewpoint was eventually vindicated when Parliament decided to make express mention of the discretion in the EPA 1987 (now section 11(3) of the EPA 1991).

In an important decision rendered in January 1988, the High Court held that if a person has been lawfully arrested the detention becomes unlawful if he or she is then seriously assaulted.[45] Hutton J, as he then was, described the remedy of habeas corpus as 'jealously maintained by courts of law as a check upon the illegal usurpation of power by the executive at the cost of the liege'. He also cited a decision from the Republic of Ireland to support his view of the law. But he cast no doubt on Lord Lowry's opinion in *Ex parte Lynch* (above) to the effect that detention does not become unlawful just because the detainee is denied access to a solicitor and barrister. He also stated, somewhat alarmingly: 'in our opinion some minor assault on a suspect such as, for instance, a kick to propel a suspect into a cell, whilst unlawful, would not of itself make the detention unlawful'.[46]

There has been a series of applications brought by prisoners for judicial review of decisions affecting them. As already mentioned, the Court of Appeal accepts the reviewability of disciplinary decisions, whether taken by prison governors or by Boards of Visitors, but the view is maintained that purely administrative decisions cannot be challenged. In *McKernan* v *Governor of H.M. Prison Belfast*[47] the Court of Appeal held that a governor's decision to remove a prisoner from association with other prisoners fell within this category and in *In re Russell's Application*[48] the Lord Chief Justice refused to review a governor's decision to confine a prisoner to his cell for 48 hours while a full-scale search of the prison was conducted. In *In re Whelan's Application*[49] the Court of Appeal confirmed that life-sentence prisoners could not be given details of the matters which might be held against them by the Life Sentence Review Board whenever it was deciding whether to recommend them for release; the need to preserve confidentiality of information was deemed more important.

In other areas the judges have afforded the citizen greater protection. According to section 12 of the EPA 1991 (formerly section 9 of EPA 1978), the onus of proving a lack of knowledge or control in relation to a charge of possessing explosives, firearms or ammunition is placed squarely on the accused. In *R* v *Killen*,[50] however, Lowry LCJ stressed that because the section 'erodes the protection of the ordinary criminal law . . . its application must be viewed in the most circumspect manner'. On behalf of the Court of Appeal he reasserted that 'the eventual duty of the tribunal of fact is to convict only where satisfied beyond reasonable doubt'. Similar statements have been made in later cases. The Northern Irish judges have also been careful not to extend unduly the conspiracy laws. They have accepted, for instance, that a member of a gang planting a bomb cannot be convicted of conspiracy to murder if he intended a warning to be given.[51] On the other hand the judges have meekly accepted the changes to the right to silence introduced by the Criminal Evidence (NI) Order 1988. In *R* v *Gamble and others*[52] Carswell J said that, if a defendant makes an admission to the police which leaves ambiguous the extent of his knowledge about the planned crime, the court is entitled, under Article 4 of the Order, to draw adverse inferences about the true extent of that knowledge from the defendant's refusal to testify at the trial.

As regards the use of lethal force by the police or army, the judges have not done all they could to make the law more protective of possible victims. To an extent they have been hamstrung by the wording of section 3(1) of the Criminal

Law Act (NI) 1967 and by the rulings issued by the House of Lords, but they have still been slow to seize the remaining opportunities for providing guidance on when potentially lethal force can or cannot be legitimately employed.[53] The fact is that only one soldier or police officer has ever been convicted of murder while on duty in Northern Ireland.[54] It was not until October 1989, in *Hegarty, Doyle and Kelly* v *Ministry of Defence*,[55] that the Court of Appeal endorsed Carswell J's more systematic approach to the application of section 3(1). This entails asking two questions (though not necessarily in every case). First, what were the facts and circumstances the police officer or soldier honestly and reasonably believed to exist at the time? Second, given that honest and reasonable belief, was it reasonable to fire in the prevention of crime or to effect an arrest? But even this new approach is unlikely to assist many plaintiffs. In the *Hegarty* case itself, where over twenty rounds were fired by UDR soldiers at a Ford Granada which was attempting to evade a hastily erected checkpoint, killing one of the five occupants and injuring two others, all the claims for compensation were rejected. Nor have the judges had the ingenuity to recommend, for example, the creation of a new offence whereby soldiers or police officers could be held to account to some degree without having to suffer the full opprobrium of a murder or manslaughter conviction.

In civil actions against the security forces for compensation the judges have recently confirmed that the burden of proving that the force used was reasonable in all the circumstances lies on the security forces. The current Lord Chief Justice has been to the fore here. In *McGuigan* v *Ministry of Defence*[56] he awarded more than £28,000 after the plaintiff had been shot by a soldier from a clandestine observation post. He decided that the soldier had no reasonable grounds for believing that the plaintiff was armed. In *Wasson* v *Chief Constable of the RUC*[57] the same judge ordered £14,050 to be paid for injuries caused by a plastic bullet because the RUC could not prove that its version of how the injuries were sustained was more likely to be true than Mr Wasson's version and in *Tumelty* v *Ministry of Defence*[58] an award of £41,000 was made to a rioter injured in the head by a plastic bullet. In each of these cases the award would have been higher (by 50 per cent in *Wasson* and 80 per cent in *Tumelty*) if the claimant had not been contributorily negligent. Although each case must be considered on its merits, these successes contrast starkly with the failure of the claim made by the mother of thirteen-year-old Brian Stewart, who was killed by a plastic bullet in 1976 (and whose case was even rejected by the European Commission of Human Rights[59]).

There has been greater judicial sympathy for the predicament of the police and Army when cases have come to court concerning deaths or injuries caused at road blocks,[60] though an increasing number of cases are occurring where damages are won in court for assault or false imprisonment and others are settled out of court on the basis of these precedents. In *Walsh* v *Ministry of Defence*[61] Lord Lowry LCJ awarded a schoolteacher £4,000 for a two-hour period of wrongful imprisonment and in *Scullion* v *Chief Constable of the*

RUC[62] Nicholson J granted a press photographer £3,000 compensation and £1,500 exemplary damages for assaults committed against him by several police officers in Dungannon on the occasion of an Orange Day parade on 12 July 1986.

Judges and politics

It would be naive to assume that Northern Ireland's judges do not give serious thought to how they can best mould the legal system so as to strike the right balance between dealing effectively with violent crime and preserving the rights of the citizen. They have, of course, maintained the English tradition of not giving interviews to the press about particular cases. Nor have they joined the small band of English judicial rebels who have spoken publicly about more general matters such as sentencing in rape cases or reforming the legal professions. Their strict silence has been further necessitated by the political sensitivity of many of the issues coming before them.

Of these none has been more controversial than the use of 'supergrasses' – witnesses who, although themselves often implicated in crime, testify against a large number of accomplices. According to the leading researcher in this area, '[b]etween November 1981 and November 1983, at least seven Loyalist and 18 Republican supergrasses were responsible for nearly 600 people being arrested and charged with offences connected with paramilitary activities in Northern Ireland'.[63] Although the supergrass trials between 1983 and 1985 involved only 12 per cent of the total number of terrorist defendants tried during this period, the use of the prosecution tactic is widely supposed to have had a profound impact on the internal organization of paramilitary groups. But there was widespread moral and political disapproval of the ploy and, although no judge openly articulated his views, the strong inference is that the early acceptability of the phenomenon among the judiciary soon began to wane. Certainly the increasing reliance on half-credible witnesses did not withstand appellate scrutiny.[64] In the words of Bonner:

> [I]n executing a difficult and unenviable task the Northern Ireland judiciary here, as in a number of other contexts, have demonstrated skill, integrity and independence of the executive. Any argument that they have rejected cases to make themselves and the process look good smacks too much of conspiracy theory for this author's taste.[65]

The task of judges in supergrass cases is, of course, essentially the same as that which they must perform in any Diplock case. In the absence of a jury it is the judge who must decide not only what evidence is admissible but also what weight to give it if it is admissible. Some commentators have suggested that this latter process tends to be conducted within too loose a legal framework and that there is a serious risk that subjective factors will influence the outcome.[66] As Korff points out: '[s]uch subjective factors need not constitute bias on the part of the judge, but may include "case-hardening": the negative effect of constant involvement in the administration of justice on the detachment and objectivity of judges'.[67] But to date there is little concrete evidence that a judge sitting alone is less effective at fact-finding than a jury of twelve lay persons. At least the judge in a Diplock Court has to give written reasons for his decisions, whereas jury determinations are totally inscrutable.

Although the judges in Northern Ireland have not spoken in public in recent years about overtly political matters, it is clear that on several legal issues of a politically sensitive nature they have made their views known to the government in private. It is an open secret that they are against the introduction of three-judge Diplock courts, that they are content to apply the new restrictions on the right to silence and that they do not want to be involved in authorizing detentions under the Prevention of Terrorism Act for up to seven days. Their intransigence on this last point seems to have prompted the government into officially derogating from the European Convention on Human Rights after having its seven-day detention power condemned by the European Court of Human Rights in the *Brogan* case.[68] The government appears to respect the independence of the judges but it often does their bidding whenever changes are being planned to the rules on trial procedures.

There is no evidence of judicial bias in legal disputes involving politicians or clerics.[69] Sinn Fein councillors have successfully challenged unionist councillors' attempts to exclude them from debates in Craigavon and Cookstown.[70] Likewise, Alliance Party councillors went to court to stop Belfast City Council from displaying a 'Belfast Says No' banner outside the City Hall.[71] In April 1991 Sinn Fein received £5,000 in compensation after Campbell J ruled that a police raid on their premises in October 1990 was unauthorized.[72] In a challenge made by Catholic bishops against those parts of the Education Reform (NI) Order 1989 which appeared to give preferential treatment to integrated schools in Northern Ireland,[73] MacDermott LJ held that the law was not discriminatory within the terms of section 17 of the Northern Ireland Constitution Act 1973 because any damage caused by it affected all non-integrated schools and not just those favouring a religious ethos.

Judges in Northern Ireland undoubtedly have their own political views. But they do not seem to let these intrude into their judicial work. If they can be criticized at all it is for their pro-Establishment attitude, an attribute which does not distinguish them from judges in most other jurisdictions. This frame of mind is, as a former Lord of Appeal, Lord Devlin, has suggested, almost a qualification for the job.[74]

Notes

1 D. P. J. Walsh, *The Use and Abuse of Emergency Legislation in Northern Ireland*, Cobden Trust, London, 1983, pp. 88–90; D. Bonner, 'Combating Terrorism: Supergrass Trials in Northern Ireland', *Modern Law Review*, 51 (1988), 23, 42–3.

2 Northern Ireland Court Service, *Judicial Statistics for Northern Ireland for 1989*, Belfast, 1990, p. 51.

3 *Report of the Commission to consider legal procedures to deal with terrorists' activities in Northern Ireland* (Diplock Report) (Cmnd. 5185), HMSO, London, 1972.

4 Northern Ireland Office (NIO), *Review of the operation of the Northern Ireland (Emergency Provisions) Act 1978* (Cmnd. 9222) (Baker Report), HMSO, London, 1984.

5 J. D. Jackson, 'Three Judge Courts in Northern Ireland' in *12th Report of the Standing Advisory Commission on Human Rights 1985–86* (HC 151, Session 1986–7), HMSO, London, pp. 63–76.

6 Baker Report (Cmnd. 9222) p. 38; W. Hellerstein, R. McKay and P. Schlam, 1988. *Criminal Justice and Human Rights in Northern Ireland*, Association of the Bar of the City of New York, p. 56.

7 M. O'Connell, 'The Case of the Armagh Four', *New Law Journal*, 139 (1989), 429.

8 K. Boyle, T. Hadden and P. Hillyard, *Law and State – The Case of Northern Ireland*, Martin Robertson, London, 1984, p. 12.

9 Sir Edward Jones, *Jones L.J. – His Life and Times*, privately published, 1987, p. 104.

10 B. Hadfield, *The Constitution of Northern Ireland*, SLS, Belfast, 1989, pp. 126–30.

11 J. A. G. Griffith, *The Politics of the Judiciary*, Fontana Press, London, 1991, ch. 1.

12 Northern Ireland Court Service, *Judicial Statistics 1989*, pp. 39 and 51.

13 NIO, *Report of the Working Party on Public Prosecutions* (Cmd. 554) (MacDermott Report), HMSO, Belfast, 1971.

14 *Report of the Law Enforcement Commission* (Cmnd. 5627), HMSO, London, 1974.

15 NIO, *Report of the Tribunal of Inquiry into Violence and Civil Disturbances in Northern Ireland in 1969* (Cmd. 566) (Scarman Report), HMSO, Belfast, 1972.

16 *Report of the Tribunal Appointed to Inquire into the Events on Sunday, Jan. 30, 1972, which led to loss of life in connection with the procession in Londonderry on that day* (Widgery Report), (HC 220, Session 1971–2), HMSO, London.

17 *Report of the Committee of Privy Counsellors appointed to Consider Authorised Procedures for the Interrogation of Persons Suspected of Terrorism* (Parker Report) (Cmnd. 4901), HMSO, London, 1972; Diplock Report; *Report of the Committee to Consider, in the context of Civil Liberties and Human Rights, Measures to Deal with Terrorism in Northern Ireland* (Cmnd. 5847) (Gardiner Report), HMSO, London, 1975.

18 NIO, *Report of the Committee of Inquiry into Police Interrogation Procedures in Northern Ireland* (Cmnd. 7497), HMSO, London, 1979.

19 NIO, *Review of the operation of the Northern Ireland (Emergency Provisions) Act 1978*.

20 K. D. Ewing and C. A. Gearty, *Freedom Under Thatcher: Civil Liberties in Modern Britain*, Clarendon Press, Oxford, 1990, ch. 7; S. Livingstone, 'Policing, Criminal Justice and the Rule of Law' in J. Hayes and P. O'Higgins (eds), *Lessons From Northern Ireland*, SLS, Belfast, 1990, pp. 87–109.

21 *McEldowney v Forde* [1971] AC 632.

22 *The Attorney-General for Northern Ireland's Reference (No. 1 of 1975)* [1977] AC 105.
23 *Farrell* v *Secretary of State for Defence* [1980] NI 55.
24 *Farrell* v *UK* [1983] 5 EHRR 466.
25 *McKee* v *Chief Constable of the RUC* [1984] NI 169.
26 *Murray* v *Ministry of Defence* [1988] 2 All ER 521.
27 *McKerr* v *Armagh Coroner and others* [1990] 1 All ER 865.
28 *Brind* v *Home Secretary* [1991] 1 All ER 720.
29 *Leech* v *Parkhurst Prison Deputy Governor* [1988] 1 All ER 485.
30 *In re McKiernan's Application* [1985] 6 NIJB 6.
31 *In re McElduff* [1972] NI 1.
32 *Ex parte Martin Henry Lynch* [1980] NI 126.
33 Ibid., at 134; See also D. Korff, *The Diplock Courts in Northern Ireland: A Fair Trial?*, Netherlands Institute of Human Rights, Utrecht, 1984, pp. 24–8.
34 In both *Hanna* v *Chief Constable of the RUC* [1986] 13 NIJB 71 and *Moore* v *Chief Constable of the RUC* [1988] 14 NIJB 39.
35 *Holgate-Mohammed* v *Duke* [1984] AC 437.
36 D. S. Greer, 'Admissibility of Confessions and the Common Law in Times of Emergency', *Northern Ireland Legal Quarterly* 24 (1973), 199; Walsh, *Use and Abuse*, ch. 3.
37 *R* v *Flynn and Leonard* [1972] 5 NIJB.
38 MacDermott, Lord, *Address to the Bentham Club*, 1968.
39 *R* v *McCormick* [1977] NI 105.
40 *Ireland* v *UK* [1978] 2 EHRR 25.
41 *R* v *O'Halloran* [1979] 2 NIJB.
42 *R* v *Milne* [1978] NI 110.
43 *R* v *McGrath* [1980] 5 NIJB.
44 Korff, *Diplock Courts*, p. 61.
45 *In re Gillen's Application* [1988] 1 NIJB 47, where the suspect allegedly suffered a perforated eardrum.
46 Ibid., 68.
47 *McKernan* v *Governor of H.M. Prison Belfast* [1983] NI 83.
48 *In re Russell's Application* [1990] 9 BNIL 71.
49 *In re Whelan's Application* [1990] 5 BNIL 91.
50 *R* v *Killen* [1974] NI 220.
51 *R* v *McPhillips* [1989] 9 NIJB 68.
52 *R* v *Gamble and others* [1989] 10 NIJB 54.
53 See *R* v *Bohan and another* [1979] 5 NIJB; *R* v *Robinson* [1984] 4 NIJB; and *R* v *McAuley* [1985] 2 NIJB 48.
54 *R* v *Thain* [1985] NI 31.
55 *Hegarty, Doyle and Kelly* v *Ministry of Defence* [1989] 9 NIJB 88.
56 *McGuigan* v *Ministry of Defence* [1982] 19 NIJB.
57 *Wasson* v *Chief Constable of the RUC* [1987] 8 NIJB 34.
58 *Tumelty* v *Ministry of Defence* [1988] 3 NIJB 51.
59 *Stewart* v *UK* Appl. no. 10044/82 [1985] 7 EHRR 453.
60 See, for instance, the joyriding case of *Magill* v *Ministry of Defence* [1987] 10 NIJB 1; and *Hegarty, Doyle and Kelly* v *Ministry of Defence*.
61 *Walsh* v *Ministry of Defence* [1985] NI 62.

62 *Scullion* v *Chief Constable of the RUC* [1989] 6 NIJB 1.
63 S. C. Greer, 'The Supergrass System' in A. Jennings (ed.), *Justice Under Fire: The Abuse of Civil Liberties in Northern Ireland*, Pluto, London, 1988, p. 73.
64 See *R* v *Gibney and others* [1986] 4 NIJB 1 (the Kevin McGrady trial); *R* v *Donnelly and others* [1986] 4 NIJB 32 (the Christopher Black trial); and *R* v *Steenson and others* [1986] 13 NIJB 36 (the Harry Kirkpatrick trial).
65 See Bonner, 'Combating Terrorism', p. 44.
66 Walsh, *Use and Abuse* pp. 94–8; S. D. Bailey (ed.), *Human Rights and Responsibilities in Britain and Ireland – A Christian Perspective*, Macmillan Press, Basingstoke, 1989.
67 See note 33 above, pp. 69–70.
68 *Brogan* v *UK* [1989] 11 EHRR 117.
69 T. Wilson, *Ulster: Conflict and Consent*, Basil Blackwell, Oxford, 1989, p. 242.
70 See *Re Curran and McCann's Application* [1985] NI 261; and *In Re Neeson's Application* [1986] 13 NIJB 24.
71 *In Re Cook's Application* [1986] 1 NIJB 89 and [1987] 4 NIJB 42.
72 *Belfast Telegraph*, 11 April 1991.
73 Unreported, October 1990.
74 Lord P. Devlin, 'Judges, Government and Politics', *Modern Law Review*, 41 (1978), 505.

10

Northern Ireland: some European comparisons

Antony Alcock

Most European states today contain ethnic or cultural minorities. In the years between the First and Second World Wars, the age of nationalism triumphant, these minorities were regarded with suspicion or outright hostility as potential if not actual threats to the security and integrity of the state, and all the more so if they formed a majority in a distinct part of the state.

For that reason few voluntary arrangements were made for the protection of minorities. On the other hand, aware of the potential threat to international peace posed by minorities thrust unwillingly by the redrawing of frontiers into states dominated by another cultural expression, the Principal Allied and Victorious Powers obliged certain states to accept measures for the protection of their minorities in the form of treaties, and placed these treaties under the guarantee of the League of Nations, or required states with mixed populations and wishing to become members of the League to give formal declarations regarding the treatment of their minorities.[1] The states concerned were resentful because of their perceived inequality in status in being obliged to sign such treaties or give such declarations, while the great European Powers on the Allied side were not obliged to give similar undertakings.[2] Indeed, a few years later fascist Italy would embark on a deliberate policy of cultural genocide of its German-, French-, Romansch- and Slavonic-speaking populations, while France refused to recognize that the *république une et indivisible* had any cultural minorities at all.

For their part, the minorities were equally resentful. The 1919 peace settlement had allegedly been made on the basis of self-determination, yet many people had been transferred to the sovereignty of another state without consultation of their wishes in the form of a referendum. It was clear that boundaries had been drawn with the object of giving the states bordering on the potentially revisionist powers of Germany and Hungary strategic or economic advantages. As a result, the whole question of treatment of minorities would fall victim to the political environment, particularly the revisionist policies of Nazi Germany.

Because exploitation of German minorities in Czechoslovakia and Poland by the Nazis was seen as a major cause of the Second World War, there was little interest to begin with after 1945 in embarking once more on special international arrangements for minority protection. The new ethos, as reflected in the United Nations Charter, the 1947 Peace Treaties, and the 1950 European Convention on Human Rights was one of equal rights and non-discrimination. Whereas the League of Nations had been an organization for the solution of political problems, the new ethos was that political problems were mostly caused by unsatisfactory economic and social conditions and non-observance of basic human rights. Everyone should be accorded the basic human rights, but it would be up to states to decide whether to grant any special rights for the minorities within their jurisdiction over and above cultural measures, relating, for example, to education and the media, either unilaterally or on the basis of negotiations with the minorities concerned and/or the kin states. Thus the 1946 de Gasperi–Gruber Agreement between Italy and Austria on South Tyrol left deliberately vague, and in most cases up to the later direct dealing between the inhabitants of the area (Italian-, as well as German- and Ladin-speaking South Tyrolese) and the central government in Rome, such matters as the status of the German language and proportional representation in public employment as well as the more delicate questions as to which legislative and executive powers might be devolved to a local South Tyrolese parliament and how the decision-making process in that parliament should operate.[3]

For many years thereafter little progress was made on international dimensions to minority problems. In 1957 the Consultative Assembly of the Council of Europe adopted a Resolution to the effect that whereas Article 14 of the European Convention on Human Rights already protected individuals belonging to minorities against discrimination, it was also desirable to protect the collective interests of minorities. However, with the issue of security still uppermost, it recommended that this should be done 'to the fullest extent compatible with safeguarding the essential interests of the states to which they belong'. As a result the Legal Committee of the Assembly was asked to prepare a report on the existing legal situation of minorities and the possible permanent supervision of minority situations. The report came out in 1959. Indicative of the times, it dealt only with minorities in member states which benefited from an international agreement. It therefore did not deal with minorities which had no kin state, such as the Bretons or Welsh; it did not deal with minorities which had a kin state but were not the object of an agreement, such as the French community in Val d'Aosta; and it did not deal with the minorities in states not members of the Council, such as the Basques and Catalans in Spain and the Swedes of the Finnish Åland Islands. In fact only five minorities were examined: the German-speaking population of South Tyrol; the Slavs of

Trieste, in Italy; the Slavs in Austria; Germans in the Danish province of Slesvig, and Danes in the West German *Land* of Schleswig-Holstein.

Furthermore, supervision was rejected on the grounds that the situation with regard to minorities in Western Europe was much more satisfactory than in the inter-war period, at least from the legislative point of view, and that the idea was too much like the League of Nations system, which was felt to have aggravated problems and not been convincing.[4] Dissatisfied with the Report, the Consultative Assembly then made an attempt to add a Protocol to the European Convention on Human Rights to guarantee the rights and privileges of cultural minorities, but that also failed.[5]

It was not until the end of the 1980s that, thanks to hard work and co-operation between the Council of Europe and the European Parliament, a European charter for regional or minority languages, having the character of a Convention, could be adopted by the former.[6] However, at the time of writing the Convention has not received the necessary number of ratifications to enter into force. Even so, in the Preamble it was stated that the Charter 'represented an important step along the road to a Europe based on the principles of democracy and cultural diversity *within the framework of national sovereignty and territorial integrity*'.

This process, however, only reflected the renaissance in the fortunes of minorities that had taken place during the previous two decades. In Italy, a tripartite agreement between Rome, Vienna and the South Tyrolese had led to a substantially improved autonomy in 1972;[7] Spain, following the death of General Franco in 1975, abandoned centralism in favour of regional government, and gave autonomous government to Catalonia and the Basque country; Belgium had taken on all the trappings of a federal state on cultural lines by 1988; in that most centralist of all Western European countries, France, the government gave Corsica a *statut particulier* in 1982 and in 1990 announced proposals to recognize the Corsicans as a people (even though only as a part of the French people); while even in that model of cultural partnership, Switzerland, the minority French-speaking and Catholic population in the north of the German-speaking and Protestant Canton of Berne was able to break away and form a new Canton of the Jura after the voters had adopted the amendment to the Constitution in 1978.

Undoubtedly the main reason for these successes was the process of Western European integration. First, with possibly two exceptions (excluding Gibraltar) state boundaries were mutually recognized and thus minorities generally ceased to be seen in terms of threats to the territorial integrity of states. Second, integration has brought with it recognition of the so-called regional factor. This has meant not only the need to remedy regional economic imbalance and improve living standards and occupational opportunities in the peripheral areas of the European Community, where many cultural minorities are to be found, but also appreciation that regions were 'heirs to the history of Europe and the richness of its culture, . . . an incomparable asset of European civilization . . . the symbol and guarantors of the diversity which is the pride of the European heritage in the eyes of humanity'. 'Every European's right to "his region" is part of his right to be different. To challenge this right would be to challenge the identity of European man and ultimately of Europe itself'. Other significant aspects of the philosophy of regionalism sweeping the Community were the demand for more popular participation in local planning and decision-making and rejection of decisions being taken in distant capitals by unsympathetic civil servants, and the view that it would be easier to promote cultural pluralism within a regional framework.[8] It was certainly helpful that three of the European Community's five leading member states – Germany, Italy and Spain – are federal or regional in character, as well as Belgium.

So confident has the movement for European integration become that discussions of the continent's future have long gone beyond economic and monetary union and begun contemplation of political union, with the federal model of government widely held to be the best, although there are differences of opinion as to whether such government should be on the basis of a Europe of the states, a Europe of the regions, or a Europe of the (ethnic) peoples. There have also been calls for the creation of a second chamber of the European Parliament along the lines of the German *Bundesrat* that is, on the basis of regions.

In contrast to these recent positive developments the experience of two European areas with culturally divided communities, Cyprus and Northern Ireland, has been disastrous. The main reason why their experience has been disastrous while similar areas have been able to solve their problems more or less satisfactorily is the doubt as to their territorial destiny. But as far as Northern Ireland is concerned this major source of instability has been compounded by three further factors: that the attitude of the British government with regard to the maintenance of the Union between the province and the rest of the United Kingdom is perceived as being unenthusiastic; that the identity of the so-called loyalist British community in the province is not perceived in the same sharply defined terms as the so-called Irish nationalist community; and that the Irish minority (in British ethnic terms) is also a minority in its homeland.

The doubt as to the territorial destiny of Northern Ireland stems from the claim of the Irish government to that territory in Articles 2 and 3 of its 1937 Constitution. Article 2 asserts that 'The National Territory consists of the whole island of Ireland'. Article 3 limits the effect of laws passed by the Irish parliament to the territory of the Republic, but, according to Article 3, without prejudice to the right of the Parliament and government established by the Constitution to exercise jurisdiction over the whole of the island.

For many years, to the anger of unionists, British political and public opinion alleged that these articles expressed merely an aspiration to Irish unity and were not a legal claim. This view was shattered by the judgment of the Dublin Supreme Court on 1 March 1990 when, in the case of *McGimpsey &*

McGimpsey v *Ireland*, the Chief Justice ruled that the true interpretation of the articles was that reintegration of the national territory was a constitutional imperative, and Article 2 was indeed a legal claim of right.[9]

Foremost in the arguments deployed by Irish nationalism for the unification of Ireland is self-determination allied to the geographical factor: that Ireland is a self-contained geographical unit, and on the island an undoubted majority of the population wishes for that unification. But another reason concerns the identity of the unionist community of Northern Ireland. Overwhelmingly its members may be of English or Scottish descent. They may be brought up to be British and to learn British history and traditions. But this is not necessarily how the Irish perceive them. The *New Ireland Forum Report* stated that unionists also 'generally regard themselves as being Irish, even if this does not include a willingness to live under all-Ireland political institutions'.[10]

Of course since the Irish language is so little used in daily life in the Republic, let alone in the North, one of the most vivid features distinguishing cultural communities from one another is lacking. It is therefore made easier for the Irish to claim that the difference is merely one of religion, and that the rightful place of the so-called unionists is in a united Ireland, representing the Protestant ethos in the island.

But is this so? As Arthur Aughey has put it, 'the identity of unionism has little to do with the idea of the nation and everything to do with the idea of the state'. Two competing views of the state are, on the one hand, that it is a structure which holds together a nation, and that a nation is defined in terms of culture, the usual symbols of which are race, language or religion; and, on the other hand, that the modern state does not need to depend on these but is an institution grounded in right and the rule of law. The relevant concept is thus not the cultural one of identity but the legal one of citizenship. For Aughey, the United Kingdom is a state which, being multi-national and multi-ethnic, can be understood in terms of citizenship and not substantive identity – the imperial notion of *civis Britannicus sum* has transformed itself into the democratic ideal of different nations, different religions and different colours, all equal citizens under one government. This was the concept to which intelligent unionism, which embraced both Protestants and Catholics, owed allegiance, and it was from this concept of a British state that twenty-six Irish counties seceded in order to found a state on the principle of national (cultural) unity.[11]

In areas with culturally divided communities reconciliation of the concept of equality of rights, on the one hand, with demands for a framework devoted to maintenance of an ethnicity, on the other, is one of the most challenging difficulties faced by those dealing with majority–minority relations. The task is rather easier in countries where one community occupies an entire area almost exclusively, as in Belgium or the Åland Islands.

The problem for Ireland, North and South, is that Protestants in the North perceive no equality of rights for their religion and culture in the South (for example, the bans on divorce and contraception) while Catholics in the North generally, as will be seen, perceive little or no equality of rights in the economic and social fields.

However, the great danger in Irish people perceiving Ulster unionists, despite their overwhelming Scottish and English ancestry, as Irish is that since they find it impossible to believe that Irish people would not want to be united the attitude of Ulster unionists can only be ascribed to a perversity of mind, bigotry, or a desire to maintain a privileged position in society rather than other more obvious reasons for unionist objections to a united Ireland, namely a probable resultant fall in living standards, the Catholic and Gaelic ethos of the state, and the Republic's neutrality status.[12] The Irish claim to Northern Ireland may have been formally presented in 1937, but few Irish persons accepted the Partition of 1922. Resentful of the failure to achieve unity through the self-determination apparently being offered elsewhere in Europe at the time, Irish nationalists and republicans tried to destroy the Northern regime in its early days by boycotts, non-co-operation, intimidation of Catholics to prevent acceptance of public appointments or police service, and even by raids and assassination. Local authorities under their control refused to recognize the Northern jurisdiction and sought only to deal with Dublin.[13]

On the other hand, it cannot be said that by and large drawing the border as it was did not correspond with the times. The traditional nine-county province of Ulster had an overall loyalist majority but the area, distinctive in historical and geographical terms, was not retained as a whole by Britain. Three counties with undoubted nationalist majorities, Cavan, Donegal and Monaghan, were allowed to go to the Republic. It is interesting to compare the Northern Ireland experience with Upper Silesia.

At the Versailles Peace Conference it had originally been decided to give that area, with its undoubted German majority, to Poland. But the British Prime Minister, Lloyd George, protested that this would create a new Alsace-Lorraine in Eastern Europe, and it was therefore decided that the area should be partitioned following a referendum on a municipal basis. The referendum duly took place on 20 March 1921 and in general the north and west of the area, which was overwhelmingly German, remained with that country while the south and east, with their Polish majorities, went to Poland.[14]

However, with a moderate government in power following victory in the civil war in the South over hard-line republicans led by De Valera, an agreement was signed with Britain in 1925 recognizing the existing boundaries between North and South, and thus *de jure* recognizing Northern Ireland. Futhermore, that agreement was registered with the League of Nations by the Irish government.[15] But when De Valera and his Fianna Fáil party took over the Irish government in 1932 nationalism revived. Dublin pursued economic policies, such as boycotts, which divided the island even more, and hit hardest border towns with majority Roman Catholic populations.[16] Thereafter, the introduction of the 1937 Constitution unilaterally abrogated the *de jure* recognition of Northern Ireland contained in the 1925 Agreement.[17]

The consequences of the pursuit of the aspiration to Irish unity, formal or otherwise, have been far-reaching. For the unionist community the immediate consequence of the Irish claim is that terrorism and economic sabotage to force them and the British government into agreeing to Irish unification and to intimidate potential supporters of maintaining the link with Britain among the minority community is blessed. Unfortunately, if terrorism is blessed, so is counter-terrorism by loyalist paramilitary organizations in the name of community self-defence, so that both communities are set against each other in distrust and alienation.[18]

Further consequences of this situation include, first, the failure to obtain political co-operation between the two communities. Regional power-sharing is an acknowledged technique of government in areas populated by culturally divided communities, and one advocated by both the British and Irish governments with regard to Northern Ireland, but it has been rejected by representatives of the main unionist parties. One strong argument is that it is clearly absurd, if not dishonest, to share power within a political framework when it is the avowed intention of the putative partner, even if only in the long run, to do away with the framework within which that power is shared.[19] Thus an attempt to set up a power-sharing administration in 1973–4 was brought to naught by a general strike organized by the Ulster Loyalist Workers' Council.

Second, there is the retaliation by members of the majority community against the minority community in the form of discrimination in jobs and housing. On the one hand, they ask why jobs and state benefits should be extended to those they suspect of wishing for and often seeking by violence the abolition of that state; on the other, there is reluctance to employ persons who might turn out, even against their will, to be a security risk. Unfortunately, if recent fair employment legislation aims to do away with discrimination it is questionable if it helps remove the cause of that discrimination, namely, the fear concerning the ultimate aims and behaviour of members of the minority community.

Third, as shown by the proceedings of the New Ireland Forum, political debate has been focused not on the terms under which the Irish community in Northern Ireland would consent to live as part of the United Kingdom but on the terms under which the unionist community would consent to live in the Irish Republic. It is symptomatic of this situation that the SDLP MP for Newry and South Armagh, Mr Seamus Mallon, continually refers on radio and television to 'the north of Ireland' when speaking about Northern Ireland, thus implicitly denying the existence of the latter.

For unionists the questioning of the territorial destiny of Northern Ireland and the consequences in terms of lives lost and economic damage are compounded by demoralization arising from the attitude of successive British governments, amounting, on the one hand, to an astonishing toleration of the Irish claim and, on the other hand, by implication, to a rejection of their kin, through a general reluctance, like the Irish in the Republic, to view the two communities in the province in anything other than religious terms.

To Articles 2 and 3 in the new 1937 Constitution, seen by unionists as a declaration of war, Professor F. S. Lyons wrote that the British government's reaction 'was phlegmatic to a degree that would have excited the envy of Phileas Fogg'. The only thing the British government was interested in was whether the new Constitution left Eire in or took Eire out of the Commonwealth. Indeed, the following year the British and Irish governments signed an Agreement under which the British evacuated the ports guaranteed them under the 1921 Partition Treaty, something that would cost them dearly in the battles of the Atlantic a few years later.[20]

And since then British governments have declared on many occasions – at the time of the 1949 Ireland Act, in the 1973 Sunningdale Agreement, and in the 1985 Anglo-Irish Agreement – that if a majority in Northern Ireland declared in favour of unification with the Irish Republic Britain would not stand in the way. Yet even this so-called 'guarantee' that as long as there is a majority in favour of remaining with Britain that wish would be respected has been condemned by nationalists as 'inhibiting . . . political progress . . . [and] removing the incentive . . . to seek a political solution' (that is, in favour of a united Ireland).[21]

Given these attitudes it is not surprising that mainland British political parties have not, until very recently, campaigned in Northern Ireland. Unionists feel that this is because it would appear to tighten links between the province and Britain, and thus incur the anger of Dublin. But the effect has been to abandon the political arena in Northern Ireland to local parties whose *raison d'être* is solely either to maintain or break the Union. In any case Labour Party policy is Irish unification by consent. Pleas, particularly by trade union circles, to set up in Northern Ireland have fallen on deaf ears. The Conservatives may have had a close relationship with the Unionist Party in the past but this was shattered by the events of the 1970s and the Anglo-Irish Agreement. Only in 1989 did the Conservatives decide officially to set up in the province, 'in order to end sectarian parties', but by then seventy years had passed since Carson's warning, and it was too late. The Liberal Democrats, for their part, leave expression of their views to the Alliance Party.

It might have been possible for Britain to exert pressure on the Irish government to drop the claim to Northern Ireland at the time both countries entered the European Community. But there is no evidence that this was considered by the British government, with the result that the process of European integration is proceeding with one member state officially claiming the territory of another member state. Nevertheless, the Irish government still felt able to sign in 1975, together with Britain, the Final Act of the Helsinki Conference on Security and Co-operation in Europe, according to which member states undertook to regard as inviolable each other's frontiers, to respect the territorial integrity of each of the participating states, to refrain from any action against the territorial integrity, political independence or the unity of any participating state, and to refrain from any intervention, direct or indirect, in the internal affairs of another participating state.[22]

The argument for change of sovereignty over certain areas of the world on grounds of geography rather than the democratic will of the population inhabiting these areas is not unknown in Europe. For example, excluding claims to enclaves such as Gibraltar, at the Versailles Peace Conference in 1919 following the First World War, the Italian government claimed from Austria not only the province of Trento, whose population of 400,000 was almost entirely Italian, but also the southern part of Tyrol, below the Brenner Pass, 85 per cent of whose population of 250,000 was German-speaking. This was despite the fact that the basis for the peace settlement was understood to be the Fourteen Points of President Woodrow Wilson, Point IX of which stated that '[a] readjustment of the frontiers of Italy should be effected along clearly recognisable lines of nationality'.

The Italians, however, wished to have a strong natural northern strategic frontier against the German world, and felt this could best be achieved by drawing the border at the Brenner rather than the Salurn Pass between Trento and southern Tyrol. In demanding the Brenner frontier the Italian government took up the arguments of Giuseppe Mazzini in 1866 that it was also the natural frontier since it lay on the Alpine chain which provided the watershed between the Black Sea, on the one hand, and the Adriatic on the other. Furthermore, the climate and flora in the southern Tyrol were distinctly Mediterranean, in contrast to those in the northern Tyrol.

In order to get around the awkward fact that if Italy succeeded in her claims it would acquire almost a quarter of a million persons of another culture, in addition to arguing that the area once belonged to the Roman Empire and had historically been populated by persons of Italian culture, the Italian government took the geographic argument a stage further. It claimed that the entire territory of both South Tyrol and Trento was geographically, historically and economically one, and that since the Italians had a majority of two-thirds therein, Italy's right to South Tyrol was a democratic one. The Italian claim succeeded, and as a result the South Tyrolese were separated from their kin.[23]

Cyprus is another area in which the geographic factor became involved. Eighty per cent of the island's population was Greek-speaking and 18 per cent Turkish-speaking, and at the time of the struggle for liberation from British rule in the 1950s the demand was for *enosis*, the union of the whole island with Greece, in accordance with the wishes of the majority. This was opposed by the Turkish Cypriots, who were not opposed to the establishment of Cyprus as an independent state (even if they were not enthusiastic) but who adamantly rejected *enosis* and proposed that if there was not to be an independent Cyprus then the island should be partitioned.[24] Their case was weakened in that geographically the two communities were very mixed: the Turkish Cypriots had enclaves, but dominated no distinct part of the island as the Germans dominated South Tyrol or the unionists the six northern and eastern counties of Ulster.

With regard to questions of identity it is usually clear to which group an individual in culturally divided areas belongs. But sometimes even the clearest of identities is not accepted. Even before the First World War certain Italians were arguing that the majority of Germans in the South Tyrol were not descended from the German migration into the area during the Dark and early Middle Ages but rather from pre-German elements which, over the centuries, under the influence of the dominating culture that demanded the use of German in schools and the administration, accepted that language and in time forgot their neo-Latin dialect. This view, rejected out of hand by most German historians, formed part of Italian official thinking under fascism and was used to justify the programme of cultural genocide instituted against the South Tyrolese in the inter-war period.[25]

The separation of the South Tyrolese from their kin in 1919 and their subsequent brutal treatment at the hands of Mussolini had a profound effect on the development of the South Tyrol question, inviting a number of comparisons with Northern Ireland.

After the Second World War the South Tyrolese were determined that Italy should never again have a say in their future and sought to have South Tyrol returned to Austria. But the victorious Allies decided to leave the area with Italy while putting pressure on the Italian and Austrian governments to provide the populations of the area with a degree of autonomy, to be drafted in consultation with the South Tyrolese.

However, the resulting de Gasperi–Gruber Agreement was received in Austria and South Tyrol with anger and bitterness. Leading Austrians and South Tyrolese insisted that the Agreement did not mean renunciation of eventual reunification of South Tyrol with Austria or renunciation of the right of the South Tyrolese to determine their own destiny.[26]

The Italians appreciated well enough the hatred borne towards them and feared that any South Tyrolese attempts to repair the economic, social and cultural ravages of fascism would be at the expense of the area's Italian community, so that any weakening or even decline in the numbers of that community would be but a prelude to calls for a referendum on the return of South Tyrol to Austria in an area where the South Tyrolese minority, unlike the Irish nationalist community in Northern Ireland, was in the majority.

The result was that the autonomy granted to the province of Bolzano (South Tyrol) in 1948 in fulfilment of the de Gasperi–Gruber Agreement, by an Italian government unequivocally determined to keep the area, was very restricted, following minimal consultation with the South Tyrolese in its preparation. First, the provincial parliament, whose composition would presumably reflect the South Tyrolese majority, was given few meaningful legislative and executive powers, and certainly none regarding the economic development of the Province. Second, South Tyrol was placed together with the province of

Trento within the larger framework of a region (Trentino-Alto Adige), and it was the region that possessed not only more powers but also the most important powers, including those relating to agriculture, tourism and industrial development. But since Trento had a larger population than Bolzano, and was 99 per cent Italian while Bolzano was only 66 per cent German, the Regional Asembly was dominated by a two-thirds Italian majority. Third, since Italy was not a federal state but a centralized state with power devolved to the regions, approval by Rome was required before any provincial or regional legislation could take effect. Fourth, if the provinces or regions had legislative power to deal with a matter, it was the state which provided – or did not provide – the money.[27]

Italy's determination to maintain South Tyrol as part of the state is seen in other ways. For example, all the leading Italian political parties campaign in the province. When, in 1968, there was a possibility that Austria might join the European Community the Italian government vetoed exploratory talks, on the ground that Austrian action against the preparation of terrorism on its soil designed to separate South Tyrol from Italy was inadequate.[28]

Article 54 of the Italian Constitution and Articles 29 and 49 of the Autonomy Statute require elected politicians and civil servants to take an oath of loyalty to the state. One consequence of this latter requirement was that in the statutes of the Südtiroler Volkspartei (SVP), a political party which regularly attracted 90 per cent of the German ethnic vote, it was stated that although it considered that the right of self-determination for the South Tyrolese people was inalienable, the SVP recognised the de Gasperi-Gruber Agreement as 'the basis for the national development of the Tyrolese minority *within the Italian state*'.[29] Not only has such a declaration not been required of the SDLP but the 'Prime Minister' of the power-sharing Executive government of 1973–4, Brian Faulkner, agreed that a long-term objective of a united Ireland was acceptable in a potential coalition partner provided that the 1973 Constitution Act was accepted.[30] Mr Faulkner was to find that such toleration was not agreeable to the great majority of his community. Is there not, however, a contradiction between an agreement to operate within the Italian state, on one hand, and a refusal to renounce the right to self-determination that might lead to separation from that state, on the other?

Traditionally, the call for self-determination has indeed been associated with, and is usually perceived by the dominant majority to be, a call for separation or secession by the minority from the host state. But in order to counter the impression that minorities have separation ultimately in mind, as well as to get round answering the awkward question as to whether the principle of self-determination (which is accepted as applying to whole peoples) should also apply to ethnic minority groups, the right to self-determination has been recently reinterpreted to mean the right of a people or group to decide freely what legislative and administrative powers in the cultural and possibly other fields it might be necessary to have in order to enable it to maintain its cultural characteristics, separate identity and continued existence, and to demand these from the host state. Separation would then only be sought as a last resort if the latter denied these legitimate demands.[31]

In May 1955 the Four-Power occupation of Austria ended with the signature of the Austrian State Treaty. Article 5 laid down Austria's frontiers as those of 1 January 1938, and, in guaranteeing these frontiers, the Powers made it clear that a return of South Tyrol to Austria was no longer a possibility, and thus confirmed, after ten years of doubt, the territorial destiny of South Tyrol as part of Italy.

It was thus possible for Italy, despite an outbreak of terrorism that owed its origins to the extremely restrictive application and interpretation of the 1948 Autonomy Statute, to negotiate with Austria and the South Tyrolese a vastly improved statute. Coming into effect in 1972, it transferred most of the important powers relating to the economy from the region to the province, allowed for increased access of the South Tyrolese to public employment, and provided the province with greatly increased sums of public money with regard to sectoral expenditure.[32]

On the other hand, doubts about the territorial destiny of Cyprus quickly led to the collapse of the Republic. The state was created by outside pressure, and accepted reluctantly by the people of the island, with the Turkish Cypriots fearing the alternative of *enosis* and Greek Cypriots fearing the alternative of partition, and both the Greek and Turkish governments fearing that a deterioration in their relations might lead to ejection from NATO, loss of American military and economic aid, or even war.[33] But inter-community hostility was not stilled by independence. Each side believed that the other considered the situation as temporary and suspected it of preparing for its own preferred solution.

Greek Cypriots considered the constitutional arrangements of the state as a separatists' charter rather than a formula for harmonious integration of the two communities, particularly the fact that important Bills in the House of Representatives required separate majorities in order to become law and that the Greek Cypriot President and Turkish Cypriot Vice-President had extensive powers of veto. Their fears seemed to be justified when it was found impossible to agree on customs and taxation laws. Soon government was paralyzed, and the Greek Cypriots pressed for amendment of the Constitution with abandonment of both the respective veto rights and the principle of separate majorities, proposing instead one new unitary sovereign state with powers emanating from the people, who would be entitled to decide by majority the future on the basis of self-determination.

Turkish Cypriots rejected these proposals. Their attitude was that the Republic was based on the existence of two communities, which were co-founders of the state rather than a 'majority' and 'minority' community.[34] Self-determination was perceived as leading eventually to *enosis*. Interestingly, the Turkish Cypriots' view that they are co-founders of their state and not a mere 'minority' is one shared by Swedes in the Finnish mainland, French Canadians, and French- and Flemish-speaking Belgians with regard to their respective countries.

With the rejection of the proposals, bitter communal war broke out. The Turkish Cypriots were driven into their enclaves and a United Nations peacekeeping force had to be sent to the island.

In 1974 a *coup d'état* was mounted against the Cyprus government by members of the extreme Greek Cypriot nationalist and terrorist movement, EOKA, with the connivance of the Greek government in Athens. At the invitation of the Turkish Cypriots, a Turkish army landed in Cyprus to prevent the Greek Cypriot National Guard from taking over the island, and occupied the northern and eastern third of the island containing most of its economic strength. Some 200,000 Greek Cypriots fled from the area. Efforts to unite the island with Greece, the presumed wish of the majority community, thus led to its being effectively partitioned, the solution sought by the minority Turkish Cypriot community.

By contrast, the fact that the territorial destiny of the area was settled quickly led to a solution of the Åland Islands question that has been hailed as one of the most satisfactory for a minority anywhere in the world.

As with the rest of Finland, the islands were ceded by Sweden to Russia in 1809. Sweden claimed the islands back unsuccessfully in 1856 following the Crimean War, and then again at the end of the First World War at the behest of the islanders, who feared possible threats to their Swedish culture at the hands of the newly independent Finns, and sought the right of self-determination. The Finnish government, however, argued that the issue was an internal problem and hoped that a far-reaching autonomy would induce the islanders to drop demands for reunification with Sweden.

The matter was submitted to the League of Nations, which decided in 1921 that since the islanders represented 10 per cent of the Swedish population of Finland they could not claim the right of self-determination which applied to national groups as a whole. The League recommended that Finland should have sovereignty over the islands but that special guarantees on the islanders' language and culture should be provided. Shortly afterwards, Finland and Sweden reached an agreement under which the former undertook to preserve not only the Swedish language and culture of the islanders but also the Swedish character of the islands. In accepting the decision of the League Sweden automatically withdrew its claim to the Islands. A very generous autonomy was then introduced which gave the islanders absolute control over their own affairs subject only to the maintenance of the integrity of the Finnish state. Among other things, the individual islanders enjoy Åland regional citizenship and only such citizens can acquire land, vote, or carry on a business in the islands, although the regional government can make exceptions.

So successful has the autonomy been, in an area of Finland 98 per cent

Swedish, that only once did the islanders express a wish to reunite with Sweden. This was at the end of the Second World War when it seemed that Finland might be incorporated into the Soviet Union or become a satellite state like so many other Eastern European countries. Sweden, however, immediately rejected the islanders' overtures.[35]

The issue of territorial destiny may be the deciding factor in relations between majority and minority in an area which is the homeland of both cultural communities, but is by no means the only issue. One issue is the process of government itself. Power-sharing was institutionalized in both South Tyrol and Cyprus. In the former case it has succeeded so far; in the latter case it failed.

In South Tyrol government at provincial level must be shared on the basis of linguistic proportions. This raises questions about whether the representatives of the two communities are obliged to adopt a common programme and what decision-making process is best able to defend the rights of the minority community.

In fact, in South Tyrol it has always been possible to put together a German-Italian coalition. Usually the SVP governs in a coalition with the ideologically similar Christian Democrats, together with the Social Democrats and Socialists. But should, for example, the SVP decide on a policy with which the Italian members of the coalition disagree, there is nothing to prevent it, with its overall parliamentary majority that has been enjoyed since 1948, from putting through the necessary legislation. Democratic government by parliamentary majority thus operates, and the only check on that majority is if a Bill is held to violate the equality of the rights of citizens of one language group. In that case, according to Article 56 of the improved Autonomy Statute, a majority of the deputies of that group may call for a vote by language groups, and if the Bill is thereafter passed despite two-thirds of the members of the language group that called for the vote voting against it, that group can contest the law before the Constitutional Court. While the appeal is in progress, however, the law passed (if also approved by Rome) remains in force.

The danger is that one day the language groups in South Tyrol may come to be represented by parties with much more sharply differing ideologies and programmes. For a short time in the 1970s it seemed possible that the Italian community would be represented by the Communists. In the 1980s and 1990s, as dissatisfaction with the revised Autonomy Statute has risen among the Italian community, the neo-fascist Movimento Sociale Italiano (MSI) has seen its share of the vote rise sharply. The programme of the MSI includes abolition of the Autonomy Statute, that is, the internal framework within which power is shared.[36]

An alternative to the system in South Tyrol is to provide the minority community in the area with the power to block a parliamentary majority or simply to veto proposals by the majority. This occurred in Cyprus, where the 1960 Constitution required that important Bills received majorities among both the Greek and Turkish Cypriots in the House of Representatives. Furthermore, if decisions in the Cabinet could be taken by majority vote the Greek Cypriot President or the Turkish Cypriot Vice-President could veto any decision relating to foreign affairs, defence or security, and a number of decisions required the agreement of both, including the promulgation of legislation, implementation of Cabinet decisions, and the appointment of senior members of the armed forces, the judiciary and the civil service.[37]

Since the fifty-seat House was filled on a basis of thirty-five Greeks and fifteen Turks, this meant that eight Turkish votes (16 per cent) could block a bill approved by forty-two deputies. This was seen by the Greek Cypriots as simply undemocratic. It could not be considered simply a defence against discrimination, since Article 6 of the Cyprus Constitution forbade discrimination against either community or any citizen, and legislation deemed discriminatory could be challenged before the Constitutional Court.

Giving power to a minority which is also a majority in its homeland in order to enable it to have a large say in its economic, social and cultural development through regional-type government is a traditional way of compensating it for separation from its kin. The problem for Northern Ireland is that its Irish community is also a numerical minority, and if the question of territorial destiny is solved in favour of the unionists and devolved government returns to Belfast it is likely that ways will have to be devised to enable the Irish community to develop its interests, in the confidence that these will not be thwarted by the votes of a numerical majority convinced of decision-making in those terms because of its own position and traditional British practice.

In conclusion, it can be said that until the territorial destiny of areas with culturally divided communities is settled relations between those communities and their kin states (if any) will be difficult.

With regard to Northern Ireland, unionist representatives have declared that they will agree to little so long as Articles 2 and 3 of the Irish Constitution as presently formulated remain in place. For them, only the Irish people can disarm the IRA, by changing or removing the articles. And, as debates in the Dáil in December 1990 on a motion to amend the articles have shown, there is a growing realization in the Republic of the offensiveness of these articles to the unionist community and that it is these articles that are the stumbling block to political progress in the North rather than the guarantee by successive British governments that as long as a majority of the people of Northern Ireland wished to remain part of the United Kingdom that wish would be respected. In the event, the motion to amend the articles was defeated by 74 votes to 66, partly on the grounds that the eventual Irish negotiating position might be compromised in talks between Ireland and Britain, on the one hand, and between parties in the North on the other, and partly because it might dishearten the minority community in the North and weaken the constitutional wing of Irish nationalism there to the advantage of the extremists. But a more general reason for rejecting the motion was the feeling, shared also by

Fianna Fáil's coalition partners, the Progressive Democrats, that the whole 1937 Constitution required amendment, not merely Articles 2 and 3.[38]

In South Tyrol, the Åland Islands, Corsica and the Basque country the message is that security for the national majority in terms of the integrity of the state is one side of a coin whose other side is the ability of the minority to carry out in confidence economic, social and cultural activities designed to enable it to flourish and develop its distinguishing characteristics. Only then can the partnership essential for peace at both local and international level be expected to succeed.

Notes

1 For example, the so-called Minorities Treaties between the Principal Allied and Associated Powers and Poland (28 June 1919), Czechoslovakia and Yugoslavia (10 September 1919), Rumania (9 December 1919), Greece (10 August 1920), and the final peace with Turkey, signed at Lausanne (24 July 1923); declarations made by Finland (27 June 1921), Albania (2 October 1921), Lithuania (12 May 1922), Latvia (7 July 1923) and Estonia (17 September 1923).

2 T. H. Bagley, *General Principles and Problems in the International Protection of Minorities*, Geneva, 1950, pp. 73–5.

3 Text of the Agreement in A. E. Alcock, *The History of the South Tyrol Question*, Michael Joseph, London, 1970, pp. 473–4.

4 Council of Europe, Consultative Assembly, *Report on the Position of National Minorities in Europe* (M. Struye), Doc. 1002, Strasbourg, 30 April 1959.

5 H. Lannung, 'The Rights of Minorities' in *Mélanges offerts à Polys Modinos* (Problèmes des Droits de l'Homme et de l'Unification Européenne), Pedone, Paris, 1968, pp. 181–95.

6 Council of Europe, Standing Conference of Local and Regional Authorities of Europe, 23rd Session (15–17 March 1988), Annex to Resolution 192 on Regional or Minority Languages in Europe.

7 A. E. Alcock, *Geschichte der Südtirolfrage – Südtirol seit dem Paket 1970–1980*, Braumüller, Vienna, 1982, pp. 1–25.

8 Council of Europe, Convention on the Problems of Regionalisation, Bordeaux, 30 January – 1 February 1970.

9 K. Maginnis, *McGimpsey & McGimpsey v Ireland*, Tyrone Printers, Dungannon, 1990, p. 10.

10 New Ireland Forum *Report*, Stationery Office, Dublin, 2 May 1984, p. 21.

11 A. Aughey, *Under Siege – Ulster Unionism and the Anglo-Irish Agreement*, Blackstaff, Belfast, 1989, p. 19.

12 A. E. Alcock, *Northern Ireland – Problems and Solutions*, Libertas, Sindelfingen, 1985, pp. 28–35.

13 Presbyterian Church in Ireland, *Loyalism in Ireland*, report presented to the 1975 General Assembly, Belfast, 1975, 23.

14 G. Kaekenbeeck, *The International Experiment of Upper Silesia*, Chatham House, London, 1940.

15 Northern Ireland Assembly (NIA), Committee on the Government of Northern

Ireland, *First Report*, Vol. 1, Belfast, HMSO, January 1986, p. 34. See also F. S. Lyons, *Ireland since the Famine* (revised edn), Fontana/Collins, London, 1973, p. 492.

16 Presbyterian Church in Ireland, *Loyalism*, 24.

17 NIA, *First Report*, p. 35.

18 Alcock, *Northern Ireland*, pp. 21–2.

19 Ibid., p. 22.

20 Lyons, *Ireland since the Famine*, pp. 521–2.

21 *New Ireland Forum Report*, ch. 5, para. 4, 10.

22 Text of the Helsinki Final Act in *Keesing's Contemporary Archives*, 1975, pp. 27301ff.

23 Alcock, *History*, pp. 11–21.

24 Report by the UN Mediator on Cyprus (Mr Galo Plaza) to the Secretary-General, UN Doc. S/6253 of 26 March 1965, para. 10.

25 Alcock, *History*, pp. 14 and 33–40.

26 Ibid., pp. 139–40.

27 Text of the 1948 Autonomy statute in ibid., pp. 475–92.

28 Ibid., p. 434.

29 Alcock, *Geschichte*, pp. 164 and 180 (emphasis added).

30 B. Faulkner, *Memoirs of a Statesman*, Weidenfeld and Nicolson, London, 1978, pp. 195–6.

31 Professor Theodore Veiter in *Das Menschenrecht*, Vienna, April 1970.

32 Text of the improved Autonomy Statute in Alcock, *Geschichte*, pp. 239–74.

33 R. Stephens, *Cyprus – A Place of Arms*, Pall Mall, London, 1966, pp. 157–9.

34 A. E. Alcock, 'Three Case Studies in Minority Protection: South Tyrol, Cyprus, Quebec' in A. C. Hepburn, *Minorities in History*, Arnold, London, 1978, p. 205.

35 Details of the Autonomy Statute in *The Autonomy Act for Åland*, Mariehamn, Åland Tidnings-Tryckeri, 1978; see also T. Modeen, 'The International Protection of the National Identity of the Åland Islands', *Scandinavian Studies in Law* (Stockholm), 1973, 179–200.

36 A. E. Alcock, 'South Tyrol' in Minority Rights Group, *Co-existence in Some Plural European Societies*, Report no. 72, London, 1986, 6.

37 Alcock, 'Three Case Studies', pp. 205–6.

38 *Irish Times*, 13 December 1990.

11

Government and politics in the Irish Republic: judicial activism and executive inertia

James Casey

In terms of religion the population of the Republic of Ireland[1] is plainly more homogeneous than that of Northern Ireland.[2] Its political system has traditionally been more stable than that of Northern Ireland, and since the 1937 Constitution came into force the state's legitimacy[3] has been questioned only by a tiny minority. These factors serve to explain, in part at least, why the Republic has been spared the security and political problems that have beset Northern Ireland in the last twenty years. But the trauma of the North has naturally had repercussions in the South, not only in the economic and political fields but also in the constitutional and legal order. The security problem, for example, although of differing dimensions in the two jurisdictions, is nevertheless common to both. And in each it has had an impact on the content and processes of the law, notwithstanding the marked differences in the two constitutional systems.

The existence until 1921 of a shared constitutional history should not obscure the fact that a constitutional revolution has occurred in both Irish jurisdictions. In the case of Northern Ireland this is obvious enough, with the suspension of the Stormont Parliament and the imposition of direct rule. It is less obvious in the case of the Republic, for its Constitution seems to replicate in many respects the Westminster model of government. But this superficial resemblance is misleading. As will be seen, the executive and legislature in the Republic are subject to constitutional constraints which do not trouble their Westminster counterparts; and this has had important consequences for the protection and promotion of fundamental rights.[4] On the debit side, however, it may sometimes have led to an excessive reliance on judicial activism for law reform, and occasionally provided politicians and administrators with an excuse for inactivity.

Overall, however, judicial review under the 1937 Constitution has been an outstanding success. The same does not hold for the other political institutions created by that Constitution. Although normally dominant over parliament, the Executive has frequently been remiss in tackling important issues. Yet its dominance has not been counter-balanced by effective mechanisms for securing accountability to the Dáil, and the Seanad has failed to find a distinctive role for itself.

The 1937 Constitution

It is well known that the 1937 Constitution was De Valera's brainchild, and largely his handiwork. The text, in several places, reflects his conservative ideas, and the Constitution was certainly not designed as a vehicle for radical new social policies.[5] Instead, De Valera's aim was, in the words of Professor Fanning, 'to enact a constitution that would satisfy what he regarded as justifiable republican aspirations and thereby secure the legitimacy of the state'.[6] This aim – largely achieved[7] – serves to explain some of the ways in which the 1937 Constitution differs from its predecessor, such as the absence of the Oath, the presence of an elected head of state and of several aspirations towards reunification. It also explains why so much of the 1937 Constitution is identical in content – and often in language – with that predecessor. But notwithstanding such similarities, the 1937 Constitution has proved a much more significant document than its counterpart of 1922. There are three interconnected reasons for this: first, amendment is possible only by referendum (Article 46); second, judicial review has flourished; and third, the Constitution has lodged itself in the public consciousness as the fundamental law of the state.

The impact of judicial review

The 1937 Constitution – again faithfully reflecting the content of its predecessor – specifically provides for judicial review of the validity of legislation. It is doubtful, however, whether anyone saw judicial review as potentially more significant in practice than it had proved since 1922.[8] But in the last twenty-five years particularly, judicial review has positively burgeoned. Its impact has been twofold: first, the courts have insisted upon the Constitution's restrictions, emphasizing that it is – *in its totality* – the basic, fundamental law of the state; and second, the Constitution has become a remarkably effective vehicle for the protection and assertion of rights.

With regard to the first point, the courts have rigorously policed, for example, the Constitution's electoral dispositions, its separation of powers provisions and its fair trial guarantees. This process has sprung some unpleasant surprises on politicians and administrators, who have found their freedom of action limited in hitherto unsuspected ways. Thus, the courts will scrutinize constituency revision Acts for constitutional compliance;[9] there are now limits on the extent to which legislative power may be delegated;[10] and parliamentary committees may not try or convict those accused of breach of privilege.[11] There is a strong presumption in favour of granting bail to an accused person,[12] who also enjoys constitutional rights to a speedy trial by a properly constituted court,[13] to legal advice,[14] and to have unconstitutionally obtained evidence excluded at the trial.[15]

This emphasis on constitutional restrictions on the exercise of power reached its zenith in 1987 in *Crotty v An Taoiseach*,[16] where the Supreme Court held, by a majority, that the Single European Act (SEA) could not – absent a constitutional amendment – be ratified. The existing text did not contemplate the surrender of sovereignty and independence in the field of foreign policy envisaged by the SEA. The sense of shock this decision provoked in some quarters may be gauged from the comments of a former Attorney General:

> what the court ruling has done is to considerably circumscribe the extent to which the Government can, even with the approval of the Dáil, ratify international agreements. The results of the majority judgment are so far-reaching that consideration may have to be given at some future time to a further amendment of the Constitution in order to restore to the government the powers that previously it was generally believed to enjoy.[17]

It is certainly true that the full implications of the *Crotty* case remain to be worked out. As Gerard Hogan has pointed out, it raises questions about the state's adherence to the United Nations Charter,[18] and on the basis of the majority's reasoning it could be argued that its adherence to the European Convention on Human Rights (ECHR) is also constitutionally suspect. For to pledge the state to 'secure to everyone' within its jurisdiction a series of rights and freedoms whose content is ultimately determined by the European Court of Human Rights may not be compatible with the sovereignty and independence proclaimed by Article 5 of the Constitution.

In relation to the second point above, the courts have in general shown themselves zealous in defence of the rights recognized by the Constitution. But they have gone further, by accepting that it protects rights other than those specifically listed. Among those so far identified are the rights of privacy,[19] of access to the courts[20] and to legal representation on criminal charges.[21] Important rights have even been spelt out of what might have seemed unpromising and socially outdated provisions. Thus, Article 41.2.2 provides: 'The State shall . . . endeavour to ensure that mothers shall not be obliged by economic necessity to engage in labour to the neglect of their duties in the home.' In *B.L. v M.L.*[22] Barr J derived from this a principle, independent of the constructive trust device, which enabled him to give the petitioner wife a 50 per cent share in the matrimonial home and its contents. This process of judicial exposition has been especially important in bringing about changes in the law which the executive and legislature – either through conservatism or pusillanimity – had failed to effect.[23]

Judicial review has also had the result of producing a heightened awareness of constitutional rights and of limitations on governmental power. Litigants have demonstrated both zeal and astuteness in exploiting the Constitution's possibilities.[24] These factors, combined with a generous approach to *locus standi*, have ushered in the strategy of the constitutional test case. This technique of using litigation to bring about change is observable as early as 1961 in the constituency revision case of *O'Donovan v Attorney General*,[25] and is exemplified also in *McMahon v Attorney General*[26] (secrecy in voting) and *McGee v Attorney General*[27] (access to contraceptives). In contrast, McCrudden has noted the absence of any such phenomenon in Northern Ireland in the 1960s.[28]

It is hardly too much to say that the 1937 Constitution is now accorded something of the reverence given to its United States counterpart. As evidence of this one may cite the events in Dáil Éireann on 29 June 1989. Following the general election – which had yielded no clear majority – a motion that Charles Haughey be nominated for appointment as Taoiseach was defeated, and the other persons proposed likewise failed to secure nomination. Initially Mr Haughey sought an adjournment until 3 July to allow for further consultations, pointing out that under Article 28.11.2 of the Constitution he and his Cabinet colleagues continued in office. But the Labour leader, Dick Spring, invoked Article 28.10:

> The Taoiseach shall resign from office upon his ceasing to retain the support of a majority in Dáil Éireann unless on his advice the President dissolves Dáil Éireann and on the reassembly of Dáil Éireann after the dissolution the Taoiseach secures the support of a majority in Dáil Éireann.

In Mr Spring's view the Taoiseach *had* failed to retain the support of a Dáil majority, and was thus obliged to resign. Mr Haughey said he had been advised by the Attorney General that immediate resignation was not required by Article 28.10. After a short adjournment, however, he made the following statement:

> It is of critical importance that we not just legally uphold the Constitution, but be seen to do so. Our people hold their Constitution to be sacrosanct. I would never wish even to appear to do otherwise than adhere strictly to the precepts of the Constitution. Accordingly . . . I now propose to go to the President and to convey my resignation as Taoiseach to him.[29]

Government and parliament

If judicial review has functioned with conspicuous success, the same can hardly be said of the other institutions created by the 1937 Constitution. The Executive, although usually dominating parliament, has frequently been slow to make and implement decisions on important questions of social and legal policy. Occasionally, this may stem from a reluctance to tackle questions with a moral dimension, such as contraception, but that cannot explain everything. Farrell has discerned 'a considerable degree of overload' at Cabinet level,[30] and this may be true of the government machinery as a whole.

There are many examples, from the most disparate fields, of inordinate delays with problems. In the early 1970s the price of building land, its effect on house prices, and the question of securing part of the increase in the value of such land for the community's benefit, came on to the political agenda. Two official reports followed, one in 1973 and the other in 1985,[31] but effective action remains to be taken.[32] Here, admittedly, a constitutional question mark, based on the property rights guarantees, many have hung over earlier proposed solutions, but any such doubts have been dispelled at least since 1985. This situation illustrates a potential disadvantage of judicial review – that it may offer an excuse for inertia. Keane J has referred to an all-purpose justification to the more inert section of our public service for not tackling seriously needed reform: 'we could run into trouble with the Constitution, Minister'.[33]

This excuse, which has also been deployed in other areas,[34] would be more plausible if the Constitution was incapable of being amended; but that, of course, is not the case.

Possible constitutional difficulties certainly cannot underlie every instance of inaction. They could not conceivably explain the failure to legislate in regard to Seanad representation of tertiary-level educational institutions. Originally, under Article 18.4, three seats were allocated to the National University of Ireland and three to Dublin University (Trinity College). In 1979, however, the Seventh Amendment of the Constitution Act allowed the Oireachtas to extend this representation to other institutions of higher education. No such legislation has yet been enacted, notwithstanding the anomaly that since 1989 two new universities have come into existence.

In Article 41 the Constitution lauds the family as a vital social institution, guarantees to protect it 'in its constitution and authority' and, particularly, recognizes a role for women as home-makers. But for decades the state failed to give practical form to these aspirations. The legislative modernization of family law began only in the 1970s, proceeded fitfully and as yet is far from complete. Reform has been achieved in regard to succession, support obligations and – in part only – the family home.[35] But in a polity which forbids divorce and in which – no doubt in consequence – the High Court's nullity jurisdiction has been increasingly invoked, development of the law in this field has been left entirely to the courts. And this despite a White Paper in 1976, a

Law Reform Commission report in 1984 and a report by a joint Oireachtas committee in 1985.[36] In 1985 also Henchy J called for 'a modern statute providing for the grant of decrees of nullity of marriage on fair, reasonable and clearly stated grounds and making due provision for the consequences of such decrees on those directly affected by them'.[37] But, like many other judicial calls for change in the law, this has gone unheeded.

At the time of writing (mid-1991), much concern has been expressed about the placing of two fifteen-year-old offenders in an adult prison. This has highlighted once again the remarkable failure to modernize childcare services and the administration of juvenile justice. The principal statute in this field remains the Children's Act 1908, which in May 1990 O'Flaherty J charitably described as 'showing its age'. Ten years ago a Task Force (no less) called for 'the introduction of a comprehensive Children Act concerned with the welfare and protection of children'.[38] Although a Children (Care and Protection) Bill was introduced in 1985, neither it nor any other reforming measure has as yet become law. In the meantime judicial decisions have exposed the frailties of the 1908 Act, and Finlay CJ has recently observed that 'the necessity for a modern Children's Act making a more efficient and simpler procedure for the protection of children available to the Courts remains one of urgency'.[39]

This phenomenon of inertia is especially noticeable in matters relating to the administration of justice. Examples are legion. In 1966 the Committee on Court Practice and Procedure recommended increases in the civil jurisdiction of the District and Circuit Courts. In 1971 the Courts Act implemented those recommendations, but in the meantime inflation had rendered the new financial limits largely out of date. A report of 1965 on jury service by the same committee was implemented by the Juries Act 1976, but only after key provisions of the previous legislation were declared unconstitutional by the Supreme Court.[40] The Bankruptcy Law Committee Report, delivered in 1973, was implemented only by the Bankruptcy Act 1988, notwithstanding that a draft Bill was annexed to the report.

The uncertainty and inconvenience such inactivity can produce has recently been graphically illustrated. In 1978 the Interdepartmental Committee on Mentally Ill and Maladjusted Persons made a series of recommendations on the treatment and care of mentally disordered persons charged with criminal offences. These included repeal of the Trial of Lunatics Act 1883; substitution of a verdict of 'not guilty by reason of mental disorder' for 'guilty but insane'; and empowerment of the courts to order appropriate measures for the care, treatment and control of persons in respect of whom such verdicts were found. The report again contained a draft Bill, but no steps were taken to implement it. In 1990, however, the matters dealt with in the report proved their practical significance. Three High Court judges had to deal with cases where persons, found guilty but insane and sentenced to be detained in the Central Mental Hospital, had, according to expert evidence, recovered from mental disorder. A sharp conflict of judicial opinion resulted. O'Hanlon J held that the Trial of

Lunatics Act 1883 was constitutional and that, in accordance with its terms, release from continued detention was a matter for the Executive.[41] Johnson J concurred in this view.[42] Keane J, however, held the 1883 Act invalid and ruled that the question of release fell for judicial determination.[43] Subsequently the Supreme Court upheld the conclusions of O'Hanlon and Johnson JJ.[44] As matters now stand, therefore, the Executive has the task of deciding whether such persons should be released. Fresh legislation has been promised,[45] but it is not yet clear what form it will take. Should the Interdepartmental Committee's recommendations be adopted, the decision on release would be transferred to the courts. This might prove a politically attractive option in terms both of public acceptability and of shifting responsibility for potentially unpopular decisions.

It is not, of course, suggested that the decision-making process systematically fails to function, but there are a worrying number of instances of decisions delayed, or indefinitely deferred, and of situations where change has been resolved upon but never implemented. The cause is presumably to be found in some defect in the machinery of government, whether it be overloading at Cabinet, or departmental level, or both.

The problem of overload can only be exacerbated by a remarkable centralization of decision-making functions. Local authorities are virtually bereft of independent financial resources, and many of their decisions are subject to ministerial sanction. J. J. Lee has commented:

> public administration has become centralised to an extreme degree by the standards of more economically advanced countries. The thrust of central government since independence has been to restrict the scope of local authorities, and to centralise control over financial resources.[46]

At the time of writing, the reform and reorganization of local government is under active examination; but that has occurred before, without any practical result.

Extensive and radical changes in the organization of central government were recommended in the Devlin Report of 1969.[47] But implementation began only in 1984, with changes in the system for making top-level Civil Service appointments.[48] Further reform – including greater budgetary responsibility and decision-making authority for Civil Servants – has been mooted, and in part achieved.[49] It remains to be seen whether the complete reform programme will be implemented, and if it is, whether it will deliver the expected improvements in performance.

The functioning of parliament

As noted above, the Executive lethargy in policy-making is *not* the product of parliamentary difficulties. Indeed, what many regard as the two most dynamic governments of the last thirty years – those of Séan Lemass, 1961–5, and of Charles Haughey, 1987–9 – both lacked an overall majority.

Although the constitutional text might suggest otherwise, the Oireachtas is not a legislature in the sense of a *law-making* body. Basil Chubb has called it a *law-declaring* body, and has described the system as one in which the government (Cabinet) makes the law with the advice and consent of the Oireachtas.[50] This, of course, has happened elsewhere but other parliamentary bodies have compensated for it by emphasizing their role of investigating policy formulation and implementation. So far, only tentative steps have been taken in this direction in the Republic. Between 1983 and 1987 a number of select committees – some of them Joint Dáil–Seanad bodies – were established, but the experiment has only been moderately successful.[51] The committees have not been organized on a departmental basis, so there has been no systematic examination of, for example, the activities of the Defence, Foreign Affairs or Justice Departments. Some, indeed, look suspiciously like devices for allowing the executive to defer decisions – such as the Joint Committees on Marriage Breakdown and on Building Land.

Reform of parliamentary procedures has been under discussion for years, but little has happened. The joint programme agreed by the Fianna Fáil–Progressive Democrat coalition now in office stated:

> At the end of 1989 the new Government will bring forward detailed proposals for the reform of the Oireachtas and in that process will examine, among other issues, the following: the procedure for the passage of legislation through the Dáil and the Seanad, the committee system, Question Time, and the *sub judice* rule. The new Government proposes that MEPs qualify for membership of the Oireachtas committees relevant to EC affairs.[52]

This undertaking has unfortunately not been fulfilled. However, Fine Gael, the main opposition party, has advanced its own proposals on the matter, and this should ensure that the question of reform is kept alive.

Recently the Seanad has been the focus of much attention, although not for the reasons its members might desire. The Progressive Democrats' proposal to abolish the chamber temporarily enhanced public interest in its role, but the greatest publicity sprang from an unedifying series of disputes between its chairman (the Cathaoirleach) and a group of independent senators. Matters came to a head in March 1990 when Senator David Norris (Ind.) was found guilty of a breach of privilege and was suspended for a week. Senator Norris claimed in the High Court that the procedures leading to this decision were unfair, and Blayney J gave him leave to apply for judicial review.[53] It subsequently emerged that the Cathaoirleach, Senator Doherty, had obtained legal advice that he should not chair the Committee on Procedure and Privileges when it considered Senator Norris's case, since he (Doherty) was the target of Senator Norris's allegations. But the Cathaoirleach omitted to mention this to the Committee, whose inquiry he proceeded to chair.[54] Senator Norris's suspension was lifted on 21 March. On 28 March a motion of no confidence in Senator Doherty as Cathaoirleach was defeated by 29 votes to 26.[55]

The Seanad, as is well known, exemplifies the difficulty of designing a second chamber for a unitary state. Although theoretically based on vocational representation, it is in reality dominated by party. Necessarily – and explicitly – given a position subordinate to that of the Dáil,[56] it has failed to carve out any distinctive niche for itself. Individual senators have made distinguished contributions, but the Seanad as a collective entity probably merits Chubb's severe judgement that 'the prestige of Seanad Éireann was, and remains, low. To most it seems a leisurely body that is merely another selection of party politicians chosen in an unnecessarily complicated and not particularly democratic manner'.[57]

The Seanad's predicament is perhaps highlighted by the fact that although reform does not necessarily involve a constitutional amendment, it has not yet found a place on the political agenda.

The electoral system

For Dáil elections Article 16.2.5 of the Constitution prescribes proportional representation (PR) by the single transferable vote (STV). This system has in fact been in use since the 1920s and its roots go back to the Government of Ireland Act 1914. (It is, of course, also the system used in electing the three Northern Ireland MEPs, the Northern Ireland Assemblies of 1973 and 1982, and the Constitutional Convention of 1975.)

The effects of this electoral system have been much debated. It can hardly be said to produce governmental instability; the three general elections in eighteen months in 1981–2 were exceptional – and perhaps avoidable. Clearly, however, PR by STV is kinder to smaller parties than the United Kingdom's first-past-the-post single-member constituency system; five organized parties enjoy substantial representation in the current Dáil. In the last decade, the voting system has combined with an increasingly volatile electorate to make it difficult for any party to win an overall Dáil majority. It has been suggested that, if present trends continue, coalition governments will be the norm in future, and that Fianna Fáil – which abandoned its historic anti-coalition stance in 1989 – is likely to be involved in them.[58]

In referenda in 1959 and 1969 the electorate rejected attempts to change the system, and it seems safe to assume that *some* form of proportional representation will endure. Indeed, the joint programme of the present government parties does not envisage any change here. But there has long been concern that the current arrangements entail serious disadvantages, including notably a degree of intra-party competition leading deputies to concentrate on constituency affairs to the detriment of their national responsibilities. It has been suggested that this need to watch one's back imposes a particularly unfair burden on ministers. It can also reduce the pool of ministerial talent available to a Taoiseach by putting a premium on the more mundane political skills.[59]

Even within the confines of the Constitution reform is possible, for the size of the Dáil could be reduced. Article 16.2.4 provides the formula of not less than one deputy per 30,000 population, and not more than one per 20,000. But it has long been the practice to opt for the figure yielding the more generous representation, and there are no signs that this will change. If over-representative by standards prevailing elsewhere, this phenomenon must be judged in the context of the extreme centralization already referred to. A former minister, now retired from parliamentary politics, has proposed a series of interlinked reforms consisting of: reformed and reinvigorated local government; a smaller Dáil, with better-paid and better-serviced members; and a revamped PR system akin to that in Germany.[60] But the prospects for change on so many fronts hardly seem bright.

The impact of the Northern Ireland situation

The problems of Northern Ireland have had an impact on the government and politics of the Republic in several different ways. Most notably, emergency powers have been invoked, though not to the same extent as in the North. Thus, internment – though readily available (the 1940 Offences against the State (Amendment) Act authorizing it may be brought into operation by Executive proclamation and Dáil approval is not required) – has not so far been employed. But the 1939 Offences against the State Act has been utilized to re-establish special criminal courts for the non-jury trial of alleged subversives,[61] and section 30 – which allows the Garda to hold a suspect for up to forty-eight hours – has been extensively used (if not, indeed, abused), as suggested by Table 11.1.[62]

The heightened security concerns giving rise to these measures coincided with a perceived rise in 'ordinary' crime. Police measures to cope with this – including extensive use of section 30 of the 1939 Act – have caused disquiet about a 'spillover' of emergency measures into the ordinary criminal law.[63] Concern has also been expressed about the treatment of persons in Garda custody, although – in contrast to the position in Northern Ireland – allegations regarding this have not been officially investigated. Separate proceedings for damages have been instituted by two individuals complaining of assault and battery while in Garda custody; but the Special Criminal Court, in reasoned judgments, has rejected their allegations in this regard, and two High Court judges have held the plaintiffs estopped from litigating the issue again.[64]

The Northern Ireland situation has also prompted Executive action, under the Broadcasting Acts, to restrict access to the airwaves by those deemed

Table 11.1 Numbers arrested and charged under the
1939 Offences against the State Act, 1980–4

	Number arrested	Number charged
1980	1874	168
1981	2303	323
1982	2308	256
1983	2334	363
1984	2216	374

Source: Speech to the Dáil by the Minister for Justice, Michael
Noonan TD, on 26 February 1985 (356 Dáil Debs., c. 741).

apologists for terrorism. In *State (Lynch)* v *Cooney*[65] the Supreme Court
rejected constitutional and administrative law challenges to this ban. There is
now, of course, a UK parallel in directives issued by the Home Secretary to the
BBC and IBA which have been upheld as lawful by the House of Lords.[66] In
neither state has action been taken against the print media. In particular,
section 10(2) of the Offences against the State Act 1939 – which makes it an
offence to publish statements emanating from an unlawful organization – has
not been invoked.

The question of extraditing alleged offenders from the Republic has long
been a major focus of concern. One difficulty is that the law on this subject has
now become quite complex. The basic Extradition Act of 1965 has been
amended by two 1987 statutes, the first of which implements the European
Convention on the Suppression of Terrorism of 1977, something long thought
to be constitutionally precluded.[67] There is, in addition, a large corpus of case
law which shows some alterations in judicial opinion. Indeed, the latest
Supreme Court decision on the subject, *Finucane* v *McMahon*[68] overrules a
prior decision of only two years' standing.[69] In the *Finucane* case also all five
members of the Supreme Court agreed that, in the light of the evidence,[70] the
applicant would, if extradited, become a probable target for ill-treatment in
prison. Consequently the court, it was held, must prohibit his extradition in
order, so far as practicable, to defend his constitutional rights.

If the shift in judicial opinion which occurred in the *Finucane* case should
extend to other aspects of extradition law, the situation would be transformed
and securing extradition could become very difficult. That the corpus of case
law will grow is inevitable; already an unsuccessful challenge has been made in
the High Court to the Extradition (Amendment) Act 1987, which gives a new
'screening' role to the Attorney General,[71] and other possible constitutional
stumbling-blocks have been suggested. Lying behind all this, of course, is a
marked difference of view between the Executive authorities in the Republic
and the United Kingdom. The former would prefer greater use of existing

extra-territorial trial machinery,[72] while the latter seem to prize effective extradition arrangements as a symbol of increased security co-operation.

If the Northern Ireland situation has produced changes in the Republic's statute book, it has had little impact on the text of the Constitution. In 1972 the Fifth Amendment of the Constitution Act altered Article 44 by removing *inter alia* the reference to 'the special position' of the Roman Catholic church. That provision – which irritated many people outside the North – had no juridical significance;[73] nor, of course, did the Church's political clout rest upon it. It is very difficult to estimate the full extent of that clout today, in the much more secularized society that the Republic has become. The Church obviously played a very important role in the adoption of the 'pro-life' amendment of the Constitution in 1983, and in the rejection of the pro-divorce amendment in 1986. But it is too simplistic to suppose that these things occurred merely because the Church so desired; both situations were much more complex than that.[74]

No change has been made in Articles 2 and 3 of the Constitution, long a source of grievance to unionists with their apparent claim of jurisdiction over the North. In 1975 the Supreme Court appeared to suggest that Article 2 was a political declaration devoid of legal effect;[75] but the more recent decision in *McGimpsey* v *Ireland*[76] repudiates this notion. There Finlay CJ, speaking for the Supreme Court, said:

> With Articles 2 and 3 of the Constitution should be read the Preamble, and I am satisfied that the true interpretation of these constitutional provisions is as follows.
>
> 1 The reintegration of the national territory is a constitutional imperative (*cf* Hederman J in *Russell* v *Fanning* [1989] ILRM 333).
> 2 Article 2 of the Constitution consists of a declaration of the extent of the national territory as a claim of legal right.
> 3 Article 3 of the Constitution prohibits, pending the reintegration of the national territory, the enactment of laws with any greater area of extent of application or extra-territorial effect than the laws of Saorstat Éireann and this prohibits the enactment of laws applicable in the counties of Northern Ireland.
> 4 The restriction imposed by Article 3, pending the reintegration of the national territory, in no way derogates from the claim as a legal right to the entire national territory.[77]

The Chief Justice went on to make it clear that the Article 3 restriction did not affect the validity of extra-territorial measures such as the Criminal Law (Jurisdiction) Act 1975.

The *McGimpsey* ruling provoked fresh calls from Northern unionists, and others, for the repeal or reformulation of Articles 2 and 3. This, however, would require a referendum and although some political parties in the

Republic favour a change, and a possible model was provided by an all-party committee on the Constitution in 1967, no government has so far been willing to move. This reticence seems prudent, for it is easy to imagine how a referendum campaign could be exploited by IRA sympathizers, as foreshadowing an abandonment of Northern nationalists. But a Dáil debate in December 1990 suggests that if current initiatives were to fructify in a new internal political settlement in Northern Ireland, this might well set the scene for change.[78]

Notes

1 'Republic of Ireland' is, by statute, the *description* of the state – its *name* is Ireland. See Article 4 of the 1937 Constitution and the Supreme Court's decision in *Ellis* v *O'Dea* [1989] IR 530.

2 The *Census of Population of Ireland 1981*, vol. 5, *Religion*, Stationery Office, Dublin, 1985, gives the Roman Catholic population as 3,204,476 – 95 per cent of the whole. The *Northern Ireland Census 1981*, *Summary Report*, HMSO, London, 1983, gives the Roman Catholic population as 414,532 out of a total of 1,481,959 – 28 per cent.

3 For a discussion of this concept, with particular reference to Northern Ireland, see R. Baxter, 'Obedience, Legitimacy and the State' in C. Harlow (ed.), *Public Law and Politics*, Sweet & Maxwell, London, 1986, pp. 3–22.

4 See further J. Casey, *Constitutional Law in Ireland*, Sweet & Maxwell, London, 1987; M. Forde, *Constitutional Law of Ireland*, Mercier Press, Dublin, 1987; J. Kelly (1984). *The Irish Constitution* (2nd edn, with supplement), Jurist Publishing Co., Dublin, 1987.

5 On the drafting process, see D. Keogh, 'The Constitutional Revolution: an Analysis of the Making of the Constitution', *Administration*, 35 (1987), 4–84; and D. Keogh, 'Church, State and Society', in B. Farrell (ed.), *De Valera's Constitution and Ours*, Gill & Macmillan, Dublin, 1988, pp. 103–22. On De Valera's conservatism regarding the position of women in society, see Y. Scannell, 'The Constitution and the Role of Women' in Farrell, *De Valera's Constitution*. De Valera's economic and social philosophy is analysed in J. J. Lee, *Ireland 1912–1985: Politics and Society*, Cambridge University Press, Cambridge, 1989, pp. 329–41.

6 Ronan Fanning, 'Mr De Valera Drafts a Constitution' in Farrell, *De Valera's Constitution*, pp. 33–45.

7 Ibid., p. 44.

8 On the slow development of judicial review see further J. Kelly, 'Fundamental Rights in the Constitution' in Farrell, *De Valera's Constitution*, pp. 166–7; and D. Barrington, 'The Constitution in the Courts' in F. Litton (ed.), *The Constitution of Ireland 1937–1987*, Institute of Public Administration, Dublin, 1988, pp. 110–15.

9 *O'Donovan* v *Attorney General* [1961] IR 114; *O'Malley* v *An Taoiseach* [1990] ILRM 461.

10 *City View Press Ltd* v *AnCO* [1980] IR 381; *McDaid* v *Sheehy* [1989] ILRM 342.

11 *Re Haughey* [1971] IR 217.

12 *People (Attorney General)* v *O'Callaghan* [1966] IR 501; *Ryan* v *DPP* [1989] IR 399.

13 *State (O'Connell)* v *Judge Fawsitt* [1986] ILRM 639; *Shelly* v *District Justice Mahon* [1990] IR 36.

14 *DPP* v *Healy* [1990] ILRM 313.

15 Ibid.; *People (DPP)* v *Kenny* [1990] ILRM 539.

16 *Crotty* v *An Taoiseach* [1987] IR 713.

17 P. Sutherland, 'Twin Perspectives: an Attorney General Views Political and European Dimensions' in Farrell, *De Valera's Constitution*, p. 185.

18 G. Hogan, 'The Supreme Court and the Single European Act', *Irish Jurist* (n.s.), 22 (1987), 55–70.

19 *Kennedy* v *Ireland* [1987] IR 587.

20 *Macauley* v *Minister for Posts and Telegraphs* [1966] IR 345; *State (McEldowney)* v *Kelleher* [1983] IR 289; *Cashman* v *District Judge Clifford* [1989] IR 181.

21 *State (Healy)* v *Donoghue* [1976] IR 325.

22 *B.L.* v *M.L.* [1989] ILRM 528.

23 Examples are *Byrne* v *Ireland* [1972] IR 241, which established the state's liability in tort; and *McGee* v *Attorney General* [1974] IR 284, which struck down statutory restrictions on access to contraceptives.

24 Consider *Murphy* v *Attorney General* [1982] IR 241, which effectively ended the situation where a married couple, both working outside the home, could pay more in tax than a similarly circumstanced – but unmarried – couple.

25 *O'Donovan* v *Attorney General* [1961] IR 114.

26 *McMahon* v *Attorney General* [1972] IR 69.

27 *McGee* v *Attorney General* [1974] IR 284.

28 C. McCrudden, 'Northern Ireland and the British Constitution' in J. Jowell and D. Oliver (eds), *The Changing Constitution* (2nd edn), Clarendon Press, Oxford, 1989, pp. 310–11.

29 *Dáil Debs.*, vol. 391, 29 June 1989, col. 58.

30 B. Farrell, 'Ireland' in J. Blondel and F. Müller-Rommel (eds), *Cabinets in Western Europe*, Macmillan, London, 1988, p. 46.

31 *Report of the Committee on the Price of Building Land* (the Kenny Report) (Prl. 3632) Stationery Office, Dublin, 1973; *Report of the Joint Committee on Building Land* (Pl. 3232) Stationery Office, Dublin, 1985.

32 The Local Government (Planning and Development) Act 1990 has, however, restricted the circumstances in which compensation is payable where planning permission is refused.

33 R. Keane, 'The Constitution and Public Administration' in Litton, *Constitution of Ireland*, p. 141.

34 It was used to resist proposals for amending adoption law by bringing some legitimate children within the categories eligible to be adopted. This matter was considered in the *Report of the Review Committee on Adoption Services* (Pl. 2467) Stationery Office, Dublin, May 1984, pp. 11–14. The committee favoured changing the law, and admitted that constitutional uncertainty did exist; but it suggested this could be resolved if the relevant Bill were referred by the President to the Supreme Court under Article 26 of the Constitution. This course was eventually followed, and the Bill was upheld: see *In re Article 26 of the Constitution and the Adoption (No. 2) Bill 1987* [1989] IR 656.

35　See P. O'Connor, *Key Issues in Irish Family Law*, Round Hall Press, Dublin, 1988, *passim*.
36　*The Law of Nullity in Ireland*, Office of the Attorney General, 1976; *Report on Nullity of Marriage* (LRC 9 – 1984); Report of the Joint Committee on Marriage Breakdown (Pl. 3074) Stationery Office, Dublin, March 1985.
37　*N. (orse. K.)* v *K.* [1986] ILRM, 75, 89.
38　Task Force on Child Care Services, *Final Report* (Prl. 9345) Stationery Office, Dublin, September 1980, p. 265.
39　*MF* v *Superintendent, Ballymun Garda Station* [1990] ILRM 767, 769.
40　*de Burca and Anderson* v *Attorney General* [1976] IR 38.
41　*DPP* v *Ellis*, Law Report, *The Irish Times*, 7 May 1990.
42　*DPP* v *Gallagher*, *The Irish Times*, 15 December 1990.
43　*People (DPP)* v *Neilan* [1991] ILRM 184.
44　*DPP* v *Gallagher*, *The Irish Times*, 13 February 1991.
45　A report in *The Irish Times*, 14 February 1991, said that the drafting of legislation was at an advanced stage.
46　Lee, *Ireland 1912–1985*, p. 559.
47　Public Services Organisation Review Group 1966–1969, *Report* (Prl. 792).
48　See Lee, *Ireland 1912–1985*, pp. 548–57.
49　The Minister for Finance announced this on 7 September 1989: see *The Irish Times*, 8 September 1989. The new system has already been implemented in the Department of Social Welfare: See *The Irish Times*, 5 July 1990.
50　B. Chubb, 'Government and Dáil: Constitutional Myth and Political Practice' in Farrell, *De Valera's Constitution*, p. 98.
51　See J. F. Zimmerman, 'An Oireachtas Innovation: Backbench Committees', *Administration*, 36, 3 (1988), 265–89.
52　*The Irish Times*, 13 July 1989.
53　*The Irish Times*, 17 March 1990.
54　*The Irish Times*, 21 March 1990.
55　*The Irish Times*, 29 March 1990.
56　See Article 13.1.1° (only the Dáil nominates the Taoiseach); 17 (estimates presented only to the Dáil); 20–24 (limited role of Seanad in legislation); 28.4.1° (government responsible only to Dáil); 28.7.2° (not more than two senators in Cabinet); 28.5 (international agreements to be laid before, and approved by, the Dáil alone).
57　Chubb, 'Government and Dáil', p. 94.
58　P. Mair, 'The Irish Party System into the 1990s' in M. Gallagher and R. Sinnott, (eds), *How Ireland Voted 1989*, Centre for the Study of Irish Elections, University College Galway, 1990, pp. 219–20.
59　T. Garvin, 'Change and the Political System' in F. Litton (ed.), *Unequal Achievement: The Irish Experience 1957–1982*, Institute of Public Administration, Dublin, 1982, pp. 25–7.
60　G. Hussey, 'Fantasies of a Reformed Political System', *The Irish Times*, 17 August 1989.
61　See G. Hogan and C. Walker, *Political Violence and the Law in Ireland*, Manchester University Press, Manchester, 1989, ch. 10.
62　The Emergency Powers Act 1976 authorizes detention for seven days; although not currently in force, it may be brought into operation at any time by government order.

63 Hogan and Walker, *Political Violence*, p. 277. See also D. Walsh, 'The Impact of the Antisubversive Laws on Police Powers and Practices in Ireland', *Temple Law Review*, 62 (1989), 1099.

64 *Kelly* v *Ireland* [1986] ILRM 318; *Breatnach* v *Ireland* [1989] IR 489.

65 *State (Lynch)* v *Cooney* [1982] IR 387.

66 *Brind* v *Home Secretary* [1991] 1 All ER 720.

67 See Hogan and Walker, *Political Violence*, p. 287.

68 *Finucane* v *McMahon* [1990] ILRM 505.

69 *Russell* v *Fanning* [1988] ILRM 333.

70 In particular, successful Northern Ireland High Court proceedings by a prisoner alleging ill-treatment: *Pettigrew* v *NI Office* (1989) 3 BNIL 83.

71 On which see Hogan and Walker, *Political Violence*, pp. 293–5. A constitutional challenge to the relevant provisions was rejected by the High Court in *Wheeler* v *Culligan* [1989] IR 344.

72 See C. Campbell, 'Extradition to Northern Ireland: Prospects and Problems', *Modern Law Review*, 52 (1989), 616–17.

73 *Quinn's Supermarket Ltd* v *Attorney General* [1972] IR 1.

74 See Lee, *Ireland 1912–1985*, pp. 653–7; and T. Hesketh, *The Second Partitioning of Ireland, The Abortion Referendum of 1983*, Brandsma Books, Dun Laoghaire, 1990.

75 *Re Article 26 and the Criminal Law (Jurisdiction) Bill 1975* [1977] IR 129.

76 *McGimpsey* v *Ireland* [1990] ILRM 441.

77 Ibid., at 449.

78 In that debate a Workers' Party Bill to amend Articles 2 and 3 was defeated by 74 votes to 66. But the government's objections to the Bill stressed that it was premature in the light of current negotiations: see the speech of the Taoiseach, Mr Haughey, in *Dáil Debs.*, vol. 403, December 1990, cols 1307–19. And the Progressive Democrats' leader, Mr O'Malley (the Minister for Industry and Commerce) supported change, but only in the context of more general constitutional reform: *Dáil Debs.*, vol. 403, December 1990, cols 2288–95.

Index